The Subject of Film and Race

The Subject of Film and Race

Retheorizing Politics, Ideology, and Cinema

Gerald Sim

B L O O M S B U R Y

NEW YORK · LONDON · NEW DELHI · SYDNEY

Bloomsbury Academic
An imprint of Bloomsbury Publishing Inc

1385 Broadway	50 Bedford Square
New York	London
NY 10018	WC1B 3DP
USA	UK

www.bloomsbury.com

Bloomsbury is a registered trade mark of Bloomsbury Publishing Plc

First published 2014

Library of Congress Cataloging-in-Publication Data
Sim, Gerald.
The subject of film and race : retheorizing politics, ideology, and cinema / Gerald Sim.
pages cm
Includes bibliographical references.
ISBN 978-1-62356-753-8 (pbk. : alk. paper) –
ISBN 978-1-62356-184-0 (hardback : alk. paper)
1. Minorities in motion pictures.   2. Racism in motion pictures.
3. Ethnicity in motion pictures.   I. Title.
PN1995.9.M56S56   2014
791.43'9529–dc23
2014003692

ISBN: HB: 978-1-6235-6184-0
       PB: 978-1-6235-6753-8
     ePub: 978-1-6235-6135-2
     ePDF: 978-1-6235-6347-9

Typeset by Newgen Knowledge Works (P) Ltd., Chennai, India
Printed and bound in the United States of America

Contents

List of Illustrations

Acknowledgments

I share this book with those who contributed mightily or offered invaluable support. Mitsuhiro Yoshimoto and Louis-Georges Schwartz were dialectical and iconoclastic interlocutors: one's sheer economy set off the other's gripping excess. Rick Altman's advice and example always kept production on schedule. David Depew is an insightful and catholic muse, and a great coffee companion who "will discuss Hegel anytime and any place." Paula Amad's input was honest, direct, and valuable. Always pick up her gauntlets. My conversations with Michael Meneghetti and Christopher Babey echo throughout these passages; this project was conceived from shared affinities and frustrations. Nicole Brenez was generous with the readings she offered of early chapters. Ed Buscombe's affection for the Western and Bryan Gilliam's energy for film music were highly influential. James Tweedie is one of the good guys in this racket; I am endlessly grateful for his counsel. Toward the end, Jon Lewis and Rosalind Galt helped to unravel what seemed like impenetrable mysteries. Deep thanks of course go to my editor Katie Gallof and her staff at Bloomsbury for their faith and investment in this project, and to the anonymous reviewers who strengthened it.

Part of Chapter 4 was published as "Said's Marxism: *Orientalism's* Relationship to Film Studies and Race," in *Discourse: Journal for Theoretical Studies in Media and Culture*, 34.2–3. It appears here with the kind permission of Wayne State University Press. I am grateful to its editors and blind reviewer for supporting the work, and reserve special thanks for Genevieve Yue's editorial labors.

Eric Freedman and Chris Robé handed me my first job and that will always mean something to me. I have shared an office wall with Stephen Charbonneau for six years, and still cannot believe my luck: *This stuff just flies through the air . . . You just gotta know how to grab it.*

Thanks to all my students who kept faith with Adorno, namely Chris Vanderwall whose comment in Introduction to Critical Reading and Viewing smoothed out one of the final creases in Chapter 5. Iowa was indeed a great place to be, especially with colleagues like Jay Beck, Jennifer Fleeger, Dennis Hanlon, Kevin Mcdonald, Linda Mokdad, Jennifer Proctor, and Prakash

Younger. My corner is overpopulated with friends and colleagues who offered support in many forms and at all hours. Thank you, Andy Brodie, Scott, Kristin, and Jack Christopherson, Emily Light, Carol Schrage, Jesse Sheedy, and Sophia and Dhelia, partners in crime.

Peter Sim once mused that tobacco taxes are effectively a levy on the poor because "the rich don't have the kind of problems that smoking provides relief for. They don't need to smoke, but poor people do." My father smoked a pack-a-day from boyhood. The habit did his pulmonary health no favors, but to this day secondhand smoke smells like memories. His ruminations on tobacco policy represent my first and abiding lesson in class-consciousness. Looking back, I have to think that my worldview was shaped by the profundities that cut through those plumes. No one taught me more about alienated labor, use and exchange value, and species being more than he, not with those words but no less plainly. I will forever remember the lessons that his face imparted on the sublimities of Hitchcock, Tashlin, and Donen, on how to enjoy political rallies like stand-up comedy, how to treat every moment as parody, and the advice said and unsaid about how important it is to live happy.

Introduction: What is Critical Race Film Studies?

"Is it racist?" We still often ask that question about popular culture, in which cinema continues to provide abundant kindling for racial controversy. As history evaluates whether Barack Obama's promise of a post-racial America has been fulfilled, a mere glance at the multiplex can disavow that notion. Although films such as *The Blind Side, Precious* (both 2009), *The Help* (2011), and *Django Unchained* (2012) were either critical or commercial successes, the film reviews and social commentaries they engendered evince that race remains a highly contested issue. Film culture is a prominent forum for that public debate. Its audiences appear to possess keen awareness of ideology's presence in films as well, within the stereotype but also beyond. In these four films, empathy and identification lie unmistakably with the victims and not the perpetrators of racial prejudice who are punished by narratives' end. None of them can be accused of encouraging racial animus outright in the way that *The Birth of a Nation* (1915) clearly does. But the popular criticism proved sufficiently sophisticated to ponder other factors at play. They asked why black triumphs are inevitably facilitated by white saviors (Figure I.1). Is that racist? Are any ideological failings attributable to white directors? Are they racist? Are they morally or experientially authorized to tell these stories? Questions like these stand as a testament to the striking success of film theorists and critics who have taken on cinema's relationship to race. Their ideas are discernibly active in public discourse, and the influence of their enterprise on both film scholarship and popular criticism is clear.

That work within film studies can be understood within the wider political struggles for racial equality. In the aftermath of the tumultuous 1960s, film criticism began a battle of its own. However, even after the election of America's first African American president, the political outcomes of that era remain mixed. The political importance of passing civil rights legislation is tempered by stark reminders for instance, of the failure to eradicate the minority underclass. Correspondingly significant levels of social change did not accompany the

Figure I.1 Django (Jamie Foxx) and his white savior, King Schultz (Christoph Waltz). Is it racist? (*Django Unchained*, 2012).

hard-won constitutional protections. But tumultuous political events eventually turned attention toward mass media's complicity with racial ideology. What I call "critical race film theory and criticism" gathered momentum in the early 1970s. Where sit-ins, boycotts, and marches to change racist social practices left off, the critical movement to alter public minds picked up. With this book, I propose to interrogate that film criticism that concerns itself with race. I examine the ground that the project has covered and the direction it has taken. I launch my proposition from the field's political context because in the end, political efficacy is essentially the final measure by which these endeavors will be judged. One assumes that this is how those projects would wish to be considered. Basically, critical race film studies analyze how cinema communicates racist values to individual spectators and society at large. Its exponents theorize textual operations to analyze cinematic racism. To wit, they apply critical theory to explain how the medium carries racist ideology. How have the fortunes of critical race film theory fared as a result of being tethered to those ideas? How politically effective then, are those ideas?

The term, "critical race film studies" borrows its nomenclature from critical race theory. First developed in legal scholarship, critical race theory is a multidisciplinary corpus of theoretically oriented research that, according to its eminent exponents Richard Delgado and Jean Stefancic, is "interested in studying and transforming the relationship among race, racism, and power."[1] It views racism as an ideological function, socially constructed, normalized, and thus unnoticed. It also believes that racism is materially determined, which is to say, race is mobilized to advance economic interests. Finally, critical race theorists invest in the notion that persons of color experience oppression uniquely, and thus possess an innate competence to speak about race and racism.[2] According to these tenets, "critical race" is thus an apt moniker for film scholars concerned with race-centered analysis, due to their shared interests in examining ideology, discourse, and identity. Over approximately four decades of Anglo-American scholarship investigating how concepts and questions centered on race and ethnicity are represented and articulated in the cinema, these themes from critical race theory have endured in its sister discipline from film studies.

A further note on nomenclature: I use the terms "film criticism" and "film theory" interchangeably for the following reasons. While I would, in general circumstances, accept Dudley Andrew's definitions of film criticism (as ideas that pertain to single films or a group of films) and theory (as that which speaks of cinema as a whole),[3] insofar as issues of race occur in films beyond those that deal explicitly and thematically with them, we might therefore be dealing in fact with all films. This is because on any given issue, while the immediate object at hand may be a solitary film, the specter of race exists far beyond its borders. From a certain point of view, to speak of race is to possibly speak of most if not all films. Treating theory and criticism as one is also historically practical because time and canonization often transform and even "elevate" criticism into theory; take for example, the writing of Sergei Eisenstein whose work championing montage in film culture is now the core of formalist film theory.

As we shall discover, critical race film studies is marked in large part by a few objectives and theoretical precepts summarized by the following: stereotype studies, discourse analysis, and fragmented subjectivity. This hews closely to what Delgado and Stefancic call the "idealist" camp of critical race theory, to which "racism and discrimination are matters of thinking, mental categorizations, attitude, and discourse." By contrast, the "realist" school of critical race theory approach racism as economic determinists who privilege material and class concerns.[4] Critical race theorists including Delgado have observed that the idealist mode of discourse analysis came to dominate critical race theory. Education theorist Mike Cole contends that critical race theory, arising out of critical legal theory, broke away because the latter was too class-based and underestimated race as the primary axis of social oppression.[5] Indeed, the following chapters show that critical race film studies have followed suit and not attended sufficiently to class issues, essentially assuming the idealist position at the expense of the materialist one. In revealing these leanings, this book seeks to correct that bias. The urge to remind the field about critical race theory's materialist wing is but one reason to do so. This is because I believe that the return to economic concerns is actually induced by contradictions within film studies' own existing methodology on race. In particular, I find that critical race film theory's antihumanist assumptions do not comport with its reliance on unified bourgeois subjectivity that is more familiar to Neo-Marxism.

The faintest hint that a methodology is culling material concerns automatically signals combatants from broader and older conflicts to enter the fray. Terms such as social constructivism, discourse analysis, and fragmentation possess a distinctively poststructuralist and postmodern flavor. As such, it is easy to overlay this terrain with intellectual cartographies that do not just delineate between idealists and realists, but poststructuralists and Marxists, postmodernists and humanists, or Marxists and Post-Marxists. The general move away from class concerns in film theory and criticism is overdetermined by many developments. One could point to philosopher Jean-François Lyotard's dismay and turn of faith at Marxism's political failure during the Paris événements of 1968, as a seminal event that precipitated larger intellectual changes. Others would recognize it as a triumph of capitalism, and point out that poststructuralism's rejection of Marxism occurs just as capitalism permeates our subjective experience and embarks on global expansion and standardization.[6] That is to say, capitalist politics reify in critical theory. So-called Post-Marxists would counter that orthodox Marxism was too reductive and rigid to fully explain all of capitalism's subtleties and shifts.[7] These battle lines offer context and guidance in understanding the issue but it is important not to oversimplify. Venn overlaps exist in all these relationships. By no stretch of the imagination are all poststructuralists averse to materialist thinking, nor can one assume that a Marxist will reject postmodernism. With regard to this book's theoretical focus and deference to the unified Neo-Marxian subject, there are also many materialists who reject humanism as such. These are thinkers likely to see Marxism as one of the most important antihumanist philosophies.

Finally, of course, critiques do not extend to the personal. Just as I disagree elsewhere with those who do presume that the apolitical nature of cognitivist film studies renders its practitioners ideologically suspect, I would not accuse anyone of personally lacking class consciousness even if I criticize some critical models in use.[8] In short, from a large enough distance, this book can sound like familiar carping, and appear to be another instance of a materialist barking about how people are not talking enough about economics and class. But neither a reactionary deference toward class nor economic reductionism is what I advocate here. The goal is to clear the theoretical brush. As odd as this might sound, the desire is to simultaneously complicate, clarify, and refine.

Yet I cannot assert that my initial survey of the situation was absolutely impartial, nor can I deny being gladdened in figuring out that critical race studies was pointing in a certain direction I predicted. A Neo-Marxian theoretical foundation provides a critical backbone and default sensitivity toward class issues, and fueled my initial skepticism. That generally inclines me to give the final word on most matters to the lineage of cultural criticism defined by the Frankfurt School, the intellectual movement that sprung from the University of Frankfurt's Institute for Social Research. Neo-Marxism began as an interdisciplinary movement of the twentieth century responding to traditional Marxism's limitations in accounting for sociological developments and cultural phenomena. Its import for film and media studies arises from the conviction that mass culture serves to impose capitalism's ideological will on free individuals. How it hindered critical subjectivity was of great concern to two of the Frankfurt School's most important critics, Max Horkheimer and Theodor W. Adorno. Their legacy is best represented today by Fredric Jameson who, along with David Harvey, provide some comprehensive accounts of how postmodern capitalism cloaks itself in abstractions and incomprehensibility. They thus offer a persuasive explanation for why the critical subject's dialectical and negational capacities are so crucial. Jameson also writes in *The Geopolitical Aesthetic*:

> "Otherness" . . . is a peculiarly booby-trapped and self-defeating concept; and the slogan of "difference," while politically impeccable in all the obvious senses, is formalistic and empty of concrete social and historical specification—where it does not, indeed, relax and lend itself to the usual late capitalist celebration of multi-cultural pluralism. (It has, in short, all the ambiguity of an essentially liberal, rather than radical, value.)[9]

The passage expresses the other half of my position well—the issue is one of politics as well as its relation to theory. In the 40 years since film scholars began to address race, the field has built itself a few dominant platforms. I measure their short-term goal of general ideological and cultural criticism, as well as their objective in the long run, to deliver social justice via the intermediate desire for cultural democracy in the mass media. When scholars illuminate films to reveal the presence and workings of racial ideology, they assume that these critiques will find their way into the public consciousness, where increased awareness will force racist ideas to unravel on a larger scale, and ultimately change the way society thinks and acts. In that case, how well is critical race film studies fighting racism? Is it a problem that poststructuralist preferences for theoretical inquiries into discourse and difference define film studies' view of racial Otherness narrowly on a linguistic level or as a discursive matter? Does it distract from empirical material inequalities?

This book's Neo-Marxian "materialist" model of cultural criticism incorporates Marxist dialecticism into theorizations of culture. Like Neo-Marxism, I assume that culture shares a complex but more or less direct relationship with the economic system producing it. In this base-superstructure model of society, Marxists refer to the economic mode of production as the "base" or alternatively, the "substructure," and social constructions such as laws, religion, politics, and culture as the "superstructure." The thing is, Neo-Marxism is not normally an approach associated with critical race film studies, which has become more affiliated with the idealist camp of critical race theory. This book suggests that this elision of materialism strengthens existing power structures and limits critical race film studies' potential to produce historical and political change. Since racial conflicts are often waged over redistribution and access to resources, Neo-Marxism provides an intellectual orientation that is both fresh and well equipped to evaluate film studies' engagement with race. That sense of things is only strengthened when we discover fundamental theoretical contradictions arising when race- and identity-related concerns are privileged over paradigms based on class. For an indicative example to reinforce that assessment and the forthcoming analysis, take Daniel Bernardi's recent collection of interviews with filmmakers who are grappling with identity issues, *Filming Difference: Actors, Directors, Writers and Producers on Gender, Race and Sexuality in Film*. Its title foregrounds the popular poststructuralist trope of "difference" and excludes class-consciousness from that overview even though economics and class are frequent topics of conversations within the book.[10] My book resolves incongruities like this with critical theory, and frequently finds clues that taken together, invite us to apply the Frankfurt School when we examine film and race. It might well result in a rearrangement of the familiar quadrivirate of race, gender, sexuality, and class into a new orientation where class occupies a more privileged position. If that installs Marxism and especially Marxist humanism more prominently in critical race film studies, it would certainly not unsettle my sensibilities, but it is important to emphasize that those conclusions were not externally imposed but beckoned by what I found.

A poststructuralist regime in critical race film studies was uncovered, that counts race, gender, sexuality, and class as the constituent categories of identity. Each is seen as an axis on which social divisions have been created in the service of ideology. The differences that people come to see between haves and have-nots, white and nonwhite, male and female, or east and west, thus become sources of meaning. When these thought structures are naturalized into classism, racism, sexism, and heteronormativity, they form the premise for common sense, which then translates into everyday praxes that enable the oppression, dispossession, and pacification of minority and subordinate groups. The power of ideology is such that those axes of meaning, the binary categories themselves, are seldom questioned. Poststructuralism justifiably challenged ideology by pointing out how identities are social constructions based on difference and have no ontological status. More than that, individual subjectivity itself is deemed to have never existed. Deconstructionists took it even further; Jacques Derrida's notion of différance for example, emphasizes the fluidity and excess of unstable meanings.

Are the social categories of race, gender, sexuality, and class equivalent? I believe that class is distinctive for several reasons. Racial, gender, and sexuality differences become most consequential when they affect economic standing. Social justice only becomes an issue when they determine a person's economic class. Essentially, it is a question of economic inequality. Class identity is intractable and ontologically stable, while race, gender, and sexuality are not. A person's class identity is stable enough to resist any sort of performative subversion, a form of rebellion highlighted here because of the prominence given to it by those who examine identity and cinema. It is common to find arguments in favor of appropriation via dress, speech, behavior, and so on because it highlights the arbitrariness of normalized cultural inscriptions and underscores identity's contingency. It explains the high regard for Billy Wilder's comedy, *Some Like It Hot* (1959), a film whose cross-dressing stars Tony Curtis and Jack Lemmon's gender-bending antics turn heteronormativity on its head. But that strategy of subversion does not translate to class. Much of the comedy in *Trading Places* (1983) where a rich white businessman (Dan Ackroyd) switches places with a black beggar (Eddie Murphy) is on balance based more on race than on class. In real life, neither the rich nor the poor can pretend to be the other with the same alacrity. Of course, race, gender, sexuality, and class identities all structure our social experiences in significant ways. They collide on occasions when social conflict compels groups to choose sides. For example, during the O. J. Simpson murder trial, media attention turned to how African American women on the jury would react to revelations of Simpson's spousal abuse. The controversy played itself out publicly on talk shows, and when Simpson was acquitted, race evidently trumped gender. Notably though, the advantage that Simpson enjoyed as a rich defendant did arise, but class was ultimately undersold since the collective memory of that saga consists mostly of the racial and gender divisions.

Racism and misogyny should not be minimized, but identity politics that critical race theory fosters and as this book will show, recur in critical race film studies, cause collateral damage both inside and outside the academy. A recent skirmish that pit racial with gender interests occurred when Barack Obama and Hillary Clinton competed for the 2008 Democratic presidential nomination. Each candidate was out to achieve a milestone. He would be America's first black president and she would be her first female president. Clinton began her campaign with more African American backing. But when Obama's Midwestern victory in the Iowa caucuses legitimated his chances for victory, his support among initially cautious black voters increased and fault lines were drawn. Feminist icon Gloria Steinem published a column in *The New York Times* where she made a case for Clinton based on identity politics.[11] "Gender is probably the most restricting force in American life," she wrote, arguing also that while racist ideology has been rejected, sexist ideology remains normalized. A later paragraph's contention that she was "not advocating a competition for who has it toughest" thus rang rather hollow. Grounded as it was in feminist identity politics, Steinem's case for Clinton's candidacy only worsened factional tensions, which eventually flared up during the primary campaign. Clinton supporters accused the other side of sexism with racially loaded language; and for their part, Obama supporters were at the ready with charges of racism. It highlights how unproductive and destructive identity paradigms can be. Steinem's reliance and simultaneous disavowal of identity politics parallels the recurrent problem in critical race film studies examined in these chapters. She fully grasps the harm they can inflict but engages in them anyway. The primary election activated emotional faults that splintered social groups that probably shared much in common. In the case of the Simpson trial, they facilitated an injustice (assuming as I do that the defendant was guilty). And since both events made for gratuitous and highly profitable media spectacles, should we then ask who the ultimate victors and beneficiaries of these cultural battles are? Knowing my instincts, some will predict my answer, that profits are reaped by an economically determined power structure presiding over Late-stage or global capitalism. But throughout this book, any path to conclusions like that is accompanied by its share of surprises. The journey navigates its way through a theoretical discussion about the Western Enlightenment's unified subject—the humanist idea that each individual possesses a stable core identity and the capacity for rational thought. This individual is indispensible if we are to attempt to understand how Late Capitalism works and how it affects our culture.

Poststructuralist and postmodernist approaches behind critical race film studies challenge that subject. One of the tacts they take is to argue that unity is illusory because subjectivities are fragmented. Another approach destabilizes the subject through the notion that determinants of individual identity such as race, gender, and class, are ideological constructions. In other words, identities take form in discourse and exist only because people adopt discursive formations. While that might be true, all of these social formations are also materially and economically determined. If that is so, I find it worthwhile for political purposes to ascertain the values of each identity's valence. To wit, which category, among race, gender, and class, is most important? Such clarity is more crucial than ever, for even with an ostensibly class-based insurgency like the Occupy movement's anti-Wall Street protests in 2011, the argument that economics are paramount does not necessarily prevail. The Associated Press marked the demonstrations' first anniversary with an elegiac report that linked its diminution to social splintering. "Protesters accused each other of being patriarchal and racist and domineering."[12] Activists would defend its gains but Thomas Frank's diagnosis of Occupy's demise supports the AP's contention. He blames the movement's political and practical inaction on academic pseudointellectuals who began to populate the movement's ranks, and even singles out poststructuralists for particular lament.[13] Lest one's reservations are aroused about the opinions of cynics such as Frank and the AP, the more sympathetic assessment of those fissures by Todd Gitlin is perhaps most damning. It confirms the inviolability of class-based analysis. Class difference, he documented, was a central but unacknowledged organizational impediment to the would-be economic revolution.[14]

Disputes such as this between race and class define both contemporary politics and film studies, where the same tensions come to guide film interpretation. Consider one example, African American Studies scholar Henry Louis Gates's review of Warren Beatty's political satire, *Bulworth* (1998).[15] According to critics' general consensus, the film's socialist message rails against corporate money flooding political campaigns, a trend that disenfranchises the working-class and coincides with deregulation favoring corporate interests. Beatty's narrative unfolds in a multi-genre plot abhorring American political spectacles within a fish-out-of-water interracial romantic comedy. The protagonist senator Jay Bulworth (Beatty) is a politician borne of 1960s' idealism who becomes so disillusioned with his own political compromises over his career that he plans to commit suicide by taking an assassination hit out on himself. Liberated from mortal and political obligations, he sparks a furor by spouting politically incorrect socialism, and finds both enlightenment and redemption in hip-hop culture, and a romance with a young African American activist, Nina (Halle Berry). The racial interplay between Beatty and his black love interest, or between WASP and black culture, provides the basis of humor and spectacle.

Twentieth Century Fox advertised the film in that vein with a trailer that features prominent clips from two scenes. In the first, Bulworth exhorts to worshipers in a black church, "If you don't put down that malt liquor and chicken wings and get behind somebody other than a running back who stabs his wife, you're never going to get rid of somebody like me."[16] In the second, he declares at a Hollywood fundraiser that "my guys are not stupid, they always put the big Jews on my schedule." These two punch lines anchor the trailer, apparently the most accessible and prototypically "outrageous" gimmicks available. But more important, the preview positions race politically as a conduit toward an examination of the economic substructure. Most reviews, it seems, acknowledged that implicit message. Richard Kelly summarizes in his review for *Sight and Sound*, "only John Sayles has served up such brazen dialectical materialism in recent American cinema."[17] One can speculate as to why the studio chose to highlight remarks that are racially offensive instead of those that are capitalist-offensive. Class conscious dialogue does exist in the script. For example, Bulworth raps the following verse: "Yeah, yeah / You can call it single-payer or Canadian way / Only socialized medicine will ever save the day! Come on now, lemme hear that dirty word—SOCIALISM!" Halfway through the film, when the romantic couple are finally alone, they consummate with a political exchange where Nina delivers a crucial monologue (Figure I.2). Asked

Figure I.2 Nina (Halle Berry) provides Senator Bulworth (Warren Beatty) with a Marxist analysis of black poverty in *Bulworth* (1998).

by Bulworth about the dearth of modern black leaders, she charms him with this monologue:

> I think that it has more to do with the decimating of the manufacturing base in the urban centers. Some people would say the problem is purely cultural, by the power of the media that is continually controlled by fewer and fewer people, add to that the monopoly of the media, a consumer culture that's based on self-gratification. You're not likely to have a population that wants leadership that calls for self-sacrifice. Senator, an optimistic energized population throws up optimistic, energized leaders and when you shift manufacturing to the Sun Belt and the southwest, you destroy the blue-collar core of the black activist population. But the fact is that I'm just a materialist at heart. If I look at the economic base, high domestic employment means jobs for African Americans.

Marx, it would seem, casts a long shadow on this film.

However, Gates reads things very differently. Rather than emphasize what he noticed as the film's "bona-fide political content," his review is much more preoccupied with Beatty's awkward racial pretensions as a white liberal, and for the most part, stays mired within that displeasure. Appropriating Norman Mailer's famous essay about white hipsters who adopted swing and jazz culture, Gates is bemused and discomfited by Beatty's performance of black culture, titling his film review "The White Negro" and following with a succinct

Figure I.3 Henry Louis Gates was preoccupied with how "Warren Beatty Can't Rap" in *Bulworth* (1998).

opening sentence: "Warren Beatty can't rap." "The result is more Dr. Seuss than Dr. Dre," where the actor comes off "like a really pissed off Edgar Guest." *Bulworth's* explicit socialism or even its overt articulations of Marxist ideas did not escape Gates's mind, but why did he seem so reluctant to move past the racial dimension? Why was he so hostile toward the filmmaker's ironic masquerade of the black experience? (Figure I.3) The critique seems to have little to do with the politically loaded history of minstrelsy where the question is about who gets to enjoy the privilege of mimicking the other, merely that Beatty did not pull it off as "a white man . . . from a white part of the world."[18] If race is a discursive and performative construction, and identities are fluid, does it then make sense to base a critique on the intractable essentialism of Beatty's whiteness? That aversion surfaced more recently with critics who feel that Tarantino has no right to say anything about black history and worse, that he uses black actors in *Django Unchained* as political cover for his exploitation of the N-word and facile excursions into black culture.[19] These charges against Beatty and Tarantino comport ironically with a precept of critical race theory, that there is something exclusively unique about black subjectivity, shaped as it were, within and by the social experience of being black. It is one of the theoretical contradictions taken up by this book.

Gates, who was not in the least affronted by *Django Unchained*, became embroiled in a much more publicized and recent racial controversy. On July 16,

2009, the Harvard professor was arrested outside his Cambridge home after an altercation with a cop. Gates had returned home earlier to find his front door jammed. After entering through a back entrance, he then attempted to forcibly open the front door. When a neighbor reported witnessing a possible burglary, Sergeant James Crowley responded first to the 9-1-1 call. As he tried to verify the professor's identity, more officers arrived on the scene, an altercation broke out, and eventually, Gates was handcuffed before cameras and arrested on his front porch. Over the next few days, the incident gained national attention, culminating when now President Barack Obama responded at a press conference to a reporter's question about his thoughts by saying that the police "acted stupidly."[20] Reporting on the arrest that had focused almost exclusively on race, was flung into a more intense frenzy when Obama made his comment. Some stories highlighted concerns among Harvard's faculty that the arrest resulted from racial profiling. Media descriptions of Gates as "one of the nation's pre-eminent African-American scholars" drove the controversy further. Reports commonly cited a quote from one of his colleagues, "my colleagues and I have asked the question of whether this kind of egregious act would have happened had Professor Gates been a white professor."[21] Academic Stanley Fish's commentary in *The New York Times* reinforced the view that Crowley's actions were racially motivated, by comparing the incident to Gates's encounter with racial prejudice when both professors lived in North Carolina.[22]

The truth of what transpired that day is less relevant here than the dominant narrative the news media pushed. They politicized a racial conflict between a white cop and black suspect. Few brought up the class dynamics simultaneously at play. The police report states that Gates warned Crowley that the officer had no idea who he was messing with, and that the professor loudly attempted to summon the police chief over the phone in Crowley's presence.[23] With that alternative narrative available, why was the event not presented as a clash between an Ivy League professor and a public servant in a socio-economically divided city? Race is indeed often an inescapable part of our consciousness with real personal and social consequences, but when is it more appropriate to consider class in reading films and making sense of culture?

These brief examples from mass media foreground issues regarding the critical discourse on cinema and race highlighted throughout this book. Because of that relationship, a better understanding of critical race film studies can illuminate our social world as a whole. Furthermore, if the word emanating from the Occupy camps is accurate, that poststructuralism was in some form or other responsible for the movement's atrophy, it becomes especially urgent for us to understand these ideas that are playing an outsized role in radical politics. Nevertheless, this is "just" a book on film theory. It will not make someone suddenly care about class issues, nor will it change the mind of anyone not already predisposed or at least open to the idea of a materialist approach to understanding race. The sociological work published by those such as Max Weber, William Julius Wilson, and more recently Walter Benn Michaels's *The Trouble with Diversity*, would be far more convincing on that score.[24] But if this book enhances understanding of film, media, and theory, it should hopefully add to the critical discourse on race, which would not be insignificant since so much of that discussion nowadays takes place about the media and in the media.

This book proceeds in two-stages. The first examines the main ideas underwriting critical race film theory, and reveals key contradictions. The second is more reconstructive. The initial four chapters locate specific knots in critical race film scholarship's theoretical and political musculature. These theoretical paradoxes initially uncovered actually provide a motive force later on. Chapter 1 historicizes the major developments in critical race film studies, highlighting the origins of seminal principles and undertaking close readings of important contributions to the field by Steve Neale, Robert Stam and Louise Spence, Manthia Diawara, and Homi Bhabha. I historicize two key approaches that the field has long been identified with: a first generation of work I associate with image studies and a second generation of theory that introduced discursive analyses. As often as critical race film scholarship avows its intentions to move beyond these early methods, little progression or movement occur in practice, as my survey of the last 30 years indicates. Along the way, I pause to deliberate from a historical materialist perspective, particularly on the positions that these poststructuralist theories take on the unified subject. With these asides, momentum picks up toward eventually forming a Neo-Marxian methodology. As it were, the book's historical materialism is not an alien interjection, but an attempt to reveal Marxian ideas, including important ones governing subjectivity, that are previously either latent or elided.

Following that direction leads partly to increased sensitivity to economic issues, whose mandate includes placing greater importance on class-centered analyses of form and narrative, as well as production histories that explain the film industry's power to define images of the working-class. The field of working-class studies could be involved in this part of the project because of its mission to foster class consciousness. But its import to my study is limited because the heavy value that it assigns to "positively" representing the lived experiences of the working-class and on expressing their point of view, recapitulates the reasons relayed in Chapter 1 why critical race studies' most popular models feel well worn. Without a doubt, heightening awareness of economic inequity and of the plight of society's have-nots is important. But if we account for critical race film studies' continued overreliance on first-generation stereotype analysis, then the impetus for materialism is not simply restricted to studying the origins and persistence of damaging representations of class. This book's Neo-Marxian undertaking interrogates the politics of critical theory in addition to those of film and textual production.

The first chapter concludes by discussing how critical race film studies have splintered according to ethnicity, into independent projects with parallel trajectories. This is how critical race film studies practices identity politics, based on what I argue is an attempt to suppress contradictory theories about the individual subject. It has led to a degree of redundancy and hampers collective pan-ethnic strategies against Eurocentrism or white supremacy. The field has sometimes adopted multiculturalism as way to sidestep identity politics, but I show via political theories of "recognition" that the strategy might be lacking. Chapter 2 surveys the critical race film criticism surrounding John Ford's Western classic, *The Searchers* (1956). It is an important work as a member of the canon, as a movie whose narrative and form are driven by racial discourse, and whose director and star's reputation for reactionary politics persist to this day. Not surprisingly, it has generated much scholarship regarding its supposedly racist themes. But since its racial politics and overall ideological position are actually unclear, the film becomes a *tabula rasa* for interpretation and theorization. Although its ambivalence also threatens the film with incoherence, what prevents that from breaking out, I argue, is the reliance on the unified subjectivities of the film's author Ford and its main character, Ethan Edwards (John Wayne). This chapter acts as a key transition, using *The Searchers* as a locus where intellectual shifts in critical race film theory can be clearly observed, while I concomitantly excavate the "subject" that becomes the central topic of the next chapter, before being further coaxed out over the rest of the book.

Chapter 3 presents a theoretical discussion of critical race film studies' view on the viability of the rational bourgeois subject. Counter-intuitively, poststructuralist writing on race and cinema continues to rely on a notion of critical consciousness that greatly resembles the Neo-Marxian subject—one whom Frankfurt School critic Theodor Adorno would describe as capable of autonomy, negation, and dialectical thinking. Critical race film theory first prompts us to look in Adorno's direction, and Edward Said later affirms those instincts. From another point of view, we may begin to see how critical race film theory reinforces the very premise of Neo-Marxist criticism. This chapter defines Adorno's unified subject and argues that its persistence in the face of the poststructuralist challenge signals its strength. Ultimately, this augurs the return of Marxian class concerns. Chapter 4 then reflects on the influence that Said's *Orientalism* has maintained on critical race film studies.[25] Although that book serves as an important theoretical reference, the field's poststructuralist orientation has too frequently withdrawn the materialism and humanism of which Said had been most outspoken, in favor of the social constructivist elements of his analysis. In light of recent work outside the field that has lent credence and specificity to Said's relationship to the Frankfurt School, this chapter identifies where the misreading has been most consequential while examining how the study of race has been configured as a result. It renders the outlines of a Saidian methodology for race, but highlights an aporia ironically created by Said's adherence to Neo-Marxian critical consciousness.

By traversing Said, the book moves into an examination of postcolonial theories that film studies often uses to study race. Postcolonial criticism is much concerned with how the colonial subaltern is ideologically Othered and racialized. Its thinkers like Said, Homi Bhabha, and Gayatri Spivak are thus also prominent in critical race film studies. And since Bhabha and Spivak willingly display their debts to poststructuralism as well as postmodernism, they also provide a conceptual transition from poststructuralist to postcolonial and onto postmodern theory. Bhabha's favored trope, hybridity, is central to the final chapter's focus on multiracial discourse in contemporary Hollywood cinema. But materialists like Arif Dirlik point out that postcolonial criticism frequently tends to sublate the material conditions of postcolonial reality:

What is remarkable, therefore, is . . . that a consideration of the relationship between "postcolonialism" and Global Capitalism should be absent from the writings of postcolonial intellectuals; all the more remarkable because this relationship is arguably less abstract and more direct than any relationship between Global Capitalism and postmodernism, as it pertains not just to cultural/epistemological but to social and political formations.[26]

Dirlik's view on postcolonial research echoes Jameson's cutting critique of postmodern ahistoricism cited before. Critical race film studies, I argue, has settled into a position where it becomes an open and inviting target for such critiques.

Perhaps the book appears to have adopted a "scorched earth" policy with the past and current work on film and race, but it does not reject the need for critical race analysis at all. The intent is to shore up weaknesses so that the field may proceed forward, and not to dismantle it. Critical race film criticism is still an important undertaking as the aspiration for cultural democracy and social justice remains principled and essential. The ambition and responsibility of the final chapters are to fashion modified strategies for criticism and theory, erected over Neo-Marxist foundations. To that end, I turn a critical eye on postmodernity to chart the first phases of that future, shifting into a reconstructive phase for race-related film studies via the critical subject. The case studies in Chapter 5 of "postmodern" films and cinematic phenomena lead the way toward a conception of how critical race film criticism can more effectively operate. In particular, they examine the postcolonial and postmodern notion of hybridity. Bhabha's writing on the subject triangulates poststructuralist and postcolonial principles, condensing a mixture of ambivalence, contradiction and split subjectivity into the utopian trope of the hybrid—someone who is neither one nor the Other, and who can therefore test the limits of national or racial essentialism that is central to colonial ideology. This chapter counters Bhabha's idealism by analyzing an example of postmodern and postcolonial hybridity in contemporary Hollywood cinema, Keanu Reeves, whose hybridity courses unmistakably through his films and star persona. The actor's appeal is driven significantly by both the known fact and the symptomatic perception of his multiracial heritage and ambiguous sexuality—postmodern ambiguities circulating within and around the films. Here, the historical intersection of Late Capitalist consumerism, "Generation X" culture, digital technology, and a racial landscape created by the repeal of antimiscegenation laws provide historical context.

The culture industry presents Reeves's hybrid identity as an appeal to contemporary Generation X audiences' desire for a figure of reformed masculinity that resonates with their multicultural reality. In this way, hybridity functions outwardly as a progressive ideal. Bolstered by his penchant for roles as cyborgs, and reinforced by notions of his "stupidity" and robotic manner, critics such as Joshua Clover and R. L. Rutsky suggest that his racial ambiguity challenges Western notions of identity and the thinking subject. Following those who ask if films or film directors are racist, they ask if the traditional subject itself is a racist idea that is subverted by Reeves's discourse. In turn, others believe that Reeves's liminality opens the text to alternative readings by marginalized audiences. But once again, following the pattern uncovered in previous chapters, that hybridity discourse distracts from a compelling heuristic with regards to Reeves's films and star persona. I find that the texts actually invoke critical subjectivity on the part of both Reeves and his characters, in a way that is at odds with the split postmodern figure more commonly trumpeted. His films and star discourse seem to favor Neo-Marxist over postmodern ideals. By itself, this may present little more than an alternative reading. But nestled in a chorus of chapters, the consonance they produce renders the point more convincing. What though, explains the tendency to overestimate the transgressive value of hybrid postmodern raciality like Reeves's? After all, hybridity is not the determinant in these texts' narrative economy; rather, it is part of an intricate postmodern veneer designed and subtended by the logic and institutional force of a corporate global totality. The chapter concludes that theories of hybridity are complicit with capital, and further ratify modern consumerism.

Critical race film studies have found no embodiment of postmodern multiraciality more perfect than the cyborg. As both figure and metaphor, the cybernetic organism is also a significant part of Reeves's persona. Finally, I examine cyborg criticism's relationship with race theory and take a sustained look at the cyborg's racial metaphors in cinema. I look closest at those who posit that the cyborg's hybridity provides important ways to rethink assumptions about unified subjectivity. If there is a relative paucity of race-related analysis in this area, it is due to the privilege that feminism enjoys in writings on cyborg politics, and to the preponderance of cyborgs' presence in other textual forms such as literature, television, and the graphic novel. Applying earlier observations of Reeves's hybridity, I propose a sketch of what cyborg racial politics might look like, continuing the analysis of postmodern politics. I examine the workings of multiculturalism and its overlap with politics of a more critical or theoretical sort, where Donna Haraway's seminal essay "A Cyborg Manifesto" is inescapably central. All subsequent scholarship on cyborgs has needed to account for her Manifesto, and the present contribution is no different. It is an inescapable problem for Haraway that the traditional subject sprang from Western humanism. My alternative reading of the Cyborg Manifesto however, rejects that the subject is ipso facto a racist idea.

Before it raises suggestions for critical race film theory and criticism, the book also contributes to some other ongoing debates in film studies. Since the analysis of Keanu Reeves is essentially a star analysis, the opportunity presents itself to reflect upon the field of star studies. Research on audience consumption and interaction with stars often deal directly with issues of identification. My study of Reeves follows the recent publication of the first extensive analysis of his star discourse by Michael DeAngelis, who wrote in particular relation to sexuality studies. I am thus naturally drawn to star discourses that involve a multiethnic component such as Miriam Hansen's study of Rudolph Valentino. Both trade on the basic idea that split, contingent, or ambivalent (to use Bhabha's favored term) public personas allow fans and audiences to maintain multiple planes of identification and thus enact some form of interpretive subversion. These star studies, as with the hybridity theories described earlier, can privilege and idealize the postmodern subject (and consumer) instead of problematizing the ideological function of cinema's capitalist institutions. Emboldened by prior conclusions, I wonder if these reception studies are practicing postmodern extremism. I hope to persuade theory and criticism to incorporate a clearer consciousness of capital toward a more materialist theoretical framework for critical race film studies.

As a philosophical matter, Neo-Marxism believes unyieldingly that master narratives give great explanatory power to history. Metanarratives are anathema to postmodern cynicism and fragmentation. Nevertheless, an expansive theory about race and class that is universally applied and predeterminative would not be mobile or flexible enough to negotiate say, Josef Schumpeter's view of a highly adaptable capitalism, or Etienne Balibar and Immanuel Wallerstein's that it shapes itself to local situations. This book does not necessarily aspire to a grand theory unable to acknowledge specific histories. Critical race film studies, in trying to counter rhetorics of biological or essential determinism, has invested heavily in the notion that identities such as gender and race—especially those that have justified oppression in the past—are social and cultural fabrications lacking essential or scientific grounding, patently false, and invalid by default. But though the political meaning of race remains discursive, the political reaction must still be material. My recommendations for critical race film studies will encourage that approach, just as my theoretical conclusions will always permit it. This means placing greater emphasis on materialist considerations of class and economics. It also entails wariness of factionalism driven by identity politics, being more metacritical of stereotype studies, and treating political economy as a causal referent in textual analyses of films. The address of race issues must be materialist; any desire for social and racial change must confront a political–economic cause.

Notes

1 Richard Delgado and Jean Stefanic, *Critical Race Theory: An Introduction* 2nd edn (New York: New York University Press, 2012): 3.

2 Ibid., 7–10.

3 J. Dudley Andrew, *The Major Film Theories* (London: Oxford University Press, 1976): 4.

4 Ibid., 21.

5 Richard Delgado, "Crossroads and Blind Alleys: A Critical Examination of Recent Writing about Race," *Texas Law Review* 82 (2003): 124–25. Mike Cole, *Critical Race Theory and Education: A Marxist Response* (New York: Palgrave Macmillan, 2009): 3; Antonia Darder and Rodolfo D. Torres, *After Race: Racism after Multiculturalism* (New York: New York University Press, 2004).

6 Sean Homer, *Fredric Jameson: Marxism, Hermeneutics and Postmodernism* (New York: Routledge, 1998): 3.

7 Ernesto Laclau and Chantal Mouffe, *Hegemony and Socialist Strategy: Towards a Radical Democratic Politics* (London: Verso, 2001): viii, 24.

8 See Robert Stam's insinuation about cognitivism in *Film Theory: An Introduction* (Malden, MA: Blackwell Publishing, 2000): 240.

9 Fredric Jameson, *The Geopolitical Aesthetic* (Bloomington: British Film Institute, 1995): 188.

10 Daniel Bernardi, *Filming Difference: Actors, Directors, Writers and Producers on Gender, Race and Sexuality in Film* (Austin, TX: University of Texas Press, 2009).

11 Gloria Steinem, "Women are Never Front-Runners," *The New York Times* (January 8, 2008) <http://www.nytimes.com/2008/01/08/opinion/08steinem.html> Accessed November 16, 2009.

12 Meghan Barr, "One Year On, Occupy is in disarray; Spirit Lives On," *Yahoo! Finance* (September 18, 2012) <http://finance.yahoo.com/news/1-occupy-disarray-spirit-lives-161622760.html> Accessed April 26, 2013.

13 Thomas Frank, "To the Precinct Station," *The Baffler* 21 (2012) <http://thebaffler.com/past/to_the_precinct_station> Accessed April 26, 2013.

14 Todd Gitlin, *Occupy Nation: The Roots, the Spirit, and the Promise of Occupy Wall Street* (New York: It Books, 2012): 97.

15 Henry Louis Gates, Jr, "The White Negro," *The New Yorker* (May 11, 1998): 62–65.

16 The joke of Bulworth's impolitic utterance makes the implicit point that a great number of African Americans do believe in Simpson's guilt. The fact that most of them still felt compelled to side with the ex-football star speaks to the influence of identity politics.

17 Richard Kelly, "Film Review: *Bulworth*," *Sight and Sound* 9, 2 (February 1999): 40–42.

18 Gates, "The White Negro," 62, 63.

19 Eric Deggans, "Tarantino is the Baddest Black Filmmaker Working Today," *Salon* (December 27, 2012) <http://www.salon.com/2012/12/27/tarantino_is_the_ baddest_black_filmmaker_working_today/> Accessed April 26, 2013. Erin Aubry Kaplan, "'Django' an Unsettling Experience for Many Blacks," *Los Angeles Times* (December 28, 2012) <http://articles.latimes.com/2012/dec/28/entertainment/ la-et-django-reax-2–20121228> Accessed April 27, 2013.

20 Joseph Williams, "Obama Scolds Cambridge Police," *The Boston Globe* (July 23, 2009) <http://www.boston.com/news/nation/washington/articles/2009/07/23/ obama_scolds_cambridge_police/> Accessed November 8, 2009.

21 Tracy Jan, "Harvard professor Gates arrested at Cambridge home," *The Boston Globe* (July 20, 2009) <http://www.boston.com/news/local/breaking_ news/2009/07/harvard.html>; Abby Goodnough, "Harvard Professor Jailed; Officer Is Accused of Bias," *The New York Times* (July 20, 2009) <http://www. nytimes.com/2009/07/21/us/21gates.html?_r=1&scp=1&sq=henry%20gates%20 arrest&st=cse> Both accessed November 8, 2009.

22 Stanley Fish, "Henry Louis Gates: Déjà Vu All over Again," *The New York Times* (July 24, 2009) <http://fish.blogs.nytimes.com/2009/07/24/henry-louis-gates-deja- vu-all-over-again/> Accessed November 8, 2009.

23 Cambridge, Massachusetts Police Department, Incident Report #9005127 (July 16, 2009).

24 Max Weber, "Chapter V: Ethnic Groups," *Economy and Society: An Outline of Interpretive Sociology*, ed. Guenther Roth and Claus Wittich (New York: Bedminster Press, 1968): 385–98; William Julius Wilson, *Power, Racism and Privilege: Race Relations in Theoretical and Sociohistorical Perspectives* (New York: Macmillan Press, 1973) and *The Declining Significance of Race: Blacks and Changing American Institutions* (Chicago and London: University of Chicago Press, 1980); Walter Benn Michaels, *The Trouble with Diversity: How We Learned to Love Identity and Ignore Inequality* (New York: Metropolitan Books, 2006).

25 Edward Said, *Orientalism* (New York: Vintage Books, 1978).

26 Arif Dirlik, *The Postcolonial Aura* (Boulder, CO: Westview Press, 1997): 73.

1

Key Developments in Critical Race Film Studies

Studying cinema and race requires us to account for both the variables, "race" and "film." Alongside Anglo-American culture and societies' long and tortured history with race relations, this complex and often tumultuous period has seen race be redefined, while the socio-economic and political positions of different ethnic groups shifted. We have also witnessed cinema progressing from a technological artifact to a cheap spectacular entertainment for the masses, to a capitalist marvel, to an important ideological and marketing commodity for a global economy. Film scholarship and popular criticism have experienced growth and development as well. Once the domain of cineastes, film criticism and theory's evolution accelerated when it was introduced during the 1960s into the Anglo-American academy, where all research arguably submits to intellectual trends. During key phases of critical race film studies, what we roughly recognize as poststructuralist theory concurrently exuded a powerful presence. As it were, because much of Anglo-American film studies history overlaps temporally with the rise of critical race film studies, prominent themes in one field are predictably reiterated in the other. The key transition from stereotype analysis to discourse analysis reflects theoretical fashions in vogue at the time.

Critical race film studies conducts its business according to changes in the definition and function of race in the social world. In Robyn Wiegman's entry on "Race, Ethnicity, and Film" in *The Oxford Guide to Film Studies*, she writes that "the study of race and ethnicity in film has taken shape according to the formation of race and ethnicity in US culture more widely."[1] To be sure, the dominant definition of race in social discourse has shifted. It was once thought to be biologically determined in the way that skin color is. Subsequently over the course of the twentieth century, people gradually accepted that race is constructed in social practice and cultural discourse, which is where the content of one's character bares itself. It became less about who someone genetically is, and more about what someone culturally does.

Film studies moved as if part of the same constellation. When it became less popular to see race as an inescapable hereditary determinant of character, critical race film scholarship developed a poststructuralist suspicion of essentialism, of cinematic images, and of how they create meaning. Although race began its redefinition decades before the appearance of poststructuralism, similar if not identical political and intellectual tides exerted a force on both race and film. The predictable Marxist thing to say about this evolving landscape is that all politics and theory are intractably governed by economic structural changes, but such materialism is overly convenient and reductive. Nevertheless, how useful is Marxism for explaining these changes? What would Marxians consider to be the consequences of dealing with a film text as an open circuit of fluid discourses? What comes of reforming race into a construct of social discourse? These initial chapters float the possibility that capitalist ideology imposes a measure of its logic and values on this vast network of social and cultural phenomena. More to the point, what is its influence on criticism? The present chapter finds that critical race film studies have marginalized class-based approaches to its analysis, and lays out a prima facie case for Neo-Marxism's primacy within critical race film studies. It does so by finding a familiar, preceptual critical subject within.

Critical race film studies developed in two distinct stages, separated by crucial theoretical essays articulating seminal and frequently cited ideas that sparked turning points. The "images school" that studies stereotypes represents the first phase.[2] Its projects assume correctly that cinema is a powerful circulator of racial discourse, relying on classical realism to reinforce racist ideology. Before too long however, Steve Neale's 1979 essay in *Screen Education*, "The Same Old Story: Stereotypes and Difference" indicated that the method had run its course, and urged writers to change direction.[3] Although brief and lacking specific citations of the literature, Neale's thesis introduced key ideas to the field that remain trenchant. The new approaches that Neale advocated were more fully realized by Robert Stam and Louis Spence in *Screen*. Their essay "Colonialism, Racism and Representation" in fact recapitulates Neale's critique from four years prior.[4] Instead of a preoccupation with the sign, they paid greater attention to "textuality and intertextuality"—the processes by which film constructs point-of-view using the interaction of images through editing or that between a film and other cultural texts. Stam and Spence were eventually joined by deconstructionists and exponents of reception studies, all of whom wanted to leave simplistic stereotype and "positive image" studies behind.

I refer to that "images school" as the "First Generation" of race-oriented film criticism, and to the works that move ahead with Neale's propositions as "Second Generation" criticism. The labels serve two purposes: to order the bodies of work according to chronology and complexity. The point is to emphasize how the field has reached an impasse and been stagnant for quite some time. These labels also offer rhetorical meaning. Proper deference should be paid to the importance of "First Generation" race studies, and the term affords that body of writing a foundational and original status. Examinations of pernicious stereotypes contributed much, and present perhaps the clearest picture of cultural codes and the purest reifications of racist ideology. Likewise, the beginning of "Second Generation" study commemorates the conception of new ideas and the advancement of older ones. However, if we take second-generation criticism to have been birthed with Neale's 1979 essay, I am moved to ask why critics continued to declare image study passé for at least a decade and a half after that. It appears as though the field no doubt progressed rapidly with a burst that lasted through the early 1980s, but has not experienced remotely comparable growth since. With that assessment, I disagree with those such as Wiegman who would argue that we have seen the start of a third generation of criticism, and who consider "the most important critical emphases in the 1990s" to be the study of "whiteness, and ethnicity in the context of global media culture."[5] Those that would be third generation are so similar and implicated with "Second Generation" work, that I am reluctant to accept that they represent headway.

First-generation criticism

Before the Anglo-American academy introduced itself to it, an English art critic, Peter Noble, had already identified the issue of ethnic representation in the cinema some 20-odd years earlier. His 1948 book, *The Negro in Films*, attempts to document a quite comprehensive catalogue of black stereotypes in Hollywood and European films.[6] Noble contextualizes these depictions using a backdrop of social history, connecting the use and reuse of stereotypes to institutionalized racism in the film industry. This classic positive image study decries the association of blacks with intellectual and cultural primitivism and demands more humane and dignified black characters. At the same time, he attributes positive portrayals of black screen characters when they occurred to the personal and professional victories of industry personnel, and occasionally to the organizational strength of civil rights groups such as the National Association for the Advancement of Colored People. Edward Mapp then undertook a similar and slightly more academically oriented project in 1972. In his book, *Blacks in American Films*, Mapp recognizes a small group of unpublished master's theses and doctoral dissertations written in the 1960s that examined limited samples of films. He envisioned his contribution as an addition to Noble's, but without the social history. He compiled another comprehensive list of films that takes particular note of when black actors began to earn leading roles, as well as the professions and personal characteristics of the people they played. Mapp describes his "objective" and "systematic" methodology as one of "informal qualitative content analysis."[7] It turns out to be a scientific-sounding euphemism for a catalog.

The first lengthy piece of first-generation criticism to emerge from the academy was Daniel J. Leab's *From Sambo to Superspade*, out of research he conducted at Columbia University.[8] Compared to what Noble and Mapp had done, this work broke little new conceptual ground, but Leab provides a more detailed industrial history of Hollywood's production and distribution practices. He makes the standard connection between stereotype changes and movements in social mores, and attempts to find empirical causality in the film industry's machinations and interactions with American politics. Perhaps most significant, it articulates that history using a new vocabulary. Leab displays what is up to this point a much keener analytical eye for mise en scène and narrative structure, a likely result of film studies' ascension as a university discipline.

First-generation criticism consists of semantic analysis. Its exponents such as Noble, Mapp, and Leab consider characters or images more or less in isolation from the rest of the text, and decipher what they denote. Basically, they hold that cinematic images possess an indexical significatory relationship to reality. Therefore, films deemed guilty of ideological representation directly reflect the presence of racism. First-generation criticism has much less to say however, about the text as a whole. In this regard, Leab's book stands out to the extent that the author's analytical method accounts for some of cinema's formal and textual complexity. Even so, Neale rightly argues in "The Same Old Story" that limiting analysis to images "can easily obscure or even erase altogether those features of a text and its systems which are not only equally pertinent to the analysis but could also open up further areas of enquiry."[9] He exhibits poststructuralist instincts in faulting stereotype studies for their "inherent empiricism," disputing the belief that both reality and the text itself are straightforwardly knowable. Leading with that initial critique, Neale proceeds to find that critics of stereotypes posit an evaluative standard that is contradictory. He observes them to assume two basic positions on any film. The first measures simple legible stereotypes against a reality that in fact encompasses a much greater "heterogeneity and complexity" of individual characters and experiences. In identifying films that come up short, stereotype critics make an implicit appeal for realism. Indeed, Noble exhibits this tendency perfectly, when he supports his claim that Hollywood films were misrepresenting true reality by citing the numbers of African Americans in the various professions from statistics collected in 1940 by the Bureau of Census Statistics.[10] In a slight variation, Mapp locates the truth not in data but in the experience of the oppressed, when he writes that the issue is "the ability of white film critics to evaluate film portrayals of a black experience, alien to their own existence."[11]

Alternatively, image studies also fault stereotypes for not living up to an ideal. This also adopts an equally inflexible notion of what reality could be as opposed to what it is. Although this perspective posits films as counter-ideological interventions rather than mere reflections on society, Neale points out that the "positive" representations they advocate is an identical solution that is just as limited. "[W]hat is in fact being demanded is the replacement of one set of stereotypes with another."[12] And as a stereotype, it is easily reprocessed into yet another round of first-generation analysis. As long as racism exists, critics of racial representation can rarely find any image quite positive enough. A quote from Leab demonstrates this.

> If box-office returns are to be believed, the new stereotype of Superspade is obviously (and understandably) more pleasing to the black community than was the earlier one. Yet whether Sambo or Superspade, the black image on screen has always lacked the dimension of humanity.[13]

How does Leab define "humanity"? Can we presume that he subscribes to a liberal humanist ideal? The book will return to this question later on, but for now, the stickiness of trying to conceive of ideal representations is clearly illustrated by these conundrums. For instance, Tarantino professed that *Django Unchained* arose out of his hatred of director John Ford for promulgating toxic racial stereotypes.[14] But his attempts to reverse the effect of those images were hardly welcome, nor did they shield him from criticism (Figure 1.1). Take also the difficulties that black filmmaker Oscar Micheaux faced when he tried to tap the African American audience during the late silent and early sound era with racially conscious films centered on the black experience. Micheaux's social conscience was perturbed by hegemonic images routinely appearing in Hollywood films, as his entrepreneurial leanings also drove him to seek profits in the ethnic film exhibition market. A discussion of the racial theories within his oeuvre lies beyond the scope of this project, but Michaeux did consider it important to present ideal representations of middle-class blacks on screen. Although his earlier films experienced some success, he was eventually stymied by competition from the mainstream commercial product. His lack of production values, distribution networks, and advertising budgets became an insurmountable obstacle for his independent work. But it remains clear that one reason he failed lay in the struggle to grasp what an alternative black reality was, much less one that African American audiences would respond to. As historian Thomas Cripps writes,

> Blacks simply did not see *themselves* on the screen—even the screen of Oscar Micheaux. Mere black presence on the screen, reflecting bourgeois white aspiration, no longer was enough. The cinema remained a silent and disused tool.[15]

A similar problem complicates valuations of actor Sidney Poitier, whose fame and stardom in Hollywood were groundbreaking. Defying the buffoonery and

Figure 1.1 Quentin Tarantino's attempt to undo or reverse the racist stereotypes in John Ford's westerns with *Django Unchained* (2012).

indecency that marked southern black stereotypes, he crafted a career as a leading man with a screen persona characterized by intelligence and dignity. But as first-generation critics point out, he became an over-conciliatory symbol of middle-class values and perhaps worse, a parodic modern Uncle Tom. Mapp states that some of his roles lacked fidelity to the real black experience, and in fact criticizes them for being too racially unmarked.[16] Leab laments Poitier's on-screen typage as an emasculated, saintly commercial for civil rights, who was also palatable to white liberals.[17] These are reasonable arguments when considered by themselves, but they are paradoxical and reveal a tendency to think that no image or type is ever satisfactorily positive. Using a more recent example, consider the stereotype inversion in *Lethal Weapon* (1987), whose comedy is based on the conflict between a rigid, suburban black detective Roger Murtaugh (Danny Glover) and his white partner, the crazy, unlawful outcast, Martin Riggs (Mel Gibson). Although Murtaugh is a paragon of WASP virtue, positive image analysis does not perceive progress, but rather, the appearance of a cowardly and domesticated "tamed black man" subordinate to the white cop.[18]

Considering Neale's critique that positive images might not be the cure-all for problems in racial representation, one example of first-generation criticism stands out among the work from that early era. A careful reading of Donald Bogle's *Toms, Coons, Mulattoes, Mammies and Bucks* from 1973 reveals that its title belies how the book strays from conventional image study.[19] It distinguishes itself by problematizing reflectionism and challenging the accepted view of first-generation critics that stereotypes in the cinema have a unidirectional social and cultural impact on the audiences that consume them. Bogle presages Neale's more didactic argument that preferring positive depictions over negative ones only serves to replace one limited representation with another. In fact, he does so with a harsh value judgment of Noble's "typical, unintentionally patronizing, white liberal 'tasteful' approach."[20] In other words, Bogle recognizes that resisting cinematic racism requires more than condemning stereotypes and advocating positive images. As a primary antidote to racist ideology, positive images are both limiting and implicated in the very prejudice it seeks to challenge.

Bogle proposes instead that stereotyped roles are not as self-evident as other first-generation critics presume. For him, films generally considered racist are more open to interpretation than they might seem. Viewers who dismiss stereotypes as completely denigrating "really missed or ignored the strength of those performances, and at the same time denied black America a certain cultural heritage."[21] When black actors were presented with degrading roles as, well, toms, coons, mulattoes, mammies, and bucks, they injected elements of excess like kitsch that elevated the aesthetic value of the performances and provided resistive moments that transcend stereotypes. For example, the dimwits that Stepin Fetchit played, Bogle argues, were the product of comic genius, and in fact so over-exaggerated that they display a distinct measure of irony and detachment. Hattie McDaniel's flamboyant bossiness can be read as the expression of righteous hostility.[22] In these instances, Bogle appears to theorize performance and reception, describing how African American audiences are active readers who do not blindly identify with screen characters, and at times suggesting that film spectators from the past utilized essentially Brechtian reading strategies to enact distance from the text. Twenty years later, Bogle's would have been characterized as a reception study.

By taking broad aim at those who champion positive images, Neale's subsequent contention that "identification as the goal of an artistic practice can never be progressive since it fails to produce knowledge or to allow for the inscription of the potentiality of transformation—both of which are dependent upon the inscription of difference and of distance,"[23] appears to have overlooked Bogle's relatively unconventional thesis. Not even Manthia Diawara's 1986 essay in *Screen* on "Black Spectatorship," which proposes that "black spectators may circumvent identification and resist the persuasive elements of Hollywood narrative and spectacle," accounts for the prescience of Bogle's subtle but perceptible theory of spectatorship. Diawara is not the only one to lump Bogle with Leab, as if they were both (to borrow Neale's words) the same old story.[24] The oversight is then repeated in Stam and Spence's *Screen* essay, "Colonialism, Racism and Representation." They talk about how culturally aware audiences can perform "aberrant readings," but more or less dismiss Bogle's work as a generic stereotype study.[25]

Toms, Coons, Mulattoes, Mammies and Bucks is ahead of its time. Bogle's description of how black performers and filmgoers are alienated by racist stereotypes, and of the various ways that audiences may subvert their effects, implicitly champions a self-aware mode of consumption. While Bogle never uses the terminology as an overt Marxist, he couples alienation and transcendence in a manner that at least forces us to sit up and pay attention. By contrast, V. J. Jerome's *The Negro in Hollywood Films*, first published two years after Noble's book, was a full-throated Marxist critique. As an outspoken communist writer and cultural critic, Jerome argues that stereotypes are not part of a racist ideology, as much as the use of stereotypes is itself an ideology, designed by monopoly capitalist interests as a divisive tool to prevent a national uprising based on class consciousness against capitalism, fascism, and imperialism. He claims that racial controversies over stereotypes serve to splinter civil rights and labor groups, wedging apart black activists and white progressives, and thus preventing the formation of a powerful proletarian movement. Jerome wrote that blacks, preoccupied by white oppression, thus fail to understand "the true basis and nature of their oppression."[26] In his view, earlier virulent black images of "white supremacy" adapted themselves to become "Toms" with the aim of encouraging servility while denigrating social mobility. Films that appeared misleadingly progressive on race in fact laid the roots of black oppression completely at the feet of poor white southerners excluded from the power structure. Jerome's sociological history focuses less on the complexity of how cinema functioned as a text and an institution, than on how social groups react to them. His critique even ensnared a fellow writer. If Jerome is correct and the purpose of racist stereotypes was to ultimately deter materialist class consciousness, Cripps appears to fulfill that prognostication when he disavows efforts to cultivate a labor coalition: "During the depressed thirties blacks became the darlings of the Communist Party so that NAACP picket lines regularly drew white radicals who gave an unwarranted Marxist identity to the blacks and threatened to co-opt the issue."[27] The historian toes the bourgeois establishment line of the NAACP, viewing Marxists as threats to their righteous racial cause.

Jerome's work is not commonly cited by critical race film studies, which might have marginalized it because he did not write from within the academic establishment. In any event, Jerome's materialist concerns went unheeded in favor of race. Bogle is relatively much better known, but the field appears to have misclassified his work as image studies, and failed to register his model of critical spectatorship. In the next section's focus on critical subjectivity's presence in second-generation theory, this misperception is contextualized within the theoretical movement to decenter the subject.

Second-generation criticism

The proliferation of first-generation criticism in the 1970s is understandable given the political and accessible nature of its analysis. It also rose to meet growing interest in image culture, consisting of film and other media such as television and news photography. The range of work produced was broad and often journalistic, moralistic, and evaluative. In comparison, second-generation ideas grew out of an established academic culture, the film studies tradition in particular. Many of its significant advances came in the pages of the scholarly journals *Screen* and *Screen Education*. Writers were obviously interested in studying cinema's relationship to race, but it was not unusual for these essays to be primarily occupied with semiological issues. When the writing took a sharp theoretical turn, poststructuralism was particularly influential. Neale's essay "The Same Old Story" belongs in this category. Its critique presents a corrective to first-generation critical race film scholarship by insisting that analysis should attend to the film "text as a whole and of the global systems that traverse and articulate it." Since stereotypes are always new and different in each and every occurrence, Neale claims that negative images should not be isolated from other aspects of film structure.[28] And although each film might be different and distinctive from every other, it should be understood with regard to the discursive environs beyond the text too. Furthermore, the racism within that discourse is too complex to expect the mere study of stereotypes to illuminate the problem completely. According to Neale, images are only signifiers, but taking in the larger picture can reveal the process of signification, the discursive dynamic of racism. To him, the stereotype as an element of film language should not be seen as unchanging, that is to say, "a stable and repetitive structure of character traits that" that can link "the specific text to other texts and other discursive structures." Rather, he recommends that they be regarded in every specific instance, as part of a "discursive economy" where the difference and variation of their meanings are an intricate part of its fabric." Identifying the racism of a film thus involves seeing "if the discourse through which [the film] is read contains that term and, hence, an explicit or implicit definition of it."[29] These formulations clearly eschew stable and essential knowledge. And by also looking to context for meaning, Neale takes an unmistakably poststructuralist posture.

Neale's designs for a new approach are fully engineered in Stam and Spence's "Colonialism, Racism and Representation." In an introductory critique of preceding methodology, they too question "progressive realism," and hence the processes by which first-generation critics define positive images as good and negative images as conversely bad.[30] Those well-meaning analyses, Stam and Spence repeat, are nonetheless predicated on a bourgeois, paternalistic, and Eurocentric ideal. They essentially agree with Neale's reference to discursive economies or cultural fabrics, in arguing that any analysis must account for a film's "cultural specificity," which would require an awareness of relevant "cultural codes."[31] Stam and Spence also promise more attention to the "*mediations* which intervene between 'reality' and representation," or in other words, cinematic structure, convention, and style.[32] Unlike novels or plays, racism in the film medium possesses a "specifically cinematic" dimension, which in turn produces a unique "paradigmatic perspective."[33] To wit, Stam and Spence sought to examine how cinema's unique language articulates racial ideologies. Using Gillo Pontecorvo's anticolonial masterpiece, *Battle of Algiers* (1966) as a central example, they explain how a film's progressive or regressive attitude vis-à-vis racism can be identified in the discursive mechanisms at work within and without the text. For example, films construct points-of-view using cinematography and editing, to produce "paradigmatic perspectives" that can be divided further into physical and political forms of positioning. If first-generation stereotype studies were semantic, second-generation analysis highlights the power of film's syntax. Physical positioning refers to how spectators' visual perspectives are shaped using a combination of shot scale, mise en scène, music, and point-of-audition sounds. This places viewers in specific spots in the diegetic space. Political positioning pertains to how the same film techniques elicit sympathies and visceral reactions. Together, the resultant point-of-view determines whom audiences are likely to identify with. In *Battle of Algiers*, Stam and Spence discover political rhetoric crafted by the film's refusal to mystify and demonize Algerian rebels as faceless, irrational, and unsympathetic terrorists.

Their exposition of spectator positioning and the cinematic apparatus was followed in *Screen* shortly after by Homi Bhabha's deconstructionist "The Other Question . . .," a key text relied on by numerous works in critical race film studies for its theoretical model of race, cultural discourse, and identity.[34] Bhabha too returns to the stereotype, and although he agrees with Stam and Spence that "fixity" and essential quality of the text deserves poststructuralist scrutiny, he maintains that they do not go far enough to destabilize it. He objects to the fact that "there remains in their essay a limiting and traditional reliance on the stereotype as offering, *at any one time*, a *secure* point of identification."[35] He problematizes the possibility of subjective identification by presuming that the sign is inherently ambivalent, structured only by accepted and not stable truths. Lingering anxiety about stereotypes' truthfulness in turn requires constant discursive repetition and reinforcement. As a result, these representations of the Other are "at once an object of desire and derision, an articulation of difference contained within the fantasy of origin and identity."[36] An unstable sign produces an unstable text, resulting a state of flux that precludes stable subjectivity.

Let us return to Neale's critique and recall that he faulted first-generation criticism for wanting to say two contradictory things: that the stereotype should reflect empirical reality and a progressive ideal. While Neale sees this contradiction as an epistemological aporia and pragmatic crisis, Bhabha would probably consider it a consequence of the "play of difference" intrinsic to the stereotype. He faults Stam and Spence for operating a "passive and unitary notion of suture which simplifies the politics and 'aesthetics' of spectator positioning by ignoring the ambivalent, psychical process of identification."[37] To him, the spectator's relationship to the text is also unstable. He argues that colonial power does not express racism by merely misrepresenting the colonized Other. Rather, it actually imposes an illusory stability onto fluid fields of meaning. Alternatively, colonial discourse "is an apparatus that turns on the recognition and disavowal of racial/cultural/historical differences," hence arresting the process of subjectification.[38] Because colonial discourse articulates differences in predominantly sexual and racial terms, Bhabha likens the process to that at the scene of fetishism, where there is "a reactivation of the material of original fantasy . . . as well as a normalization of that difference and disturbance in terms of the fetish object as the substitute for the mother's penis." He thus compares the stereotype to a fetish, for doing so will illuminate the "productive ambivalence of colonial discourse," reveal its boundaries, and eventually enable "a transgression of these limits from the space of that otherness."[39]

Deconstructionist theory that attempted to lay bare the ambivalence of colonial discourse attracted others in critical race film studies, among them Richard Dyer. He expanded "White," a seminal 1988 essay in *Screen* studying white identity in cinema, into a book almost a decade later.[40] Dyer's analysis of whiteness would seem to pick up on Bhabha's claim that colonial stereotypes are "complex, ambivalent [and] contradictory."[41] Tilting that form of scrutiny onto whiteness, Dyer examines the connection between how it is signified and how that manner of signification produces a structural privilege in racial discourse. It is a position on the ethnic stereotype that follows Bhabha's; he observes that its power can be located in the ability to stabilize the sign of nonwhiteness. Dyer points out that whiteness's real power stems from its freedom to exist as an unquestioned paradox—"it both is and is not a colour, is and is not a tangible sign."[42] This capacity to exist and operate in an invisible dimension is also alluded to by postcolonial studies scholar Edward Said, whose book *Orientalism* examines the perceived neutrality of colonial discourse. Dyer avers that white masculinity in particular, has a "divided nature," contradictory in the manner that it encompasses a multitude of signs along scales of both race and gender: light and dark, masculine and feminine. It is "exceptional, excessive, marked" yet also "non-extreme, unspectacular, plain," and ordinary.[43] From this highly fluid and multifaceted state, it reaches ideological stability not by repressing excess signification, for that would deny whiteness its most potent power. Rather, it does so by denying all signification, thus adopting the character of emptiness.

If Neale chided image studies for not explaining how racism actually works, Bhabha takes a credible stab at it. But I argue that the latter's basic methodology leads to some striking paradoxes that set the stage for the rest of this chapter. His appropriation of psychoanalysis leads us possibly to a point of psychic origin, ostensibly within the unified individual subject who is able to observe the stereotype's vacillations. Bhabha contends that the colonizer does not control all colonial power and discourse because he cannot determine interpretation absolutely. The way to attack colonial ideology is to take advantage of signs' inherent instability and produce subversive readings, which is a task left to the critical individual subject. Writing about Mexican American identity and film, Juan J. Alonso has highlighted this issue in Bhabha's schema as well, but he defines that agential subject a bit differently. Alonso sees it as an ethnically delimited one whose identity is socially constructed by cultural practices and social conditions.[44] With this book, I take an extra leap in identifying this individual as a Neo-Marxian critical subject, then proceeding to employ that precept to prosecute a case for historical materialism. What is more, Bhabha happens to leave a materialist notion of reality available.

> The strategic articulation of 'coordinates of knowledge'—racial and sexual— and their inscription in the play of colonial power as modes of differentiation, defense, fixation, hierarchisation, is a way of specifying colonial discourse which would be illuminated by reference to Foucault's post-structuralist concept of the *dispositif* or apparatus.[45]

He refers to colonial *discourse* as something that is evidently separate from colonial *power*. He could have specifically defined the material conditions of that power, military or imperial, as discursively contingent, but does not. The fact that the "coordinates of knowledge" are drawn on racial and sexual axes indicates that there is a material reality in which this "play" of signification and subjectivities exists.

The importance of materialism is made clear when we apply Bhabha's method to think about *The Karate Kid* (1984), a film that is important in its own way, so popular that it is now part of the cultural lexicon. The film mixes cultural markers together. Like the eponymous martial art, the protagonist's mentor is Japanese and played by the Japanese American actor Pat Morita. But some Asian viewers could discern that he was drilling his protégé in Chinese kung-fu techniques. The 2010 remake is set in China and starred Hong Kong action star Jackie Chan but keeps the original title, and the contradiction. Ideas of ambivalence and significatory excess are immensely applicable here, where an incompatible cluster of fetishized Asian signifiers is forcibly bound to these fantasies of an imagined Asian Other. Yet the analysis is incomplete without gazing as well at the political economic context accompanying both films. The 1984 film's preponderant Japaneseness and the 2010 version's Sino-spectacle point directly to American anxieties over the respective economic challenges posed by these two countries during those periods.

If power is empirically wielded in reality, it becomes germane to consider cinema's economic and political structures. Two kinds of cinema and their modes of production raise relevant questions that should discourage us from overstating textual ambiguity as an avenue to ideological subversion. The first case is classical Hollywood cinema, especially since a work such as Ruth Vasey's *The World According to Hollywood* has described how it deliberately left films open to multiple interpretations in order to bypass censors and to maximize the market for broad-based consumption of the product. Raising the ire of foreign governments or ethnic social activists could impact a film's distribution, especially abroad. To lessen the chance that they would protest unfavorable representations of their nationalities or cultures, the studios developed a "principle of deniability" predicated on constructing an "ambiguous text."[46] Racial, ethnic, and cultural markers were often stripped of specificity as a shrewd strategy of political correctness. By using textual ambiguity to its advantage, classical Hollywood's capitalist regime stayed ahead of the game. Admittedly, this dated Hollywood practice does not necessarily invalidate Bhabha's arguments regarding ideology's function to suppress the contingency of the sign and the text. And it is not to say that anyone is going to confuse a Hollywood production, even with all the ambiguity one can imagine, with an avant-garde piece of ethno-deconstructive filmmaking such as Trinh Minh-ha's experimental documentary *Reassemblage* (1982). However, the strength of Bhabha's theory depends on its applicability to mainstream film, a model that Vasey's analysis partly dampens. In the final analysis, how distinguishable is the distinction between Bhabha's "ambivalence" and Hollywood's "ambiguity"? Hollywood's conscientious construction of indeterminacy can for all intents and purposes be identical to what Bhabha believes is the stereotype's "overdetermined" quality.[47] Can a radical reading really open up the playing field, or do we sometimes still find ourselves on the same turf laid down by the culture industry?

Bhabha's theory is also problematic for the polemical film that relies on realism as a political aesthetic, which is to say that it assumes the presence of unified, fixed, essential, and knowable categories such as nation, culture, or author. Indigenous films, Third Cinema, and expository documentaries are such genres. For a film like that, a deconstructive reading would open up the text, but would it not also disempower it and the author, in effect silencing the Other who has seized control of the mode of production? As Valerie Smith writes, black cinema is defined by the blackness of its authors.

> To the extent that it seeks to replace 'false' representations with positive, by extension 'true' or 'authentic' ones, the project of black film might thus be read as the search for an authentic black subject.[48]

With a slightly divergent view, Stuart Hall also touches upon this uneasy relationship between realism and poststructuralism.[49] He writes that the postcolonial film should not be read as a "second-order mirror held up to reflect" black diasporic identity. The variety of experiences within the black diaspora is contingent on specific social, political, and economic histories of migration. "Blackness" therefore does not have a stable meaning. If anything, he posits the theme of displacement as a common quality in those experiences and thus in black postcolonial films as well. Film images in Caribbean cinema specifically, enable postcolonial subjects to see and recognize fragments of their histories and to subsequently constitute their identity. Hall sees cultural identity as both fixed (and therefore representable) and contingent (unrepresentable), striking a fuzzy compromise in stating that the contingency only "qualifies" but does not displace the fixity of black diasporic identity.[50] As long as this position is unresolved, the intelligibility of the postcolonial artist's voice hangs in the balance. What is therefore continually at stake, in other words, is the all-important status of the individual subject.

Hall's thinking on an identity's contingency is shared by *Identities in Motion*, where Peter X. Feng's psychoanalytic method offers a similar perspective of cinema's relationship with identity.[51] Feng argues that cinema does not construct an identity that spectators either adopt or disavow. He posits instead that cinema refers to reality in a series of discontinuous representations that mobilize within spectators a formation of their ethnic and cultural identity. For Asian Americans in particular, it is an identity that is constantly "in motion"—diverse, contingent, and contradictory. Feng compares those identities to a heterogeneous collection of Asian American films, where he finds an innate awareness of and continual negotiation with Asian American social and political history. To sustain his trope of being in motion and contingent, Feng finds recourse in the work of Bhabha and Mikhail Bakhtin. Yet, in assembling a vast array of films from a great range of film genres and cinematic traditions, and in identifying the multivocal nature of the voices that can be heard articulating within each text, Feng finds his way through it all by returning to unified subjectivity in the form of authorship. *Identities in Motion* prefaces every film analysis with a biographical sketch of its author. So even when the Asian American filmmaker is assumed to possess a nonessential racial subjectivity, the artistic vision is still assumed to be relevant and of value, in some degree unified and autonomous.

That contradiction can be illustrated with the example of director Spike Lee, who I reckon shares that position with Feng. *Do the Right Thing* (1989) for example, concurs on the issue of identity. The film is oversaturated with signification, which reminds us that racial identity is contingent and constituted by these signs: kente colors, clothing, cultural iconography, and language. The glaring montage of racial slurs run off by characters from different races, do not just distance the audience because of their direct address, it forcibly separates discourse from reality (Figure 1.2). The film's jarring cinematography, audible jazz soundtrack, and psychologically ambiguous characters also serve to alienate. But while the openness of *Do the Right Thing* does all it can to destabilize conceptions of race, it belies Lee's unremitting faith in the unity of his authorial subjectivity, and assumes an equal amount of closure in that of his nemesis, Quentin Tarantino. These convictions coat his identity as an African American filmmaker, and are the premise of his objection to Tarantino's audacity to explore black identity in *Django Unchained*. How open and mobile can identities be if Tarantino's whiteness categorically shuts him off from interjecting in black discourse?

The author figure feels very much alive within these works of second-generation criticism. It undermines poststructuralist thought and prompts us to theorize unified subjectivity. Jacqueline Stewart's *Migrating to the Movies* joins Feng's reliance on individual subjectivity as well.[52] Wishing to counter inclinations to see African Americans as being passively objectified, Stewart

Figure 1.2 With direct address, Spike Lee's *Do the Right Thing* (1989) alienates viewers from racial discourse.

reminds us that they have consistently challenged racist representations of themselves as "*subjects* of their own history with mass culture."[53] She describes in equal measure how they have done so through both spectatorship and filmmaking, as "*individuals* and communities."[54] In much the same way, Daniel Bernardi's recent anthology *Filming Difference* resuscitates the significance of authorship with a collection of interviews with filmmakers. As he explains, cinema's persuasive power travels through personal communications between filmmakers and spectators. Films are pedagogical expressions that can alter perceptions and thus produce social change.[55] If the final question for films and the criticism they engender is their impact on the real world—how it can battle racism—then the only conduits between the text and social change are people, individuals who are somehow transformed. It is they who translate ontological and semiological debates into political change. By themselves, texts do not enact the final result. It is thus paramount to reflect on how spectators relate with and respond to films.

A foremost issue for reception studies is thus identification. Neale again displays foresight when he argues that complete spectatorial identification implies passivity, and thus "can never be progressive since it fails to produce knowledge or to allow for the inscription of the potentiality of transformation."[56] Unfortunately, he did not theorize active spectatorship much further than that. Although Stam and Spence elaborated on what Neale termed "the text as whole" by elucidating film's textual syntax, they still, as Bhabha concludes perhaps too harshly, espouse a fixed model of subject positioning and "aberrant readings." To counter, Bhabha splits or destabilizes the sign and builds on a call for active spectatorship. He advocates for a deconstructive reading strategy that prefigures a psychic rebellion that presumably precedes a material one. This is a key step. His idea of transgressive subjectivity makes visible the separation within the process of signification;[57] visible that is, to the critical spectator mindful of how reality is represented by textual discourse. Who else is there but such a subject to liberate the text's inherently multiple meanings from ideological suppression?

Stewart picks up where Bhabha left off, rendering a model of split subjectivities, between which black spectators "shift" and "oscillate," "creating a radically broadened freedom of identification."[58] Compared to Bhabha's psychoanalytic-deconstructive reading and Dyer's cultural studies approach, Stewart implements an interdisciplinary research method that harvests sociological conclusions from black literature. She draws a contrast between her argument and those from Diawara, James Snead, and bell hooks who merely point out the representational and ideological contradictions between films' white spectator positions and the black experience as an either/or proposition. She persuasively suggests that black spectators do not simply resist identification with oppositional readings, nor are they denied pleasure.[59] Instead, she argues that they shift fluidly between opposition and assimilation, identification and rejection, and even "between the imaginary space of the screen and the social space of the theater," resulting in a unique "array of cinematic pleasures."[60] Where else but within a unified consciousness, and who else but a critical subject can perform these oscillations?

Migrating to the Movies observes the nature of how black spectatorship was configured by the African American experience in Chicago after the Great Migration of 1916–19. Migrant southerners were brought into an encounter with modernity, but their presence in the city heightened the self-consciousness of the black bourgeoisie and petit bourgeoisie, who had struggled mightily for their social standing. Within the cinema, that anxiety manifested itself in the unease with rowdy rural and working-class blacks who did not conform to middle-class norms of silent reception.[61] All African Americans however, dealt universally with segregation and racism. In the face of these repressions and oppressions, Stewart marshals Miriam Hansen to argue that the cinema provided a "public sphere" in which marginalized, alienated, and fragmented blacks "could reconstitute themselves in(to) new public formations."[62] Black theaters offered

African Americans "reconstructed spectatorship"—the chance to become subjects of cinematic address, to experience a range of pleasures from complete identification to rejection of the screen's images, as well as the option to connect with a group identity that was familiar and new. In segregated theaters, black spectators were forced to increase their levels of black consciousness because Hollywood films centralized and celebrated whiteness while the exhibition space was configured to reinforce that ideological regime.

Whereas Bhabha only implied the need for a critical spectator who could appreciate the process of signification, Stewart is more explicit. Pressures of the black experience as she described it conferred on the African Americans concerned a "critical" and "cultivated distance."[63] Read in context with her simultaneous invocation of Jürgen Habermas's "public sphere" (by way of Hansen's reading of Habermas), we can sense Neo-Marxism nearing the vicinity. To invoke Habermas also hails Theodor Adorno via their common views on subjectivity, and while Adorno would abhor the validity of a reconstituted (American) public sphere as such, he would accept a theory of individuality.[64] Consider too, Feng's return to the author as the source of critical cultural intervention, Diawara's promotion of "active criticism" and for that matter, Jacqueline Bobo's model of spectatorship in *Black Women as Cultural Readers*, where an interplay of subjective historical discourses influence the way an audience *constructs* meaning.[65] Indeed, Bobo's viewer is able to "negotiate" the text and to control "their reactions" to mainstream cultural forms and to others' opinions about how they should react.[66] From all these second-generation models of spectatorship, ironically emerges a clear outline of what Adorno calls an autonomous subject, humanistically defined, capable of critical distance, negation, reason, perhaps even dialectical thinking when confronted by ideology and films. In spite of unstable texts, open processes of interpretation, dynamic discourses, and fluid spectatorial positions on poststructuralism's itinerary, critical race film studies still retains the idea that resistance and transformation require as its precondition, a unified subject operating outside of discourse. Edward Said, whose influence on film studies is visited later, pronounces these faculties differently and more critically—in terms of "forms and values" within texts that are "essential" for readers to engage in.

> The indeterminacy of deconstructive reading, the airy insouciance of postaxiological criticism, the casual reductiveness of some (but by no means all) ideological schools are principally at fault. While it is true to say that because a text is the product of an unrecapturable past contemporary criticism can to some

extent afford a neutral disengagement or opposed perspective impossible for the text in its own time, there is no reason to take the further step and exempt the interpreter from any moral, political, cultural or psychological commitments.[67]

Poststructuralist critical race film theory does not insist on those exemptions—it indeed counts on those "commitments." From another point of view, perhaps the persistence of these tropes suggests that Marxist humanism has to a degree been recast into a language that outwardly appears to oppose its reductive nature. Let me conclude cautiously. I do not claim that these writers are closeted Marxists. But what we have before us are not random tealeaves either. Rather, the incomplete, fossilized skeleton of a Neo-Marxian subject has been unearthed underneath a mass of contradiction, of which we have enough to move forward with inductive projections.

In summary, critical race film studies shed its sponsorship of first-generation progressive realism after understandable challenges from poststructuralism. From that moment on, its development in the 1990s took place on several fronts. Wiegman declares that the most significant critical breakthroughs for the decade took place in whiteness, ethnicity in the context of global media culture, and independent film.[68] Dyer led the way on whiteness studies, which I show to be an outgrowth of second-generation poststructuralism. Ethnicity and global media culture is a field dominated by essentially one book, Ella Shohat and Robert Stam's *Unthinking Eurocentrism*.[69] Independent filmmaking is important for the opportunity it offers the marginalized to express authentic voices that oppose ideological discourse. But as this chapter points out, authenticity is irreconcilable with decentered or split subjectivity. The field forcibly resolves the contradiction, however, with identity politics. Later in this chapter, we see how that political paradigm applies to whiteness studies and *Unthinking Eurocentrism* as well. However, the subject active in identity politics is not equivalent to the autonomous Neo-Marxian one. Nor are identity politics compatible with the Marxist faith in grand narratives. Identity politics are not the answer: they are divisive, hinder collective radicalism, and very possibly slow methodological progress.

The quagmire of identity politics gives some explanation for why despite significant strides, critical race film theory has been at an impasse. For example, the past decade has continued to witness frequent appearances of works that cling mightily to first-generation studies. In ways that are sometimes more obvious than others, these analyses continue to adopt the methods that second-generation writers like Neale have convincingly refuted. Liberalism and political correctness can be credited for positive representations these days, but film images and narratives are still held up against reality and criticized as "illusions" or "myths" if they seem to express either fantasies or fears.[70] And perhaps no "critical race" area retains an empiricist approach more than Native American criticism. As a whole, it consists almost solely of first-generation analysis. Michael Hilger's *From Savage to Nobleman* chronicles the Hollywood image of Native Americans distorted by "white American attitudes and values," with a comprehensive list of plot summaries and shot descriptions. The pervasive stereotype prompts the author to call for more "positive and realistic images of Native Americans."[71] Another book, *Hollywood's Indian* is an anthology of semi-structuralist essays focusing also on the American Western genre. It too is continually concerned with "accuracy," "authenticity," and truth in Hollywood's misconception of frontier history. Jacquelyn Kilpatrick's *Celluloid Indians* looks at how films stack up to reality as well, though she tries to differentiate her work from those "caught up in questions of 'correctness,'" "authenticity," and "historical accuracy." Drawing a fine line between those who do image studies and herself, Kilpatrick sets out to judge the realness of films' historical and sociological constructions—in other words, the social, ideological, and political history behind Native American stereotypes.[72]

From another area, Ed Guerrero's *Framing Blackness* sees the "potent ingredients of a system of social and racial signification" as the combined result of Hollywood aesthetics, economics, and politics. He tries to understand how "the recurrence of certain resilient stereotypes" and the underrepresentation of "the emotional and intellectual complexity of black life" can be corrected by a situation where blacks can find "their full potential and humanity on the big screen."[73] His concerns still center on how limited stereotypes are misrepresenting black reality. In a footnote used to cite Stam and Spence, he states:

> Many writers are now calling for a move beyond the 'reductionism' of focusing the examination of cinematic racism on stereotyping alone. They discuss the need to look at other 'mediations' and at how the 'cinematic apparatus' as a whole structures racism into its operations.[74]

The "now" he refers to here occurred 10 years earlier, and about 15 years of poststructuralist criticism is reduced to a footnote. Meanwhile, a popular anthology and university textbook published contemporaneously says about image studies: "the most current thinking exists in the earliest phase."[75] There is little reason why critical race film theory should still be running on ideas defined by Neale, Stam, Spence, and Bhabha, all published between 1979 and 1983, a fecund segment of time that is now much closer to the field's inception than it is to the present. Yet the continuing popularity of image analysis and its attendant reflectionism is undeniable, and its presence can be noted in academic writing as well as in public discourse. Its appeal, though, is understandable. Ever so often, the news will cover a protest of a film or television show that deigns to use negative stereotypes. First-generation analysis is accessible and offers the primary way that the public understands the question of racial ideology in the media. By anecdotal observation, these books on images and representation remain the most republished, worn, and dog-eared items on library shelves. But although this is an undeniable pedagogical triumph for first-generation criticism's politics, is there at the same time resistance to move on from it? The next step must be to move the tenets of second-generation thought into public consciousness. Stewart (and probably Bhabha) would suggest that it can train subjects to be more active and negational.[76]

Separate and equal: The impact of identity politics

When director George Lucas resurrected the *Star Wars* blockbuster franchise with the first of a trilogy of prequels, *Star Wars Episode I: The Phantom Menace* (1999), fans devoted to the original series did not completely warm to the digitally animated buffoon, Jar Jar Binks. Many thought that the creature was annoying and unfunny, but among the most vociferous critics were those who argued that its mannerisms unearthed memories of old African American stereotypes, a mélange of Sambo, pimp characters, and the minstrelsy of actor Stepin Fetchit. Other creatures such as the unscrupulous rhino-abundant and Yiddish-accented junk dealer Watto also aroused suspicions of anti-Semitism. The production company Lucasfilm defended the characters, suggesting that oversensitive critics were reading too much into fictional creations for a fantasy world. The controversy did little to hamper the movie's commercial success, but the charge of racism lingered into the next installment, *Attack of the Clones* (2002). This time, consternation arose about two characters, bounty hunter Jango Fett and his son Boba Fett played by New Zealand Maori actors Temuera

Morrison and Daniel Logan. While Jar Jar Binks was a new addition to the series, Boba Fett is a revered character whose origin story was eagerly awaited by fans. The ensuing reaction to Fett's "ethnicity" is thus separable from any aversion that many felt toward Jar Jar Binks as an unwelcome character in the mythology. To discuss the film's racial stereotyping *The Detroit News* convened a panel of academics and social leaders, whose opinions provoked a minor furor.[77] The news story reported Latino concern that Morrison and Logan's dark features "looked Latino." Some panelists argued that when Jango Fett is cloned in the plot to create a swarthy army of imperial soldiers, the film is essentially tapping into American paranoia regarding illegal immigration from Latin America (Figure 1.3). An Arab-American activist in the group differed, asserting that Jango Fett was not Latino, but in fact Arabic, and that the film was expressing post-9/11 anti-Arab prejudice. (Figure 1.4). After the article was published, online message boards devoted to the film lit up with incredulous fans, most of whom considered the panel's reactions misguided and a symptom of political correctness run amok.

The racial connotations identified by the panel might all be circulating in the film. Jar Jar Binks presents a sufficiently persuasive example to validate the new accusations, and the *Star Wars* series as a whole has delivered much grist for the mill of critical race studies. But the incident is more interesting in how it exemplifies the politics and methods of critical race film criticism, particularly the influence of identity politics, the political and theoretical consequences of which are the focus here. The liberty with which the critics appropriated the text also reflects poststructuralist success in decentering the text's origins,

Figure 1.3 Cloned soldiers in *Star Wars: Attack of the Clones* (2002), interpreted as an allegory for undifferentiated masses of brown immigrants.

Figure 1.4 Depending on identity politics, Maori actors (Temuera Morrison and Daniel Logan) were taken to be Latino and Arab. (*Star Wars: Attack of the Clones,* 2002).

empowering readers and locating meaning in the act of interpretation. Few panelists, if any, were constrained or fazed by the actors' Maori descent that the film made no attempt to disguise, and each felt free to wrench aspects of the film, like faces, accents, and dialogue, and then place them onto alternative contexts that created specific meanings for different ethnic groups. Elsewhere, Gabriel S. Estrada's Coyote-inflected take on the movies led him to call Jango Fett "the ultimate *coyotl*."[78] I am not inclined to diminish or dismiss these readings as others have, but take them for metacritical value.[79]

Poststructuralism has come to inhabit critical race film criticism in other ways, namely in redefining race as a social construction, and in the currency that Homi Bhabha's ideas of decenteredness has earned among subsequent studies in the field. As this book observed earlier, his preclusion of unified subjectivity problematically contradicts the implicit presence of one that is required to activate or perceive a stereotype's inherent instability. This parallels another logical knot that is created when assuming that race is a slippery discursive manifestation, because that generates friction with critical race theory's belief that race is also coherent enough to ground a unique experience and to form an identity, on which to establish a movement's oppositional actions and voices. The gist of what critical race theorists Richard Delgado and Jean Stefancic call a "somewhat uneasy tension with anti-essentialism" is referred to by Chicano film historian Chon Noriega as a paradox in critical discourse.[80] Noriega cites Rosaura Sánchez's materialist protestation that the "questioning and subsequent denial of the subject comes precisely at a moment in history when women and marginalized ethnic minorities are trying to assume their subject status to create a voice for themselves," before subsequently placing his faith for Chicano scholarship "in the uncharted spaces between cultural affirmation and the decentered subject." Likewise, Juan J. Alonso acknowledges the contradiction, but by remaining loyal to the concept of split subjectivity, he too dwells in that uncharted space. I agree with Noriega's point of view, it is an unresolved paradox. But critical race film theory has flattened the incongruity by participating in identity politics, where the subject status sought by Sánchez is a smaller and more confined racial one. That hermeneutic model was clearly at play among the critics impaneled by *The Detroit News*, since their different readings of Jango Fett's physiognomy corresponded with the identity and interests of the person who voiced them. Each was staking out a subjective space within the film's address.

Inheriting critical race theory's mode of ethnic affirmation along with the waning of its "realist" wing, critical race film studies rests similarly on racial consciousness, leading to ethnocentric paradigms at the expense of class consciousness. The elision of V. J. Jerome's study from the recognized canon of stereotype studies endorses that view. Beyond the academy in the public sphere, the same tendency manifests itself in the form of identity politics, which prefers smaller projects tactically designed to resist the oppression of groups divided along racial and gender lines, over a unified strategy against material systems behind social inequality. Identity politics unites people on the basis of shared recognition and common experiences that bond members of the group. Black activism for example, arises to counter discrimination of African Americans. Exclusionism forms the basis of identity politics, which stoked the indignation that director Spike Lee expressed about Quentin Tarantino's temerity to write African American history through a spaghetti-Western-slave-revenge movie, *Django Unchained*. The furor that Lee helped to ignite carried over to the larger conversation. Black critics who praised or liked the film had their racial identity challenged. African American commentators repeatedly wrote with great interest about the black reception for the film. One academic review even scrutinized the eponymous hero's seeming indifference to the suffering of other black characters (Figure 1.5).[81]

Identity politics can of course be class-based too. The working class can organize itself into a labor movement, and membership in that class is a form of identity. But identity politics are not commonly associated with class politics as much as with race, gender, and sexuality. Relatively newer movements mobilized around disability and neurodiversity do not buck that trend either.

Figure 1.5 One critic lamented that Django rode off and left fellow slaves behind without arming them or even looking back. Where's his black consciousness? (*Django Unchained*, 2012).

The Marxist critique of identity politics sounds a lot like Jerome's stand in *The Negro in Hollywood Films*, where he argues that race is an instrument of division exploited by capitalist interests to forestall class consciousness. This line of attack rues that identity politics are not truly radical and serve capitalist interests by marginalizing materialist critiques and exacerbating social divisions among labor. Political theorist Wendy Brown draws from Fredric Jameson to accuse identity politics of sacrificing the capacities for temporal and spatial mapping, for the more perceptible reassurance of situation and positioning. In other words, identity politics offer the comfort of filiation and community instead of "modernist communities producing collective identity" that can conduct more cutting critiques of the material world. They are therefore more allied with liberal interest group politics than with Marxian class analysis. The commodified cultures of postmodernity, Brown warns, not only subsume identity politics into its "ruptures and disorienting effects" but also displace class consciousness onto social awareness other than class.[82]

Meanwhile, in defense of politics of difference, Ernesto Laclau and Chantal Mouffe point out that identity politics are a necessary modern response when social identity and conflict are no longer fundamentally formed or played out on the axis of one's class position. Having contracted due to increased mobility, the modern world now consists essentially of "permanently changing conditions which constantly require the construction of new systems of differences." With the possibility of a fixed identity based on class rapidly foreclosing, what remains is a nexus of fluid, multiple, and often antagonistic discourses. Under these circumstances, Laclau and Mouffe claim that identity politics are inevitably more handy.[83] We thus arrive at mutually reinforcing claims. Identity politics are naturally deployed to repress theoretical contradictions, precisely because identity politics are also poststructuralism's symptomatic manifestation in modern political praxis.

The debate between materialists and poststructuralists over identity politics provides a general context for trends within both critical race film studies as well as for events in the real world of political action. As an example of the latter, the Occupy Movement sadly appears on its way to becoming a historical blip. The streets are clear and the American electorate returned Barack Obama to office for another round of neoliberal economic policy. But would it really be too glib to point out that he was re-elected with difference-making support from minority groups and women? The Occupy movement proved that class consciousness is at least possible and that a materialist understanding of Late Capitalism is entirely accessible. A sizable audience did indeed grasp their place within "the 99%." Marxist analysis, it seems, is more relevant for the present time than ever before. But if the accounts linking Occupy's splintering to the tensions and disparate demands among different interest groups are true, the Marxist warnings about identity politics' folly only strengthen. What this precedent augurs for critical race film studies is foreboding.

Once again, it would be simplistic to partition poststructuralism, identity politics, and postmodernism on one side, from Marxism, humanism, and essentialism on another. Identity politics run contrary to poststructuralists' ontological opposition to coherent subjectivities. But I highlight the tacit support for identity politics among poststructuralist works in critical race film studies in order to once more point out Bhabha's basic contradiction regarding subjectivity. Undeniably in any event, identity politics now plays a major role in organizing and shaping critical race film studies. How has the field been served by it? Practicing the politics of difference insulates ethnic subfields from each other, as illustrated in the following example. For all the salience of Neale's 1979 essay, "The Same Old Story," it is uncannily similar to a work of feminist film criticism written by Diane Waldman from the previous year in *Jump Cut*, titled "There's More to a Positive Image than Meets the Eye."[84] They are not identical but contain substantial overlap. Waldman responds specifically to Linda Artel and Susan Wengraf's book about gender stereotypes, *Positive Images,* and to other image studies. Waldman levels much the same charges that Neale articulates and oddly, in the same order. Where Neale argues that "the problem with [measuring the stereotype against what is conceived of as 'the real'] is its inherent empiricism" and where he speaks of a converse position which differs "in that it measures the stereotype not against 'the real' but against an 'ideal,'" Waldman had written, "we must ask, in ascribing 'positive characteristics' to certain depictions are we claiming a truth value for them? Do they depict things as they really are or as we think they should be?" Both writers then extrapolate the issue to discuss the process of viewer identification. Neale proclaims, "my own view is that identification as the goal of an artistic practice can never be progressive since it fails to produce knowledge or to allow for the inscription of the potentiality of transformation." And for Waldman, "if the mechanism of identification goes unchallenged, how are students to distinguish between 'positive' and 'negative' images?"[85] The strangest commonality comes at the ends of both essays, when Neale and Waldman stress the importance of incorporating stereotype analysis into a larger study of the discursive economy where ideology functions, by quoting the same paragraph from an even earlier feminist essay by Elizabeth Cowie in *Screen Education*, "Women, Representation and the Image."

> Sexism in an image cannot be designated materially as a content in the way that denotative elements such as colours or objects in the image can be pointed to. Rather it is in the development of new or different definitions and understandings of what men and women are and their roles in society which produce readings of images as sexist; the political perspective of feminism produces a further level of connotative reading.[86]

Although Cowie's primary concern was patriarchy and sexism, she intended for her discussion to be applicable to issues in racial representation as well. She embeds the political thrust of her argument in a dialogue on semiotics centered on Roland Barthes's "The Rhetoric of the Image," and takes issue with his notion of the "non-coded iconic message." She denies that meanings can possess either a literal quality or anchorage, and seeks to replace ideas of "denotative" meaning with "connotative" ones, within a hermeneutic model of interpretive "production within the image and beyond," anchored only when those reading strategies are at work.[87] Cowie's contribution can thus be considered a junction of sorts, coming as it were on the heels of Claire Johnston's 1975 meditation in *Screen* about the positive image analyses by Marjorie Rosen in 1973 and Molly Haskell's 1974 book *From Reverence to Rape,* followed by the poststructuralist psychoanalytic theory from Laura Mulvey that would depart from all of them.

After Cowie, the exploration of identities' ontology and semiology splinters into parallel highways used independently by race and gender.[88]

Introducing his essay about "Black Spectatorship," Manthia Diawara correctly observes that film theory that had "begun to focus on issues of sexuality as well as gender" use a prevailing approach centered on psychoanalytic readings that "has remained colour-blind."[89] An implication of that statement is that applying the same models to study race would manufacture new knowledge. However, the redundancy of work carried out among insulated subfields and identified earlier, might cast some doubt. Feminist and racial approaches are not all that different if they nurture similar ideas in unison. In her survey of film studies' engagement with race, Robyn Wiegman already points out that the study of race and ethnicity in film is geared to the discrete histories and political projects of specific identity sites instead of as a pan-ethnic agenda against white supremacy.[90] The fragmentation is evident to anyone who cares to stroll through the film studies section in a university library, where books about various ethnicities line up on different shelves. The Dewey Decimal System helps produce this visual array, but Wiegman's point is well taken. Critical race film scholars also self-identify according to the same classifications, and write from perspectives defined by particular racial identities. But would critical race film studies not stand to benefit from a stronger sense that the subfields are working collectively, sharing ideas and constructing pan-ethnic methodologies? Demonstrating the importance, David Palumbo-Liu shows how crucial it is to understand Asian American stereotypes in relation to other ethnic representations. The "model minority" myth is inherently connected to black stereotypes because its currency swelled during the upheavals and African American pushes for civil rights in the 1960s. It served to instruct other minorities to emulate Japanese American assimilation, since their success "proved" that urban poverty and violence were the result of personal weakness and not institutional racism or economic violence.[91] It is thus possible to further refine Wiegman's statement, in that a pan-ethnic agenda can radicalize a critique of both white supremacy and the economic substructure.

If we question why such projects do not materialize more frequently, potential clues ironically lie nestled within what has been attempted in this regard. Two magisterial volumes fall into this category, Richard Dyer's *White* and Ella Shohat and Robert Stam's *Unthinking Eurocentrism*. In one form or another, both sanction multiculturalism's hegemony, trusting that it could be part of a solution when it is an ideology that unfortunately helps to maintain the status quo's predilection for identity politics. Insights from another discipline, political theory, suggest that it is impossible to endorse multiculturalism without also acquiescing to identity politics.

Dyer in fact rejects the politics of difference, fearing that *White* would be hijacked by white male paranoia, then wedged under "White Studies" and inserted into identity politics.[92] This is why he assiduously avoids constructing a typology of white representations. *White* idealizes "postmodern multiculturalism" somewhat, and "genuine hybridity, multiplicity without hegemony" as well, which in light of Dyer's abhorrence of centrality and authority, makes "postmodern" the operative term. When he criticizes discourses of whiteness for lending whites the ability "to speak for the commonality of humanity," he does not mean that whites should not have that privilege, but rather that no one can or should possess it.[93] Accordingly, *Unthinking Eurocentrism* subscribes to a radicalized political-theoretical model, "polyvalent multiculturalism," one that accounts for social power and histories of oppression in ways that traditional multiculturalism does not. Shohat and Stam also lean on it to transcend narrow definitions of identity politics because it enables more affiliations and shared identifications across cultures.[94] Like Dyer therefore, Shohat and Stam share a hope that their iteration of multiculturalism can avoid identity politics, this time by folding Bakhtinian theory into an unrelenting faith in poststructuralist views on language and representation. Ultimately, neither makes a convincing case to have had threaded that needle.

Unthinking Eurocentrism lays bare Eurocentric constructions with an awe-inspiring offering of examples. Stam's earlier collaboration with Louise Spence, "Colonialism, Racism and Representation," exerts an evident influence over how the book treats film texts, but the essay's formalism contrasts with *Unthinking Eurocentrism*'s more robust theorizations, where Mikhail Bakhtin features heavily. Stam is greatly responsible for the Russian's import to film studies. His book, *Subversive Pleasures*, mobilized Bakhtin's concept of the "carnivalesque" to explain Brazilian film culture. Those ideas surfaced once more in *Reflexivity in Film and Literature* as a model with which to discuss anti-illusionist modernist films.[95] Shohat and Stam define the relationship between individuals, discourse, and reality, by fortifying poststructuralist film criticism with Bakhtin's view that discourse is historically determined and man's only conduit to the real world.[96] Historically situated spectators do not interact directly with the world because they are doubly mediated by social and cinematic discourse. Under these terms, art is a socially situated utterance, made up of a complex of signs uttered by socially situated subjects to other socially situated subjects. Bakhtin's position on artistic representation thus posits constant reminders about historical circumstance and social contingency. It enables Shohat and Stam to avoid the pitfalls of both stereotype analyses' "referential verism without falling into a 'hermeneutic nihilism' whereby all texts become nothing more than a meaningless play of signification."[97] Most important, it accounts for differentials in social power. The objective of criticism therefore, is to unravel all the threads in a media object's discursive fabric, reveal imbalances and histories of disempowerment, accord epistemological advantage to those who have suffered, and service a radical ethic to empower, disperse, and redistribute. In a nutshell, *Unthinking Eurocentrism*'s variant of multiculturalism takes conscientious pains to distinguish itself from liberal pluralism and to avoid the trapdoor of identity politics. The latter's pull, however, might just be too strong.

Suspicions of multiculturalism and identity politics are not necessarily just founded on a fear of relativism and flattened differences, played out for example in the Occupy movement's employment of hierarchy-averse political "horizontalism." Nor do they purely worry, as Shohat and Stam rightfully are, about insular immaterial preoccupations with cultural history. Debates in political theory around "recognition" for example, dwell instead on the very possibility of grasping the link between culture and structures of power, let alone the prospect of correcting imbalances after that occurs. Political philosopher Charles Taylor believes that democratic societies have increasingly engaged in the politics of recognition since the middle of the twentieth century. In contemporary politics, the demand for recognition is prominently foregrounded in multiculturalism. Recognition, the act of acknowledgment or respect, pertains to how an individual treats another but is also an important part of how a person shapes one's own identity. According to Taylor, we are driven to define our identities fully, and the process depends crucially on dialogical relations with others.[98] These cross-cultural dialogues occur with the assumption that people share a basic set of commonalities, but have different experiences and perspectives of them. The dialogical processes lead to conclusions about the value or worth of each culture.[99] Taylor's framework is remarkably symmetrical with how Shohat and Stam depict polycentric multiculturalism, where central and marginal groups voice themselves as "active, generative participants at the very core of a shared, conflictual history," before those who succeed in negotiating both center and margin earn the authority of an "epistemological advantage."[100] And by outlining identity formation as a dialogical process, Taylor further affirms an antiessentialist view of identity similar to Shohat and Stam's.

In political theory, the most skeptical questions to challenge the politics of recognition (and thus multiculturalism) originate from materialists such as Nancy Fraser who argues that they reify identities into rigid simplifications. If recognition is understood as cultural and thus distinct from the socio-economic structure of society, it may also decouple from the need redistribute capital, resources or power. Worse, recognition might supplant redistribution as the most pressing injustice requiring remedy. Recognition thus becomes the ends and not merely the means. Even with the more moderate critique from Lois McNay, she directs consternation at whether recognition is tied to sufficiently detailed understandings of social relations and power. For Fraser and McNay, these dangers are heightened by the reality that global capital is steadily subsuming and commodifying every part of our social and cultural lives.[101]

These cautionary alarms do more than undermine multiculturalism or dampen its optimism; they permit us to make sense of why identity politics, in the form of disparate ethnic agendas in critical race film studies, endures with such strength. These works repeat the basic vocabulary of recognition, betraying an ongoing desire for their very existence to be recognized and validated. To take just one example, Charles Ramirez Berg's *Latino Images in Film* is cognizant of how the field has, methodologically speaking, moved on from stereotype analysis. Undeterred, he presses on with the image study, compiling a comprehensive litany of Latino representations, with a fairly uncommon empirical approach via social psychological research to explain how stereotypes function. The most pressing injustice the book seeks to redress remains the falsehoods perpetrated by stereotypes. The real Latino community, therefore, has been unrepresented, invisible, and ignored—unrecognized. So Berg's wish to "legitimize" Chicano- and Latino-related film criticism, as well as endorse Chicano cinema as a "valid form of cultural production," powerfully hints at an underlying need to simply affirm their social and political presence.[102] Critical race film studies continues to be replete with ethno-specific projects like this that want to as Lester B. Friedman puts it, "demand equal access to the symbolic order."[103] The story is of course far from finished. We cannot infer that these repeated demands for equal access to the symbolic order equate to satisfaction with it. But for all the multicultural equivocations, McNay and Fraser's admonitions become progressively more persuasive, at least until pan-ethnic agendas catch on or when critical race film studies immerse themselves more deeply in materialist analysis. Multiculturalism might not be forestalling identity politics at all, but hardening around them.

To be absolutely clear, I am not saying in this instance, that Chicano American film criticism has no claim to a place at the table or that it has no value. No one can hesitate to open up parts of film culture previously unseen, even (or especially) if the methodology is well worn. Consider Christine List's essay on Cheech Marin's ethnic stereotype, which harnesses a theory of performance very similar to Donald Bogle's. Grounded in a knowledge of comic traditions, Chicano artistic practice, and ethnographic theory, she teases out a persuasive interpretation of Marin's comic style, and asserts that his one-dimensional Chicano stereotypes act as parodic satire that actually encourage audience incredulity while subtly critiquing ethnocentrism."[104] Bogle wrote of a similar subversion on the part of African American actors.

> The very best black performers played their types but played against them. They built and molded themselves into what film critic Andrew Sarris might call nondirectorial *auteurs*. With their own brand of outrageousness, the blacks created comic worlds all their own in which the servant often outshone the master.[105]

List's essay is valuable for what it reveals about Chicano culture, but it expended minimal effort to place the article within any pan-ethnic context or that of critical race film methodology. The critical environs around the piece are occupied by Chicano interests. In light of this, critical race film studies could be more methodologically aware of its history. Alternatively, it might choose to heed Fraser's advice, to ensure that recognition becomes more resiliently affixed to a redistributive mission. For film criticism, that directly entails greater interest in cinema's mode of production.

Finally, what of Jango Fett? A materialist interpretation that approaches through production history, takes the actors at face value: as Maoris. Major production and postproduction work on the three *Star Wars* "prequels" took place at Fox Studios in Sydney. Since the mid-1990s, Hollywood studios have increasingly recognized both Australia and New Zealand for its balance of modern facilities, skilled labor, attractive locations, and above all, lower wage and production costs. That combination of incentives now makes it very cost-effective for effects laden productions to locate in Oceania. The trend is a natural progression of Hollywood's move to decentralize their production base away from southern California, beginning with the establishment of satellite locations in Canada and Mexico. At the same time, Australian and New Zealand actors and other personnel who move rather freely across the blurry borders dividing the two film industries are enjoying new opportunities in American and transnational productions. Before, actors and directors attempting to enter the Western market would need to be noticed in a film that could do well in the festival circuit and then find moderate commercial success in the United States and Western Europe. After decentralization, it became exponentially easier for them to obtain exposure without the need for a "calling card" film.[106] Therefore, Temuera Morrison's presence in *Attack of the Clones* is less a symbol of an alien invasion of America and more empirically explained by Hollywood colonization of a developing film industry to establish a satellite base of production, or more generally as an illustration of multinational capitalist expansion.

Notes

1   Robin Wiegman, "Race, Ethnicity, and Film," *The Oxford Guide to Film Studies*, eds. John Hill and Pamela Church Gibson (Oxford: Oxford University Press, 1998): 158.

2   Wiegman, "Race, Ethnicity, and Film," 159.

3   Steve Neale, "The Same Old Story: Stereotypes and Difference," *Screen Education* 32, 3 (1979): 33–37.

4   Robert Stam and Louis Spence, "Colonialism, Racism, and Representation," *Screen* 24, 2 (1983): 2–20.

5   Wiegman, "Race, Ethnicity, and Film," 166.

6   Peter Noble, *The Negro in Films* (London: Skelton Robinson, 1948).

7   Edward Mapp, *Blacks in American Films: Today and Yesterday* (Metuchen, NJ: The Scarecrow Press, 1972): 7.

8   Daniel J. Leab, *From Sambo to Superspade: The Black Experience in Motion Pictures* (London: Secker and Warburg, 1973).

9   Neale, "The Same Old Story," 33.

10 Noble, *The Negro in Films*, 11.

11 Mapp, *Blacks in American Films*, 247.

12 Neale, "The Same Old Story," 35.

13 Leab, *From Sambo to Superspade*, 5.

14 Quentin Tarantino, "Tarantino Talks to Gates: A Podcast Special," *The Root* (December 26, 2012) <http://www.theroot.com/multimedia/tarantino-talks-gates-podcast-special> Accessed June 27, 2013.

15 Thomas Cripps, *Slow Fade to Black: The Negro in American Film, 1900–1942* (New York: Oxford University Press, 1977): 186–89.

16   Mapp, *Blacks in American Films*, 152–62.

17   Leab, *From Sambo to Superspade*, 223–30.

18   Stephanie Greco Larson, *Media & Minorities: The Politics of Race in News and Entertainment* (Lanham: Rowman & Littlefield, 2006): 27.

19   Donald Bogle, *Toms, Coons, Mulattoes, Mammies and Bucks: An Interpretive History of Blacks in American Films* (New York: The Viking Press, 1973).

20   Ibid., ix.

21   Ibid.

22   Ibid., 43–44, 86.

23   Neale, "The Same Old Story," 35.

24   Manthia Diawara, "Black Spectatorship: Problems of Identification and Resistance," *Screen* 29, 4 (1986): 70. Valerie Smith, ed., *Representing Blackness: Issues in Film and Video* (New Brunswick: Rutgers University Press, 1997): 3.

25   Stam and Spence, "Colonialism, Racism, and Representation," 18.

26   V. J. Jerome, *The Negro in Hollywood Films* (New York: Masses and Mainstream, 1952): 10.

27   Cripps, *Slow Fade to Black*, 68.

28   Neale, "The Same Old Story," 35–36.

29   Ibid., 33, 36, 37.

30   Stam and Spence, "Colonialism, Racism, and Representation," 8.

31   Ibid., 10.

32   Ibid., 11.

33   Ibid., 3, 6.

34   Homi Bhabha, "The Other Question. . ." *Screen* 24, 6 (1983): 18–36. The model it offers is crucial to books by Juan J. Alonso and Peter X. Feng, discussed below.

35   Ibid., 22.

36   Ibid., 18–19.

37   Ibid., 22.

38   Ibid., 18, 23.

39   Ibid., 19, 26.

40   Richard Dyer, *White* (London: Routledge, 1997) was preceded by his "White," *Screen* 29, 4 (1988): 46–65.

41   Bhabha, "The Other Question . . ." 22.

42   Dyer, *White*, 47.

43   Ibid., 28, 222.

44   Juan J. Alonso, *Badmen, Bandits, and Folk Heroes: The Ambivalence of Mexican American Identity in Literature and Film* (Tuscon, AZ: University of Arizona Press, 2009): 3, 10–11.

45   Bhabha, "The Other Question . . ." 26.

46   See Ruth Vasey, *The World According to Hollywood* (Madison, WI: University of Wisconsin Press, 1997): 104, 107.

47   Bhabha, "The Other Question . . ." 24.

48   Smith, *Representing Blackness,* 1.

49   Stuart Hall, "Cultural Identity and Cinematic Representation," *Framework* 36 (1989): 68–81.

50   Ibid., 80.

51   Peter X. Feng, *Identities in Motion: Asian American Film and Video* (Durham, NC: Duke University Press, 2002).

52   Jacqueline Najuma Stewart, *Migrating to the Movies: Cinema and Black Urban Modernity* (Berkeley, CA: University of California Press, 2005).

53   Ibid., 6, her emphasis.

54   Ibid., 6, 23, my emphasis.

55   Daniel Bernardi, *Filming Difference: Actors, Directors, Writers and Producers on Gender, Race and Sexuality in Film* (Austin, TX: University of Texas Press, 2009): 3.

56   Neale, "The Same Old Story," 35.

57   Bhabha, "The Other Question . . ." 18.

58   Stewart, *Migrating to the Movies*, 98–99. She also adds an extra dimension to "intertextuality" by bringing attention to James Snead's description of how "spectatorship might be affected by the organization of multiple films in a single program."

59   Stewart mentions James Snead, "Spectatorship and Capture in *King Kong*: The Guilty Look," *White Screen, Black Images: Hollywood from the Dark Side*, ed. Colin McCabe and Cornell West (New York: Routledge, 1994): 1–27, and bell hooks, "The Oppositional Gaze," *Black Looks: Race and Representation* (Boston, MA: South End Press, 1992): 115–31. Diawara is cited earlier.

60   Stewart, *Migrating to the Movies*, 104.

61   Ibid., 108.

62   Ibid., 101, 109. See Miriam Hansen, *Babel and Babylon: Spectatorship in American Silent Film* (Cambridge, MA: Harvard University Press, 1991).

63   Ibid., 98, 106.

64   Adorno's sentiments are projected in Martin Jay, *Adorno* (Cambridge, MA: Harvard University Press, 1984): 120–21.

65   Diawara, "Black Spectatorship," 76. Jacqueline Bobo, *Black Women as Cultural Readers* (New York: Columbia University Press, 1995).

66   Jacqueline Bobo, *Black Women as Cultural Readers*, 88.

67   Edward Said, "Politics of Knowledge," *Race Identity and Representation in Education*, ed. Cameron McCarty and Warren Crichlow (New York: Routledge, 1993): 312.

68 Wiegman, "Race, Ethnicity, and Film," 166.

69 Ella Shohat and Robert Stam, *Unthinking Eurocentrism: Multiculturism and the Media* (New York: Routledge, 1994).

70 See for example, Brian Locke, *Racial Stigma on the Hollywood Screen from World War II to the Present: The Orientalist Buddy Film* (New York: Palgrave Macmillan, 2009): 5. Diane Negra, *Off-White Hollywood: American Culture and Ethnic Female Stardom* (London: Routledge, 2001): 2.

71 Michael Hilger, *From Savage to Nobleman: Images of Native Americans in Film* (Lanham, MD: The Scarecrow Press, 1995): 2, 15.

72 Peter C. Rollins and John E. O'Connor, ed., *Hollywood's Indian: The Portrayal of the Native American in Film* (Lexington, KY: The University Press of Kentucky, 1998); Jacquelyn Kilpatrick, *Celluloid Indians: Native Americans and Film* (Lincoln, NE: University of Nebraska Press, 1999): xv.

73 Ed Guerrero, *Framing Blackness: The African Image in Film* (Philadelphia, PA: Temple University Press, 1993): 7.

74 Ibid., 220n16.

75 Lester Friedman, ed., *Unspeakable Images: Ethnicity and the American Cinema* (Urbana, IL: University of Illinois Press, 1991): 5.

76 Her quote is more precisely, "by charting black spectatorship in relation to the negative and 'negating' representational politics of individual film texts, scholars have made a variety of claims about how black viewers have worked to subvert an otherwise degrading viewing experience (99)." I emphasize her verb choice.

77 Michael H. Hodges, "Critics say 'Clones' has Racial Stereotypes," *The Detroit News* (May 18, 2002).

78 Gabriel S. Estrada, "Star Wars Episodes I-VI: Coyote and the Force of White Narrative," *The Persistence of Whiteness: Race and Contemporary Hollywood Cinema*, ed. Daniel Bernardi (New York: Routledge, 2008): 69–90.

79 See Christopher Deis's apologia for the films' progressive politics, "May the Force (Not) be with You: 'Race Critical' Readings and the *Star Wars* Universe," *Culture, Identities and Technology in the Star Wars Films: Essays on the Two Trilogies*, eds. Carl Silvio and Tony M. Vinci (Jefferson, NC: McFarland and Company, 2007): 77–108.

80 Richard Delgado and Jean Stefanic, *Critical Race Theory: An Introduction* 2nd edn (New York: New York University Press, 2012): 10; Chon Noriega, "Introduction," *Chicanos and Film: Representation and Resistance*, ed. Chon A. Noriega (Minneapolis, MN: University of Minnesota Press, 1992): xiii; Rosaura Sánchez, "Postmodernism and Chicano Literature," *Aztlán* 18, 2 (1992): 6.

81 Kristen Warner, "Django Unchained as Post-Race Product," *Antenna* (December 28, 2012) <http://blog.commarts.wisc.edu/2012/12/28/django-unchained-as-post-

race-product/>; Salamishah Tillet, "Quentin Tarantino Creates an Exceptional Slave," *CNN in America* (December 25, 2012) <http://inamerica.blogs.cnn.com/2012/12/25/opinion-quentin-tarantino-creates-an-exceptional-slave/>; Hillary Crosley, "'Django Unchained': A Postracial Epic?" *The Root* (December 25, 2012) <http://www.theroot.com/views/django-unchained-postracial-epic>; "Michael Eric Dyson Blasted in Open Letter for Defending 'Django Unchained,'" *EurWeb* (December 30, 2012) <http://www.eurweb.com/2012/12/michael-eric-dyson-blasted-in-open-letter-for-defending-django-unchained/>; All accessed June 27, 2013.

82   Wendy Brown, *States of Injury: Power and Freedom in Late Modernity* (Princeton, NJ: Princeton University Press, 1995): 35, 60.

83   Ernesto Laclau and Chantal Mouffe, *Hegemony and Socialist Strategy: Towards a Radical Democratic Politics* (London: Verso Press, 1995): 137–38.

84   Diane Waldman, "There's More to a Positive Image than Meets the Eye," *Jump Cut* 18 (1978): 31–32. Linda Artel and Susan Wengraf, *Positive Images: A Guide to Non-Sexist Films for Young People* (San Francisco: Booklegger Press, 1976).

85   Neale, "The Same Old Story," 34, 35. Waldman, "There's More to a Positive Image than Meets the Eye," 32.

86   Elizabeth Cowie, "Women, Representation and the Image," *Screen Education* 23 (Summer 1977): 19.

87   Cowie, "Women, Representation and the Image," 20, 22.

88   Claire Johnston, "Feminist Politics and Film History," *Screen* 16, 3 (Summer 1975): 115–24. The feminist equivalent to Stam and Spence's "Colonialism, Racism and Representation" should probably be Laura Mulvey's "Visual Pleasure and Narrative Cinema," in the same issue of *Screen*: 6–18. See also Marjorie Rosen, *Popcorn Venus: Women, Movies and the American Dream* (New York: Coward McCann and Geoghegan, 1973); Molly Haskell, *From Reverence to Rape: The Treatment of Women in the Movies* (New York: Holt, Rinehart and Winston, 1974).

89   Diawara, "Black Spectatorship," 66.

90   Wiegman, "Race, Ethnicity, and Film," 158.

91   David Palumbo-Liu, *Asian/American: Historical Crossings of a Racial Frontier* (Palo Alto, CA: Stanford University Press, 1999): 171–72. See Peter X. Feng, ed., *Screening Asian Americans* (New Brunswick: Rutgers University Press, 2002): 2.

92   Dyer, *White*, 10.

93   Ibid., 2–4.

94   Shohat and Stam, *Unthinking Eurocentrism*, 46–49.

95   Robert Stam, *Subversive Pleasures: Bakhtin, Cultural Criticism and Film* (Baltimore, MD: Johns Hopkins University Press, 1989), and *Reflexivity in Film and Literature: From Don Quixote to Jean-Luc Godard* (New York: Columbia University Press, 1992).

96 Shohat and Stam, *Unthinking Eurocentrism*, 179, 183.

97 Ibid., 180.

98 Charles Taylor, "The Politics of Recognition," *Multiculturalism: Examining the Politics of Recognition*, ed. Amy Gutmann (Princeton, NJ: Princeton University Press, 1994): 25, 32, 34.

99 Ibid., 66–67.

100 Shohat and Stam, *Unthinking Eurocentrism*, 48.

101 Nancy Fraser, "Rethinking Recognition," *New Left Review* 3 (May/June 2000): 107–19. Lois McNay, *Against Recognition* (Malden, MA: Polity Press, 2008).

102 Charles Ramirez Berg, *Latino Images in Film: Stereotypes, Subversion and Resistance* (Austin, TX: University of Texas Press, 2002): 34.

103 Friedman, *Unspeakable Images,* 5.

104 Christine List, "Self-Directed Stereotyping in the Films of Cheech Marin," *Chicanos and Film: Representation and Resistance*, ed. Chon A. Noriega (Minneapolis, MN: University of Minnesota Press, 1992): 183–94.

105 Bogle, *Toms, Coons, Mulattoes, Mammies and Bucks*, 37.

106 New Zealand's *Once Were Warriors* (1994) for example was a festival hit and the "calling card" film for Morrison, supporting actor Julian Arahanga who appeared in *The Matrix (1999),* and director Lee Tamahori who began working in Hollywood.

2

Theorizing Race with a
Wide-open Text: *The Searchers*

John Ford's critically and institutionally revered Western, *The Searchers* (1956) is a useful linchpin with which to survey critical race film studies, whose key debates are reified in the intriguing web of issues spinning through the film. It seems almost natural to discover the metacritical questions of interest to this book take cinematic form since the film's critical discourse is powerfully governed by authorship and stardom, as well as by mythologies of genre and social history. With its captivity narrative, first-generation critiques of Native American representations obviously abound, but upon closer examination the film contains enough ambiguity to thwart attempts to hold it down for simplistic and definitive interpretations about its racial ideology. Is it racist? Yes, in a way, but maybe not. Some of its more recent criticism tackle the film's uncertain meanings head on, but like the prominent sandstone buttes so ever-present throughout the film, whose repetition can make it seem like John Wayne spent years just circling Monument Valley, the trail of ideas lead ultimately back to authorial subjectivity as a dominant heuristic paradigm.

A project to chart the tendencies of critical race film studies against the stable axis provided by a single film, might also be expected to select D. W. Griffith's *The Birth of a Nation* (1915). It is the focus of numerically more writing on race, probably more than any other film. It is indeed pondered at length in several works discussed earlier, namely Robert Stam and Louise Spence's "Colonialism, Racism and Representation" and Manthia Diawara's essay on "Black Spectatorship." For Stam and Spence, the film's "flawed mimesis" misrepresents slavery and slaves, providing an imperialist "paradigmatic perspective," while Diawara outlines how African American audiences would find it difficult to fall in line with the film's construction of pathos—the "dominant reading" of a "dominant film."[1] At the core of critical race criticism on *The Birth of a Nation*, lies the film's vile stereotypes of African Americans, the visual impact of which is borrowed by Stam, Spence, and Diawara in the movie stills of bug-eyed white actors in blackface that illustrate their essays. Although he does not treat the film with a great degree of detail in *White*, Richard Dyer also takes it on in a separate essay, "Into the Light: The Whiteness of the South in *The Birth of a Nation*."[2] Dyer argues that the technical conventions developed for lighting and cinematography—practices that highlight the visual whiteness of white actors' skin—worked in conjunction with the Hollywood star system to reaffirm "white" ethnicity in a film narrative predicated on anxieties about the instability of racial categories. All these accounts are unified by the common understanding that *The Birth of a Nation* is indubitably racist and a pernicious carrier of evil ideology and political bias. Clyde Taylor, in fact, asserts that Griffith's racism and the film's ideology are so intrinsic that they cannot and should not be separated from aesthetics.[3] He considers film studies' tendency to detach the film's racism from its technical achievements and aesthetic significance, as weak attempts to condone the immoral ideology and to cloak the conflation of aesthetics with white bourgeois values. Nevertheless, it is the very absence of ambiguity in *The Birth of a Nation* that devalues it for the purposes of my analysis.

In contrast, the relative ambiguity if not ambivalence of *The Searchers*—a comparable member of the film canon—offers a text that is more open to critical reflection. Where critical race writing serves merely to elucidate *The Birth of a Nation*'s self-evident ideology, the ideological content of *The Searchers* is more available for debate. John Ford's Western thus presents a more contingent and provocative set of ideas. Eventually, the manner in which critical race films studies orient themselves within the film's ambiguity is emblematic of their most significant trends. What *The Searchers* says about its criticism is as important as what the writing reveals of the film. Against stereotype analyses of the film, second-generation methods started to rock the premise of a stable, knowable "bad image," and provided new insights about the text's discourse that make the film's racial ideology out to be more complex than originally thought. As the film became increasingly ambiguous and almost profligate with meaning, critics came to rely on the author figure as a constraint. This unified subjectivity is embodied not only by the director Ford outside the text, but within it by Wayne as well. Their influence as such even survives a challenge from film criticism that approached race from the counter-authorial view of genre, which privileges structuralism and myth. Although structuralism's understanding of culture through "structures" of underlying meanings is antithetical to the authorial position, the latter still maintained its bulwark.

The Searchers takes place over five years starting and ending in Texas, from 1868 to 1873. The title refers to a pair of frontiersmen, Ethan Edwards (Wayne) and Martin Pauley (Jeffrey Hunter), who spend those five years searching for a Comanche chief, Scar. Near the start of the film, Scar leads a murderous raid on their family's homestead, and kidnaps the youngest child, Debbie. When the film begins, the ex-Confederate soldier Ethan arrives at his brother's Aaron's home three years after the end of the Civil War. Aaron lives with his wife Martha—with whom Ethan shares an unverbalized but evocatively suggested past—their children Lucy, Ben, and Debbie, and Martin, an eighth-breed Cherokee orphan the family adopted after he was found by Ethan. On the next day, Comanches steal some livestock to draw all the men in the vicinity away from the homestead, leaving only Aaron, his wife and children essentially defenseless against a raid. Everyone but Lucy and Debbie are murdered, and the ranch is set ablaze. The posse returns, buries the dead, and sets out to find the missing girls. Lucy is soon found raped and killed. Ethan and Martin continue the long search for Debbie. When they eventually find her, Debbie is fully assimilated into Comanche culture and refuses to leave. But she later changes her mind and is brought back to white society.

The most evident racial issues coursing through the film are miscegenation and cultural assimilation. Ethan is an avowed racist. Soon after he appears on screen, we observe him at the dinner table hatefully glaring across at Martin, an Indian integrating himself into Ethan's family. It is later revealed that Ethan's search for his nieces is motivated by his wish to murder them because they have had sex with an Indian. By the end of the film however, Ethan's vicious attitudes toward Martin and Debbie evidently change. He bequeaths the Edwards estate to Martin and in the final shot willingly shepherds him and his Nordic fiancé Laurie Jorgensen over the domestic threshold. He relents completely on the crazed mission to kill Debbie, and literally carries her home.

Critics have described in detail how neither the psychological reasons nor the timing of Ethan's change of heart is made overly apparent. *Variety*'s 1956 review goes so far as to call the film "somewhat disappointing" because of Ethan's unclear motivations and the "subtleties in the basically simple story that are not adequately explained . . . Wayne is a taciturn individual throughout and the reasons for his attitude are left to the imagination of the viewer."[4] Ironically then, the racial component of the film's narrative is at once glaringly prominent and undeniably vague. As a result, doubts creep into what looked at first like clear and egregious depictions of Native Americans as brutal savages. Given this inherent lack of clarity, critics have addressed the issue in two ways. One group tackles the basic question of whether *The Searchers* is a racist film to begin with. And if it is, in what manner does the ideology manifest itself? In other words, is the film racist and how? The second critical approach, influenced by structuralism, debates the racial referent. To which ethnic group, if any, does the racial dimension of the film apply? That is to say, who is being victimized by its prejudice? Structuralist readings of the film see broad applicability for its myth, and believe that its racism reflects much more than anti-Native-American sentiment alone. Collectively then, the film's critical discourse reveals a pattern of thinking that metatextually reflects and allegorizes some important but fluid issues at stake. As opinion on racism in *The Searchers* shifts, its hermeneutic possibilities spread wide. What prevents them from spilling over into incomprehensibility is the unified authorial subject.

Searching for closure, Ford, and Ethan

The foremost evaluation of *The Searchers's* ambiguity has been undertaken by Peter Lehman, for whom the film is unusual because in spite of its classical quality, it stubbornly refuses to offer clarity and closure in the manner that classical narrative style often guarantees. For Lehman, classical narrative structure dictates that the film should lead toward the revelation of truth, of what has happened. But "in some ways, *The Searchers* tests the limits of epistemological assumptions within the classical narrative style."[5] From that observation, Lehman launches two major claims. The first is that the film's lack of clarity in a classical sense is belied by the prominence of pregnant visual motifs, such as the doorway and Ethan's lifting gesture. The film opens and closes with shots through a doorway from the interior. In between, it constantly frames characters through similar thresholds and cave openings. Two of Ethan's scenes with Debbie are conjoined by an identically staged and composed action of Ethan lifting the girl by her armpits and pausing at the top. According to Lehman, this visual rhyme confers a structure onto the film that encourages the audience to read the film using specific cues even when a thorough understanding is not forthcoming.[6] Secondly, Lehman argues that this epistemological quagmire is interwoven into the very fabric of the film. Most of the characters for instance, are prevented from knowing Ethan's activities between the end of the War and the narrative present. Details about what the Comanches perpetrated on their victims are also withheld. Lehman points out other examples of how characters are constantly caught in misrecognition: Aaron questions his eyes when he spots Ethan riding toward the house; with the opening line of the film, he asks no one in particular, "Ethan?" On the next day, the posse is misled into finding stolen cattle by the Comanche's effective plan to lure the men away from the settlements. In the subsequent search for the two missing Edwards sisters, Brad Jorgensen misrecognizes a Comanche "buck" dancing in Lucy's dress as his fiancé. And when Laurie reads Martin's letter out loud, the three characters listening to her interpret what they hear in radically divergent ways. This, Lehman argues, emphasizes how inaccessible reality is. Therefore both the spectators and characters of *The Searchers* are confronted with the "nature and limits of knowledge."[7]

The theoretical implications of Lehman's analysis for critical race film theory are numerous and significant. He shows that embedded within such a visually stunning film—with scenes so memorable that they were recreated by New Hollywood directors in movies such as *Taxi Driver* (1976) and *Star Wars* (1977)—is a sharp critique of the image's epistemological contingency. As Brad fatally discovers, what one sees is not what it seems. During the search, he returns from a scouting run and declares excitedly that he has spotted Lucy. Ethan explains to him that what he saw was not Lucy but a buck wearing her dress. Ethan then admits that he had found the girl when he split from the party to inspect a Comanche trail earlier in the day, and that he had buried her in his coat. When Brad presses for details—"Did they . . .? Was she . . .?"—Ethan rebukes Brad for asking him to recount the horror of what he saw. Overcome with emotion, Brad charges the Comanche camp vengefully and is killed almost immediately by gunfire offscreen. The lesson that Brad learns in death echoes Steve Neale's in "The Same Old Story": stereotypes do not denote or connote identical and repeatable meanings in every case either. Brad's misrecognition reflects that folly. Some second-generation critics argue that the stereotypes must be dealt with in context, and furthermore, dwelling on them might be redundant. These critiques of image studies are given a voice in *The Searchers*.

Figure 2.1 Ethan (John Wayne) asks, "What do you want me to do? Draw you a picture? Spell it out?" (*The Searchers*, 1956).

Pestered by Brad about what he saw of Lucy, Ethan might be speaking for more than himself when he screams a rebuke to that obsessive curiosity: "What do you want me to do? Draw you a picture? Spell it out? Don't ever ask me! Long as you live, don't ever ask me more." (Figure 2.1).

These epistemologically uncertain qualities, however, go largely ignored by critical race writings that undertake first-generation analysis of *The Searchers*, which generally tend to overlook its ambiguity. Much of their interest consists solely of how it represents Native Americans, and how those representations defy historical accuracy to express racist ideology. The following three examples epitomize that position. Maryann Oshana condemns the discrepancy between the "depth and richness" of women's roles in Native American society with the "narrow and distorted" view of them in films. For her, Ethan and Martin's cruel treatment of Look, an overweight Comanche squaw whom Martin accidentally marries, is unquestionably racist.[8] Michael Hilger writes that tracing "the images of the Savage and Noble Red Man" reveals little about Native American people, "but a lot about the evolution of white American attitudes and values." He cites *The Searchers* as a "prime example of the racism behind portrayals of the savage Native American as defiler of white women."[9] Indeed, despite second-generation challenges to that paradigm, critics of "Hollywood's Indian" such as Ken Nolley insist on judging the film—and the rest of Ford's oeuvre—for its racist images.[10] Film historian Richard Maltby for one, attempts to steer the issue away from racial misrepresentation, and toward that of genre and myth. He does not perceive Westerns and the Native American stereotypes contained within them to be the result of white anti-Indian racism alone. These films are permeated by generic discourse intertwined with a historical discourse. This "historical" narrative or cultural discourse is in turn a national allegory, a "myth of Origin," an "imperial narrative." By slightly shifting the debate like this, Maltby suggests that obsessing over on whether Native American portrayals are correct might be a "banal" exercise.[11] Still, Nolley remains adamant that even if it is merely discourse, historical discourse carries historical consequences.[12] Furthermore, he maintains that Ford is a filmmaker who is clearly concerned with history and who often bases his films on historical events; *The Searchers*, he adds, contains an event that resembles Custer's massacre of Black Kettle's group of Cheyenne at Washita in Oklahoma in the fall of 1868.[13]

Not all Native Americanist critics of *The Searchers* merely participate in image analysis. Nor are they in absolute agreement about the film's racism itself. Several writers use second-generation analysis to examine how various formal aspects of the film create paradigmatic perspectives and subject positions. Hilger attends to shot scale and angle when describing the viewer's first sight of Scar, a low-angle close-up that makes "the savage character deeply threatening. He also describes the editing strategy during the Comanche raid on the Edwards home, explaining how the horror is intensified by cutting from the posse's realization that it has been decoyed from the helpless family at the farm. By focusing on the victims' reactions and by not showing the attack, Ford magnifies the terror and produces a "classic example of manipulation."[14] Meanwhile, Kathryn Kalinak's musical breakdown of Max Steiner's score identifies both "Indian" musical stereotypes as well as discursive channels opened up by the extratextual elements of songs chosen for the film. Her semiotic approach finds that the soundtrack constructs a musical discourse that serves the common Othering function typical of imperialist ideology. The soundtrack, she suggests, positions the audience within a Western European subjectivity. Although Kalinak concedes that the musical attention that Steiner paid to Native Americans "opens up space for a more nuanced reading," the film still "clearly falls into racist stereotypes."[15] Both Hilger and Kalinak therefore take different paths before arriving ultimately at the same conclusion and emphasis on the film's racist stereotyping.

But most of all, consider Tom Grayson Colonnese's surprise and bemusement at the results of his reception study. He finds that his Native American contemporaries actually have enthusiasm for this Western's presumably painful depiction of them, when he had expected that it would inflict an experience on them akin to Jews watching films about the Holocaust.[16] Colonnese discovers that some Native Americans' aberrant or subversive readings produce a definite ambivalence toward the film. Often, his sample Native American audience even expressed affection for it. *The Searchers*'s racism is not self-evident after all. We cannot count on film's power of subjective interpellation since the spectator's subjective position can neither be easily explained nor simply dismissed as racist. Further applications of second-generation discourse analysis and reception study continue to turn away from easy interpretations of images sealed off from the rest of the film's discourse. Much of the reason to assume that *The Searchers* is racist rests on the assumption that the spectator identifies stably and unquestionably with Ethan and his hatred of Indians. Following Hilger's assessment of how the Comanche raid is edited to intensify the horror of the Comanche attack, the crucial close-up of Ethan over the back of his horse as he stares plaintively offscreen toward the direction of his brother's farm apparently reinforces the proposition that spectators are indeed encouraged to see those events through his eyes. To adopt the character's visual perspective is often to also do so socially and politically. This is a highly reasonable proposition, given the strength of John Wayne's star persona at the height of his career. However, just as Lehman alludes to the film's "profound ambiguity," *The Searchers* resists oversimplification of its subjectivity and racial ideology.[17] One can easily question the degree to which Ethan's perspective is one that audiences will automatically assume. As an antihero, Ethan is not the morally pure character that typifies most classical Hollywood protagonists. Even if we assume that American culture in the 1950s was more racially intolerant, does it necessarily mean that audiences identified with Ethan's maniacal desire to hunt for Scar and murder Debbie? As Colonnese's observations also suggest, *The Searchers* has cultivated a loyal following among a diverse audience demographic with varied and opposing ideological sympathies.

Charles Ramirez Berg adds to the nuance and complexity with which second-generation critics have come to read the film. His interjection in fact schematizes poststructuralist and postmodern ideas of decentering and of margins. Berg argues that Ford advances multicultural politics and suggests that the film's diverse reception can be explained by dissecting the textual discourse.[18] He praises *The Searchers*, as part of Ford's oeuvre, for occupying the point of view of oppressed minorities and marginalized outcasts. It presents a distinctive "multicultural vision" that is at certain points "among the most emotionally unsettling and ideologically clear-sighted moments in American cinema."[19] Berg identifies at the base of Ford's films a conflict between the simultaneous needs to celebrate and criticize the American Mainstream's racial value system. "Ford's paternalism and his condescension toward and stereotyping of people of color are incontestable." But Berg credits Ford narratively, "his films emanate from the position of that oppressed ethnic minority and his stories typically focused on marginalized outcasts."[20] The director even evinces a social constructionist definition of race.

> Ford's culturism is multiple not only because numerous ethnicities are sympathetically represented, but because Ford shows ethnicity to be a hybrid property . . . Ford regarded cultures not as autonomous, static, or fixed states, but rather as fluid, evolving, and organic ones that were inextricably intertwined.[21]

Berg illustrates his argument on Ford's evidently postmodern attitudes on ethnicity with the following examples from *The Searchers*. First, after her rescue, Debbie is returned not to the "WASP mainstream" but to the Jorgensens who as European immigrants occupy the "margins" of American society. Second, the film's multicultural perspective overpowers the temptation that spectators have to fully identify with Ethan. The narrative, Berg argues, raises a significant "cultural question" of whether Ethan can overcome his racism. Third, Ethan is indeed expelled from the multicultural margins in the famous last shot of Wayne swiveling off one foot and walking away from the domestic threshold as the door closes on him.[22] Extrapolating from Berg, one can make a strong argument that the moral center of the film is in fact provided by the racial hybrid Martin Pauley. Ed Buscombe notes that "throughout the picture Marty, in Jeffrey Hunter's unselfish and sympathetic performance, represents the voice of decency, the standard against which Ethan's actions are judged."[23] Douglas Pye's position on the audience's unstable relationship with the character is even more detailed and persuasive. He writes that while "in ways that seem entirely controlled, the film detaches us from Ethan so that we are required to perceive the neurotic and irrational nature of his attitudes and actions," at the same time *The Searchers* does not alienate viewers from its antihero permanently.[24] The film is perfectly willing to make Ethan a monstrous figure but relies on Wayne's magnetism. This also makes it difficult for the audience to detach themselves from other white characters' racial hatred.

Figure 2.2 Audiences are not asked to identify with Ethan's racism, expressed at the dinner table by his cruel comments and glare. (*The Searchers*, 1956).

Pye believes that these toggling perspectives are being used to examine the central issue of the film, miscegenation, and that this contradictory multitude of positions forms part of the film's mystery. Ethan's abhorrence of interracial sex is not an attitude that spectators can ignore (Figure 2.2). In addition to the power of Wayne's charisma and star persona, the narrative does independently encourage viewers to identify with him. But simultaneously, *The Searchers* undertakes a critique of white racism. Pye cites the episode with Look as one whose politics are almost impossible to comprehend. Martin betrays no humanitarian response to Look; and when his kick sends the helpless woman tumbling violently down a hill, the audience's intended reaction—whether or not Ethan's laughter is supposed to be shared in or condemned—is indiscernible.[25] From personal experience, at every screening of the film I have attended, the audience feels conflicted at that moment. They invariably laugh at the gag, but follow up immediately and often in mid-chuckle with groans or gasps about its brutality and misogyny. In another scene at the army camp where Ethan and Martin encounter some white captives rescued during a military raid on a Comanche village, Pye observes that even though Ethan's disgust and hatred at the sight and sounds of those women alienate us further from him, we are still asked to believe that the captives' trauma and madness resulting from their sexual experience with Indians are objectively true. Ultimately, these conflicting points of view produce a text whose "incoherence is an essential aspect of its greatness."[26]

I venture that Homi Bhabha would approve of how effectively *The Searchers* decenters its visual, narrative, and political points of view. He argues that discussions of subjective, spectatorial or rhetorical positioning entail an enforcement of arbitrary and thus ideological fixity onto inherently unstable signs. Although the overall body of criticism on *The Searchers* seems to have taken those theoretical ideas to heart in its continued wrangling over the racial significance of the film, Bhabha's call for deconstructionist politics goes unheeded. Pye is exceptional in that most writers do not treat the film's ambiguity or ambivalence as an ideal example of how it should establish and encourage what Bhabha would call a "play of difference."[27] Rather, they predominantly try to stabilize meaning with an authorial anchor. It is the common recourse they take in response to the film's lack of clarity and closure. After identifying or conceding to the overarching elusiveness of truth in the film, when closure proves elusive, they turn to the preeminent director and assume that John Ford the author can provide intelligibility. This book has witnessed the propensity before.

These personal invocations of Ford extend beyond the customary linguistic shorthand of film criticism that gives the director a nonchalant possessory credit. The writing of Pye, Kalinak, and Lehman explicitly invoke his vision, creative interventions, biography, and oeuvre. Pye concludes his essay by characterizing *The Searchers's* "complexities" and "incoherence" as the product of Ford's individual "dialogue" and response to generic traditions, and the director's subsequent wrestle with the Western's attendant racism and sexism. He does hint at a poststructuralist conception of individuality by mentioning biographical evidence that suggests that "he was as contradictory as any of us," but soon reverts to auteurism by stating that "Ford internalized the 'language' of the Western" before articulating his "artistic or political response."

Kalinak also ties down swirling discourses to an authorial base. Although she underscores how the soundtrack mobilizes Native American stereotypes, she declares a willingness "to acknowledge that *The Searchers's* representation of the Indians is more complicated than it seems on first hearing." But after doing so, she proceeds immediately to cite Berg's possessory argument for Ford the auteur's multiculturalist vision, where, with implicit authorial discourse he attributes Ford's sensibility to a "sociohistorical context"—the director's experience in the Irish Catholic immigrant class at the start of the twentieth century: denigrated, discriminated against, and marginalized by the WASP establishment.[28]

To Lehman, Ford also underwrites what he identifies as the film's "profound ambiguity." He explains how "two other Ford films helps to bring this unique aspect of *The Searchers* into focus," by citing *Fort Apache* (1948) and *The Man Who Shot Liberty Valence* (1962) for how those films deal with "epistemological issues."[29] In *Fort Apache*, Captain Kirby York recounts a history of Lieutenant Colonel Owen Thursday that represses Thursday's dark character and his military failures. In *Liberty Valance*, Ransom Stoddard reveals that the legend that propelled his political career was false, and that Valance was in fact killed by another man, Tom Doniphon. It leads the editor of *The Shinbone Star* to utter the famous line, "When the legend becomes fact, print the legend." Both films therefore depict reporters who knowingly or otherwise print misleading versions of heroic legends, and thematize Ford's predilection for epistemological murkiness. *The Searchers* though, arguably does so to a greater degree since the audience is not privileged with an omniscient narration. The textual indeterminacy of *The Searchers* is comparable to that of *Touch of Evil*, a film that Bhabha pays closest attention to in "The Other Question." Both films encourage a "play of difference" and destabilize both the sign and the audience's subjective position. Just as the book pointed out earlier that Bhabha's argument fundamentally assumes the presence of an autonomous, critical spectator capable of deconstructive interpretation, Lehman's essay—in which he stresses that meaning is contingent, multiple, and unstable—makes a similar move. Counterbalancing an implicit reference to *The Searchers* itself as a work of poststructuralist criticism, he nonetheless relies on authorship, where the director stands as the autonomous, unified artist from whom creative inspiration springs.

What is more, this need and desire for unified subjectivity is I argue, inscribed into *The Searchers* itself. These are related symptoms, shadows of a figure that never really went away. According to Lehman, despite its ambiguity, the film is nevertheless obsessed with knowability—knowing the unknown—a preoccupation shared by both its audience and characters. And when coherence starts to disintegrate, the characters also look to an authorial figure. Where the critics use the classical auteur Ford to close open circuits, the film's characters rely without question on Ethan for clarity. It is here that the film begins to tell us something about the critical discourse it engenders. The main narrative structure of the search for Debbie leads a secondary exploration into

Ethan Edwards's psychology and past. That journey, I suggest, metanarratively prefigures auteurism's standard practice of contextualizing a work as part of an oeuvre, and then with references to an artist's personal, professional or (in Berg's words) "sociohistorical" background.

Kalinak and Lehman both point out that the lyrics we hear of the theme song set up a mystery for the narrative to solve, even before the film's first image. Ethan's unknown past is alluded to as Stan Jones's theme song proffers questions with its opening lines. Kalinak uncovers clues about Ethan's motivations within the lyrics when she compares the verses of the theme that were used in the film with the full version. Only the second and seventh made the final cut.

> What makes a man to wander
> What makes a man to roam
> What makes a man leave bed and board
> And turn his back on home.
>
> A man will search his heart and soul
> Go searching way out there
> His peace o' mind, he knows he'll find
> But where Oh Lord, Lord where.

Kalinak just about collapses Ford into Ethan when she speculates that because "it is just like Ford to avoid the obvious," he purposefully excluded the first verse, which fills in what is merely suggested to us about Ethan's love for Martha and how that unfulfilled romance motivates his actions after her rape and murder.[30]

> The horizon's like a woman
> With her arms flung open wide
> And a man that's tryin' to fill his heart
> Ain't got no place to hide.

The song's tune is next heard under the next mysterious allusion, when Ethan hands Aaron some gold coins, that his brother notices are "freshly minted, ain't got a mark on 'em." The scenes in the Edwards homestead during Ethan's first evening back undulate tensely because both characters and audience remain in the dark about where he has been since the war ended. He declares that he has not been in California where his family expected him to have been. His nephew Ben innocently asks why he took three years after the end of the Civil War to make it home. Martha quickly ushers the boy out of the room to defuse the awkward moment. This unknown period in Ethan's life is probably where he learned so much about the Comanche, As Scar later observes. "You speak good Comanche. Someone teach you?" (Figure 2.3). The next morning, before the posse leaves to recover the stolen cattle, Ethan demurs that he cannot take Captain Clayton's oath to be deputized as a Texas Ranger. Then even without any knowledge of the unblemished gold coins in Ethan's possession, Clayton asks if he is wanted for a crime, but queries no further. Everyone appears to adopt a conscientious attitude of knowing ignorance about Ethan's activities.

Like the author, Ethan is treated with great curiosity, respect, and authority. His point of view is not to be adopted, but simply understood and obeyed. He possesses tremendous knowledge of the frontier and of Comanche customs and language. Neither Martin nor the audience gets to see Martha and Lucy's corpses up close, but Ethan does. And before the unscrupulous trader Jerem Futterman attempts to rob and kill Ethan and Martin, Ethan has already anticipated the unscrupulous plot. The humor of the scene with Martin where Ethan stokes the campfire in order to lure Futterman into his own trap, emphasizes Ethan's omniscience. Critics locate so much of the film's unknowable quality in the director's vision, which is where they look for clarity and closure. With the characters, a very similar impulse is directed toward Ethan, an allegorical author. The film establishes early on that Ethan's command of the frontier should be abided by if Debbie is to be found, an imperative complemented

Figure 2.3 Scar's (Henry Brandon) retort: "You speak good Comanche. Someone teach you?" (*The Searchers*, 1956).

Figure 2.4 The briefly visible inscription of Ethan's mother's tombstone. (*The Searchers*, 1956).

by the narrative drive to illuminate his inscrutable thoughts. As Martin says in voiceover during a flashback to when Ethan maniacally slaughters a herd of buffalo to deny the Comanches food: "Somethin' happened that I ain't got straight in my own mind yet." We ain't got it straight in our minds either, but as audience members we are just as curious as Martin. It motivates and prompts us to notice details about Ethan's life story that serve to both solve and feed the mystery. For example, the inscription on Ethan's mother's tombstone, the one little Debbie is instructed to hide behind when the Comanches attack, is visible only for a second in the final cut. "Here lies Mary Jane Edwards/ Killed by Comanches May 12, 1852/ A good wife and mother in her 41st year." (Figure 2.4). This backstory offers a better understanding of Ethan's hatred for Indians and the Comanche in particular, over and beyond his Confederate allegiance. The drive to fully grasp Ethan is a textual operation that parallels auteurist reading strategies, whose cultural logic is reified in the text.

The mystery gathers momentum as we gradually collect hints from Ethan's past. His familiarity with the Comanches laces his hatred with irony. In another parallel, Ford's prized authorial vision is similarly marked by contradiction. On one hand, all his films may be accused of using transparently racist and sexist images and characterizations. This is congruent with common perceptions of him as an abrasive, patriarchal, and paternalistic Richard Nixon supporter. On the other hand, he was also sympathetic to Franklin D. Roosevelt, the New

Deal, Native Americans who worked on his sets, and is widely perceived to have made some of his final films—namely *Sergeant Routledge* (1960), *Two Rode Together* (1961), and *Cheyenne Autumn* (1964)—to atone for the sins he committed against the image of Native Americans. Unlike D. W. Griffith, the highlights of Ford's biography provide a host of ways to redeem him, and film historians have rarely refused the opportunity to do so. Berg's study of Ford's "nuanced" and "richly textured" "multicultural vision" is one example.[31] Geoffrey Nowell-Smith has noted that *The Searchers*, the quintessential Ford film, is inexorably tied to Ford.

> It is in fact the film which, to anyone who knows (and loves) Ford's work, contains at the same time the most concentrated expression of his themes and the revelation of their tragic flaw . . . No criterion other than an auteurist one gives an account of the intelligibility of the film such as would justify giving it pride of place either in a private pantheon or in historiographic or pedagogic practice.[32]

Indeed, in choosing a pre-eminent classical director's most acclaimed work, I should probably not be surprised to discover that the scholarly discourse reflects the film's status as such. Together, the film and director's reputations probably pushed the critical narrative somewhat. But auteurism also faced a substantive assault on two flanks, from structuralism in addition to the one from poststructuralism. So the fact that it survives and indeed forcefully persists in that hostile climate instead of receding is more than noteworthy. Structuralism's contribution to critical race criticism of *The Searchers* indeed arises from the author versus structuralism debate.

Represented here by interventions from Brian Henderson and Richard Maltby, it offers another framework with which to contest the unified subject, but also additional means with which to ask some foundational questions about critical race film theory. Henderson's much anthologized 1981 essay, "*The Searchers*: An American Dilemma" looks away from authorship and toward structuralism, genre, and myth. Outwardly assuming the intellectual tradition occupied by Vladimir Propp and Claude Lévi-Strauss, he moves to consider *The Searchers* as a film-myth. He bemoans a "preoccupation with Ethan and his motives" which he suspects is "a ruse of the text (though not of its makers) to deflect attention from more important and hidden matters"—those that are neither the psychological operations of a text nor the artistry of a director.[33] Henderson treats *The Searchers* as a structural myth, "a collective phenomenon" pertaining to the contemporaneous issues confronting mid-twentieth-century spectators who responded to the film because it corresponded with an aspect of their current existence. It resonated emotionally because of social context, where acute anxiety existed about black–white relations.[34] Maltby adopts a similar methodology in his essay, "A Better Sense of History." But in contrast to Henderson's text-culture contemporaneous reflection theory, he finds the film's Native American representations to be part of the pioneer narrative at the core of America's national identity and historical imaginary.[35] The frontier myth that informs the overdetermined conventions of the Western consists of an opposition between white civilization and the savage Other, Native Americans in this case, whose political weakness left their representation especially vulnerable to appropriation. As they gained control of their identity, Westerns began depicting nobler and more civilized Indians, indirectly compelling the imperial narrative to migrate into other genres.[36] Maltby and Henderson also concur on the use of Freudian models.[37] Breaking the unified subjectivity of Ethan, the nation's surrogate, Henderson layers a Freudian psychoanalytic framework onto Lévi-Strauss, associating myths with an unconscious component that performs psychic work. In this interpretive schema, Scar's rape of Martha represents Ethan's forbidden libido. Because the libido is unrepresentable, Scar's crimes are never seen. His murder of Martha is also equivalent to violating Ideal Law, which enables Ethan to displace his repressed desires onto a rage toward the racial Other. Scar's miscegenation, the enactment of forbidden desires, must be repressed psychically and thus physically destroyed by Ethan, thereby reconstituting the male self.[38]

Steve Neale accuses Henderson's structuralist methodology in particular of ahistoricism and of adding insult to genocide by enacting critical and historiographical obliteration after Native Americans have suffered a stage of physical and cultural extermination.[39] Furthermore, he argues that Henderson recontextualizes *The Searchers* onto the separate context of black history too easily, suggesting "the propensity for allegorical readings and for the location of ethnic stand-ins to be limited to Westerns and to Native Americans."[40] Maltby already ventures that the myth of national master narratives require Native American images to serve as "empty signifiers," while Henderson argues *The Searchers* myth only becomes "explicable" when Indians are taken to mean something else.[41] One can add that the psychic narrative elides Indian suffering by taking the initial Comanche attack to be unprovoked, rather than retaliatory for Scar's slaughtered sons.

I believe that the charge of historical effacement is a valid one, and points to Native Americans' political weakness especially in comparison to African American prominence in the discourse of racial debates. It acts as a reminder that politically inclined film criticism has an inherent duty to balance intellectual priorities with political ones. However at the same time, shifting focus onto myths and structure does not automatically erase Native American history. It can well represent a move away from image studies. Moreover, insisting on Native American specificity carries just a whiff of identity politics, which once again raises the need for the previously mentioned pan-ethnic critical project, a more collective effort on behalf of all groups.

What I find most interesting about the author-structure bipolarity is the resemblance that it shares with the consent-descent opposition formulated by Werner Sollors—the two ways that race can be defined.[42] The consensual approach to race considers it the result of a socializing process, and suits the idea that race is a social construction. If one's race is a set of inherited attributes on the other hand, then it is obtained through descent, a definition more aligned with racial essentialism. In short, is racial identity inhabited or inherited? Transposing that question onto a film, we are led to ask where a text's racial ideology originates. Correspondingly, is a film's racial meaning inherited through the myths that structure its genre, or is it ascribed to the actions, attitudes, and creative choices of the author? I acknowledge that conflating race and cinema may seem arbitrary and capricious, but the analogy between the two binaries resonates in this instance with *The Searchers*'s most prominent themes: miscegenation and cultural assimilation. By way of a conclusion, it might just once again be worthwhile to ask what this historically and culturally important film can tell us about theory.

For both Henderson and Pye, the film poses many of these questions through Martin, the quarter-breed Cherokee adopted by Aaron and Martha Edwards. Henderson writes that as a myth *The Searchers* spoke in 1956 to racial anxieties over American society's impending desegregation of the races, while also articulating lessons to nonwhites about the social standards expected of them when they enter white society.[43] The biracial Martin and his relationship with the Edwards family, offer an example of unproblematic integration. But opposition to Martin's induction into the Edwards clan comes from Ethan, who constantly berates his adopted nephew and reminds him continually of his otherness. He refuses kinship with Martin, dismissing the idea that he was destined to find the boy after he was orphaned in an Indian massacre. "It just happened to be me. No need to make more of it." He encourages Martin to forego his search for Debbie:

Ethan: . . . I'm pushin' on tomorrow.
Marty: Well, I sure ain't gonna stay here. I started out lookin' for Debbie. I intend to keep on.
Ethan: Why?
Marty: Why? Well because she's my . . .
Ethan: She's your nothin'. She's no kin to you at all.
Marty: Well, I always kinda thought she was. The way her folks took me in and raised me.
Ethan: That don't make ya no kin.

Martin's Cherokee extraction is a major sticking point for Ethan, and why he initially refuses to accept him as a nephew. To Ethan, Martin's descent is essentially his identity. When Martin suspects something amiss when the first posse is out looking for the missing cattle, Ethan reacts without hesitation, "That's the Indian in ya." We know from Martin that he is an eighth Cherokee, with the rest Welsh and English. But Ethan adheres to the "one-drop rule," which decrees that even one drop of ethnic blood is enough to designate otherness. He refers to Martin as "half-breed" or "quarter-breed" interchangeably.

The film's emotional sympathies are contrary to Ethan's, however. As viewers, we never doubt Marty's familial bond with the family. His character is in fact ennobled by his persistence in finding Debbie. To Henderson, "Marty wins the argument," and shows that integration is an inevitable and positive part of the future. Ethan himself comes to realize that. He sees fit to bequeath his possessions to Martin, right before the latter performs the ultimate initiation rite of murdering Scar (Figure 2.5). When the film introduces Martin, he is isolated in a medium shot and physically marked by dusky skin. Jeffrey Hunter's complexion was darkened with makeup, as (German actor Henry Brandon) Scar's was as well. It does not stop Ethan from eventually accepting Martin as a nephew. Much of Ethan's psychology does remain murky, but if he is an intratextual authorial subject who judges Martin to have overcome his Native descent through the younger's actions on behalf of the Edwards family, Ethan is to be obeyed and his authority cements the recognition of consent as the definition of race. Many rightly see the final shot of Ethan walking away from the Jorgensen house as the door closes behind him, as the tragic fate deserved by a man who is punished for his sins. Westerns often include this poignant

Figure 2.5 Ethan eventually bequeaths his possessions to Martin, acknowledging that he is kin. (*The Searchers*, 1956).

inevitability for its antiheroes, whose savagery that tamed the frontier also excludes him from the rewards. But the sequence also articulates an element of Ethan's power. As he looks off-screen at the family finally united, his gaze contains both longing and approval for what he sees. It is Ethan who made it possible and validates that milieu.

Pye's essay, "Miscegenation and Point of View in *The Searchers*" traces the origin of the film's racist ideology to generic tradition. White supremacist attitudes and points of view naturalized in the Western genre, present a distinct generic discourse. Those conventions produce a resultant narrative voice, with which the author engages in dialogue. According to Pye, Ford's specific critique is driven by his concern with tradition's contradictions in general—a preoccupation that manifests itself thematically in his films. So where structuralist genre critics will generally disregard the authorial voice completely, Pye begins his analysis focused on genre, but he ultimately retains the author as figure whose own discourse pointedly competes with generic meanings. Pye's argument further supports the idea that action and performance can surmount textual heredity and structural meaning. Ford does not simply reproduce generic conventions, he inflects on them. Martin does not passively accept Ethan's attempts to exclude him; he earns membership in the family by contesting what is supposedly genetically pre-established. The film's dominant metatextual trope is the autonomous and critical subject, which "consent" foregrounds. Its capacities materialize again and

Theorizing Race with a Wide-open Text

again, most prominently in Martin's conquest of biological racial essentialism. Characters and spectators of the film also assume the presence of unity in Ethan's subjectivity; our need to comprehend it helps drive the narrative. Likewise, we see Ford's autonomy arising in his authorial confrontation with genre traditions and mythic ideology. So when *The Searchers* teeters on the edges of ambiguity, ambivalence, even incomprehensibility, it is what critical race film theory turns to as well.

Notes

1 Robert Stam and Louis Spence, "Colonialism, Racism and Representation," *Screen* 24, 2: 6; Manthia Diawara, "Black Spectatorship: Problems of Identification and Resistance," *Screen* 29, 4 (1986): 67.

2 In *Dixie Debates: Perspectives on Southern Culture*, ed. Richard H. King and Helen Taylor (New York: New York University Press, 1996): 165–76.

3 Clyde Taylor, "The Re-Birth of the Aesthetic in Cinema," *Wide Angle* 13, 3/4 (July–October 1991): 12–30.

4 *Variety*, March 14, 1956: 6.

5 Peter Lehman, "'You Couldn't Hit It on the Nose': The Limits of Knowledge in and of *The Searchers*," *The Searchers: Essays and Reflections on John Ford's Classic Western*, ed. Arthur M. Eckstein and Peter Lehman (Detroit, MI: Wayne State University Press, 2004): 243.

6 Ibid., 251–54.

7 Ibid., 261.

8 Maryann Oshana, "Native American Women in Westerns: Reality and Myth," *Film Reader* 5 (1982): 125–31.

9 Michael Hilger, *From Savage to Nobleman: Images of Native Americans in Film* (Lanham, MD: The Scarecrow Press, 1995): 1–2, 8.

10 Ken Nolley, "The Representation of Conquest: John Ford and the Hollywood Indian, 1939–1964," *Hollywood's Indian: The Portrayal of the Native American in Film*, ed. Peter C Rollins and John E. O'Connor (Lexington, KY: University Press of Kentucky, 2003): 73–90.

11 Richard Maltby, "A Better Sense of History: John Ford and the Indians," *The Book of Westerns*, ed. Ian Cameron and Douglas Pye (New York: Continuum, 1996): 35, 37, 39, 44, 49.

12 Nolley, "The Representation of Conquest," 77.

13 Ibid., 74–75.

14 Hilger, *From Savage to Nobleman*, 11–12.

15   Kathryn Kalinak, "'Typically American': Music for *The Searchers*," in Arthur M. Eckstein and Peter Lehman, *The Searchers: Essays and Reflections on John Ford's Classic Western*: 130.

16   Tom Grayson Colonnese, "Native American Reactions to *The Searchers*," in Arthur M. Eckstein and Peter Lehman, *The Searchers: Essays and Reflections on John Ford's Classic Western*: 335, 338.

17   Lehman, "You Couldn't Hit It on the Nose," 259.

18   Charles Ramirez Berg, "The Margin as Center: The Multicultural Dynamics of John Ford's Westerns," *John Ford Made Westerns*, ed. Gaylyn Studlar and Matthew Bernstein (Bloomington, IN: Indiana University Press, 2001): 75–101.

19   Ibid., 75, 96.

20   Ibid., 75.

21   Ibid., 76.

22   Ibid., 90.

23   Edward Buscombe, *The Searchers* (London: British Film Institute, 2000): 50.

24   Douglas Pye, "Miscegenation and Point of View in *The Searchers*," *The Book of Westerns*, ed. Ian Cameron and Douglas Pye: 229.

25   Ibid., 213.

26   Ibid., 233, 235.

27   Homi Bhabha, "The Other Question," *Screen* 24, 6 (1983): 22.

28   Kathryn Kalinak, "Typically American," 130; Berg, "The Margin as Center," 77.

29   Lehman, "You Couldn't Hit It on the Nose," 259.

30   Kathryn Kalinak, "Typically American," 113.

31   Berg, "The Margin as Center," 75.

32   Geoffrey Nowell-Smith, "Six Authors in Pursuit of *The Searchers*," *Screen* 17, 1 (Spring 1976): 28. See also *Screen Education* 17 (1975/76).

33   Brian Henderson, "*The Searchers*: An American Dilemma," *Film Quarterly* 34 (1981): 10–11.

34   Ibid., 12, 19.

35   Richard Maltby, "A Better Sense of History," 37.

36   Ibid., 49.

37   Ibid., 45.

38   Henderson, "*The Searchers*: An American Dilemma," 12, 14.

39   Steve Neale, "Vanishing Americans: Racial and Ethnic Issues in the Interpretation and Context of Post-War 'Pro-Indian' Westerns," *Back in the Saddle Again: New Essays on the Western*, ed. Edward Buscombe and Roberta E. Pearson (London: British Film Institute, 1998): 21. See also Jon Tuska, *The American West in Film: Critical Approaches to the Western* (Westport, CT: Greenwood Press, 1985): xix, 57–58.

40 Henderson, "*The Searchers*: An American Dilemma," 10.

41 Maltby, "A Better Sense of History," 49; Henderson, "*The Searchers*: An American Dilemma," 19.

42 Werner Sollors, *Beyond Ethnicity: Consent and Descent in American Culture* (New York: Oxford University Press, 1986).

43 Henderson, "*The Searchers*: An American Dilemma," 22.

3

Poststructuralism and
the Neo-Marxian Subject

The preceding chapters primarily conclude that second-generation critical race film criticism's focus on discourse analysis and reception studies produces a contradiction. Poststructuralist influence prompts it to reject the critical unified subject in favor of an individual whose consciousness is decentered, split, or one that otherwise never existed. But the traditional subject remains indispensible to their methodology nonetheless, judging from the degree to which critical race writing clings to romantic conceptions of authorship, personal vision, and alienated spectatorship. Some have tried to reconcile the discrepancy by reconstituting a more limited version of subjectivity that rests on a framework informed by the uniqueness of ethnic experience. This is the basis of identity politics, which now provides a popular paradigm for academic and political praxis. From an organizational perspective, identity politics has not served critical race film studies well and has done little to allay materialist intuitions regarding its efficacy for radical critique. My case for a more materialist approach to critical race film criticism now comes into closer view. It entails greater attention to cinema's mode of production as well as a push to theoretically presuppose the abiding existence of a critical subject.

Part of this book's architectural effort over the next two chapters is to start building the bridge from the opposite side, so to speak. On the basis of current evidence, the critical subject gradually taking shape bears more than a passing resemblance to the one lodged at the base of Frankfurt School critical theory. This chapter engages in the exposition of that Neo-Marxian subject by condensing it out of the orthodoxy of Theodor Adorno and the critic who has largely inherited his mantel, Fredric Jameson. When that critical subject is fully before us, it will then instruct us on how to approach cinema from a critical race perspective. I follow the leads headed toward Adorno and Jameson's direction not just because earlier analysis of second-generation theory uncovered clues that point their way. As the subsequent chapter will reveal, the alienated subject posited by this specific sector of the Frankfurt School is also the unheralded force behind one of the most important voices in critical race film studies, Edward Said. The uncanny similarities that it shares with the agential figure projected from second-generation theory could be more than ironic, given the antihumanist pogroms to bring about the bourgeois subject's demise. They perhaps hint at a Neo-Marxian backbone entrenched deep within critical race film theory.

The subject however is accompanied by essentialist claims. Do we risk falling into the territory of racial essentialism and therefore racial determinism? How may we understand the relationship between critical subjectivity and the culture in which they are embedded? The chapter concludes with that discussion. To ascertain if and how the Neo-Marxian subject is constituted with a racial identity, the inquiry will be facilitated by textual analyses of Michael Mann's *The Last of the Mohicans* (1992) and Todd Solondz's independent films, especially the work from 2004, *Palindromes*.

Critical subjects, cinema, and the culture industry

Many philosophers from the Enlightenment to modernist eras assume the presence of the liberal subject, an individual that possesses a given rationality and morality, capable of independent action and thought, unaffected by social determination. Taking its lead from Marx's earlier writing in the "Paris" *Economic and Philosophical Manuscripts of 1844* that was premised on the idea of alienated labor, Marxist humanists concur with that position. Believing similarly that subjects are conscious beings and historical agents, the Frankfurt School belongs to this tradition. But Marxists such as Louis Althusser maintain that the posthumously published Paris manuscripts do not represent Marx's fully developed ideas. He rejects traditional humanism in favor of a brand of Marxism based on a structuralist form of humanism. To him, the notion of a subject itself is a social construction and an ideological illusion. One's subjectivity, one's notion of self, is always mediated by ideology. According to

Robert Sklar, film studies swiftly latched onto Althusser's notion of "ideological state apparatuses"—institutions of religion, education, family, and law—to explain how ideological instruments like the cinema interpellate individual subjects. The signifying function of film texts is said to influence the spectator to such a degree that it effectively constitutes his or her consciousness. Sklar criticized this interpretation of Althusser as one that does not do justice to his actual insights. It rendered, Sklar wrote, "questions of historical agency, of conflict and transformation . . . more or less immaterial."[1] In any event, Althusserian Marxism came to offer a significant and influential model of the relationship between ideology and subject, and provided the theoretical basis for critics wishing to elucidate the mass media's effects. Critical race film criticism cited in previous chapters evinces Sklar's description of how film studies appropriate Althusserian thinking as a base to discuss cinema's method of transmitting racist ideology. For example, Robert Stam and Louise Spence's essay, "Colonialism, Racism and Representation" describes how point-of-view, shot scale, narration, and musical underscoring come together to situate spectators in a colonial "paradigmatic perspective." Similarly, Kathryn Kalinak's musical analysis of *The Searchers* concludes that Max Steiner's score offers an imperial European subjectivity that the film's audience is encouraged to assume.

A step further away from Enlightenment thinking and Marxist humanism, the most direct assault on the subject comes from poststructuralism and postmodernism. Lacanian psychoanalysis challenges the subject's unity, or decenters human identity, by splitting it between a knowable, conscious side and a less accessible unconscious where psychic drives reside. That is to say, the subject is thought to be marked by a fundamental lack. Both Jacques Lacan and Althusser regard the subject as an illusion. But according to Sean Homer, whereas Althusser retains some notion of its unity, Lacan does not in emphasizing its divided nature.[2] Among the critical race film critics discussed earlier, the deconstructionist Homi Bhabha stands as the prominent proponent of this view. In "The Other Question . . ." he underscores ambivalence in the text, or, of the object. While valorizing Stephen Heath's treatment of Orson Welles's *A Touch of Evil* (1958), he singles out Heath's analysis in *Screen*, of Michael/Miguel Vargas, a character with a double name and for that matter, a contradictory physical appearance, played by the white Charlton Heston in Chicano hair and makeup.[3] Vargas's racial hybridity, a metaphor for his divided or split subjectivity, presents an intense point of interest, as an allusion to the United States–Mexico border that also highlights the innately fluid and contradictory nature of colonial language and discourse. Bhabha's opposition to unified subjectivity is exemplified by a statement in *The Location of Culture* that agency only acts from the "kinetic tension between the contingent as the contiguous and the indeterminate."[4] Indeed, he likens the colonial subject's "scopic space"—especially his construction of the colonized other—to the Lacanian subject's formation of a self and other in the Imaginary during the pivotal mirror phase.[5]

Perhaps most dramatically, beyond descriptions of the subject as split, divided or decentered, stands Fredric Jameson's elegiac autopsy of the autonomous individual. After surveying the realm of the postmodern aesthetic and conducting a materialist periodization, he is struck by the relative emptiness of pastiche, in which he fails to identify unique styles attributable to individual artists or unified subjects. He thus records the subject's time of death at the emergence of late capitalism.[6]

> It is, of course, no accident that today, in full postmodernism, the older language of the 'work'—the work of art, the masterwork—has everywhere largely been displaced by the rather different language of the 'text,' of texts and textuality—a language from which the achievement of organic or monumental form is strategically excluded . . . The autonomous work of art thereby—along with the old autonomous subject or ego—seems to have vanished, to have been volatilized.[7]

For Neo-Marxism, the loss of the individual subject equates to the passing of historical agents, and along with it, the possibility of revolutionary politics. Transposing that stance onto the Frankfurt School's analysis of the culture industry results in an analogous argument about modern culture and society: the absence of the subject precludes the presence of original artists, their ability to produce radical or (in Adorno's terms) autonomous works of art, and the capacity of audiences and consumers to recognize and dialecticize. In Adorno's important essay "On the Fetish-Character in Music and the Regression of Listening," he critiques the circumstances under which consumers declare their preference for popular, contemporary "light music." Their critical autonomy to discern and choose is, in his estimation, sharply declining.

> Between incomprehensibility and inescapability, there is no third way; the situation has polarized itself into extremes which actually meet. There is no

room between them for the "individual." The latter's claims, wherever they still occur, are illusory, being copied from the standards. The liquidation of the individual is the real signature of the new musical situation.[8]

Adorno's absolutism about popular culture is perhaps a defining characteristic. To him, mass entertainment's pseudo-individualization and overwhelming level of standardization demean and cheat those who consume it. The masses' eagerness to believe that the culture industry caters to their individual tastes in fact represents the ultimate triumph of commodified culture, as well as capitalist ideology's success in eliminating alienation and resistance.[9]

However, it would be precipitous to interpret Adorno and Jameson's claims about the "death of the subject" at face value. I suggest that their prose should not be interpreted literally, and propose instead to take its turgidity to function as a method of hailing critical subjects. The overall thrust of their claims, once fully contextualized this way, actually indicates the contrary. In different ways, both authors cling desperately to the notion of subjective autonomy, particularly in the critic. This is substantially more crucial to how Jameson is understood, because his position on postmodernism—and thus on the "death of the subject"—is more ambiguous. His perspective is somewhat less dismissive and more sympathetic. He discovers a Utopian dimension in popular culture, as well as the presence of class consciousness able to aestheticize the commodity. Still, to say that he celebrates the situation, however, would be premature. After explicating Adorno and Jameson's view of critical subjectivity and mass culture, I intend to reflect on the significance that the autonomous individual's continued viability poses to second-generation critical race film theory. Namely, does the Neo-Marxian individual's similarity to critical race film theory's implied subject make them kin? This book's analysis of Edward Said's *Orientalism* suggests that it does. The connection provides a portal between Neo-Marxism and critical race film studies, and strengthens the case for the Frankfurt School to be an important contributor to the field.

I sample Adorno's writing with a strong preference for that which addresses cinema most directly. Although he wrote extensively about mass culture, he directed a relatively insignificant portion of those efforts toward cinema. He seems much more fervently invested in music, and addressed film mainly through that art form. His mother and aunt nurtured his lifelong fascination from an early age, and he cultivated the devotion both as a musician and theorist.[10] It would not be surprising that his most extensive treatment of the cinema materializes in *Composing for the Films*, a 1947 critique co-written with composer Hanns Eisler of the musical scoring conventions and techniques adopted by commercial cinema, especially classical Hollywood.[11] Its basic analysis borrows heavily from Adorno's prior writings on music, namely "On the Social Situation of Music" published in 1932 and "On the Fetish Character in Music" six years after that.[12]

Among the Frankfurt School Critical Theorists who thought about film, Adorno remains one of the biggest skeptics, even after some have recently taken note of his softened, less dismissive stance in later writings about cinema's potential. Adorno biographer and scholar Martin Jay characterizes Adorno's slight turnaround almost as part of a weary impulse to seek relief from the suffocating effects of the culture industry.[13] Andreas Huyssen describes the more recent work as a "shift in emphasis" from elitist moralizing.[14] Miriam Hansen goes so far as to call for a more complete reconsideration of Adorno's supposed elitist dismissives.[15] These arguments only serve to slightly moderate Adorno's contempt for film's commercial imperative toward illusionism and false identification. On that score, he is opposed by Siegfried Kracauer, who harbored greater sympathy for cinema. Kracauer feels that traditional definitions of art are too inadequate to accommodate film's aesthetic possibilities, the most significant of which is the power to capture physical reality. Counter-intuitively, he thought that film's technology in fact rescues the physical world from industrialization, and from the rationalization of modern science and technology.[16]

But Adorno's most noted adversary is Walter Benjamin, whose encounter with the Soviet montage artists forms the evidentiary spine of his celebratory valuation of film as a quintessential form of "the age of mechanical reproduction," where art without the burden of an aura or of institutional and discursive structures of authenticity possesses no distinction between high and low, which Benjamin thinks empowers mass audiences to harness art's potential for progressive politics.[17] For those very same reasons, Adorno reaches a very different conclusion—he abhors film because of how it limits individual expression. Adorno separates art forms into constituent parts, with each offering different possibilities for subjective and structural influence: technique and technology. A work's technique is its innate characteristics malleable by the aesthetic desires of an artist, while technology pertains to its means of re/production. In the essay "Transparencies on Film," Adorno writes that cinema is devoid of subjective creation and input, and its effects are solely determined by its technology.

> Film suggests the equation of technique and technology since, as Benjamin observed, the cinema has no original which is then reproduced on a mass scale: the mass product is the thing itself.[18]

Therefore, film audiences are constantly consuming ideology and technology in a most insidious form, while the culture industry filters the whole world for consumption, constantly seeking to seamlessly duplicate real-life experiences and eventually invading the process of empirical observation. *Composing for the Films* argues that cinema executes these directives most effectively with the continuity principles of classical Hollywood, which developed a style that effaced the medium's artifice and construction, and that seeks to institute "psychological continuity" between parts of the film and between the film world and real world.[19] Discouraged or prevented from imagination and reflection, viewers lose their individual capacities for spontaneity and spontaneous response. To wit, the subject is eroded. Like other products of the culture industry, films harness all the means at its disposal to construct and affirm a cinematic totality that is as rationalized as that which exists in our social realm.[20]

For Adorno, music interjects in the midst of cinema's subsumptive and sophisticated fabrication of totality. Since it predates the technology of film, music possesses autonomous techniques, intrinsic qualities that existed prior to both cinema and mechanical reproduction. Kracauer's exhortations for physical realism does value music to a limited extent, in that it would in the end serve the image and the self-evident visual reality that it accesses, but Adorno's view of film's structure magnifies the musical score's power as cinema's most likely conduit to the irrational, to dialecticism, and hence to aesthetic as well as subjective autonomy:

> Music is supposed to bring out the spontaneous, essentially human element in its listeners and in virtually all human relations. As the abstract art *par excellence*, and as the art farthest removed from the world of practical things, it is predestined to perform this function. The human ear has not adapted itself to the bourgeois rational and, ultimately, highly industrialized order as readily as the eye, which has become accustomed to conceiving reality as made up of separate things, commodities, objects that can be modified by practical activity.[21]

It is important to remember that Adorno would most probably privilege a very specific form of musical practice, one that draws a clear distinction between art and social reality, sustains the subject, speaks of a different world and calls up a Utopian dimension. That is to say, a progressive practice of film music must not in his view suffer from the standardization and fetishism that afflicts popular music or the rest of mass culture.

Composing for the Films posits objections on an institutional level in addition to the aesthetic. Fundamentally though, it takes most issue with the limitations imposed on individual autonomy. Adorno and Eisler dislike Hollywood film music practice for its wholly industrialized organizational structure. Studios in the classical era divided the cinematic terrain into niche markets and developed individual house styles. Production was planned and executed by a stubborn bureaucracy through strict divisions of labor. Composers functioned in that hierarchy, with procedural rigidity and efficiency as the order of the day.[22] As a rule, composers in the music department did not have a collaborative relationship with writers or directors, and for the most part, music departments would receive a final cut of the film and have no more than a few days to manufacture a score. Under such conditions, the blueprint for operations was based on classical practice that instituted film music's specific role, function, and form in any given film (con)text.[23] On the basis of those aesthetic reasons, Adorno and Eisler express the bulk of their apprehension. They seek to protect an ideal where the musical composer stands as an autonomous artist whose work needs to be integrated via what Adorno termed "free planning" into the production process from the start. We would have expected this brand of auteurism, given Adorno's distaste for the sort of rationalized production documented by Max Weber.[24] Nevertheless, what is perhaps most notable about Adorno's attitude is his obstinacy, which I take to reflect the high valuation that he places on the musician or artist's critical subjectivity. From a broader view, Adorno and Eisler also implicate film music practice in the larger context of popular culture. The Culture Industry amalgamates traditional autonomous art into entertainment in the fashion of Wagnerian totalities.[25] Hollywood scoring is based on the Wagnerian paradigm, and the musical leitmotif's function within the grand opera is itself an important metaphor for the vital but fixed and restricted role of music in Hollywood realism. In both cases, the system and its components share an ostensibly interdependent but ultimately restrictive relationship. The Wagnerian opera depends on its constituent and rudimentary leitmotifs, which in turn require a large musical canvas to attain a structural meaning.[26] Likewise, Hollywood's leitmotifs serve important significatory functions, but are ultimately limited to what the ideology of mass culture permits.

It is safe to say that these particular critiques of the Hollywood style originated from Adorno rather than Eisler because of the substantial overlap between the references to Richard Wagner in *Composing for the Films* and the rhetorical thrusts made by Adorno's more directed assessment of the composer, *In Search of Wagner*. There, Adorno takes aim at Wagner's reconception of opera into a "total art work"—the *gesamtkunstwerk*—a synthesis of multiple art forms where the composer exerts complete control over all those elements of the opera. On the face of it, one can expect Adorno to appreciate Wagner's commitment to the artist when the latter defines the work as a coherent expression of artists' unified subjectivity, and he directly states as much:

> Wagner's works provide eloquent evidence of the early phase of bourgeois decadence . . . [However], there is not one decadent element in Wagner's work from which a productive mind could not extract the forces of the future. The weakening of the monad . . . is not just representative of a doomed society. It also releases the forces that had previously grown up within itself, thus turning the monad into the 'phenomenal being' as conceived of by Schoepenhauer . . . Hence Wagner is not only the willing prophet and diligent lackey of imperialism and late-bourgeois terrorism. He also possesses the neurotic's ability to contemplate his own decadence and to transcend it in an image that can withstand that all-consuming gaze.[27]

For the most part, Adorno admires these hypothetical possibilities mostly for strengthening subjectivity within the *gesamtkunstwerk*. But he finds Wagner's practical execution lacking in that particular regard. His valuation of Wagner is especially negative in comparison to his position on Beethoven. Jay argues that when Adorno compares Wagner's work to Beethoven's symphonies, which are "coherently totalized works in which strong subjects realized their subjectivity in objective form, he finds that Wagner's operas lack any real principle of development or genuine subjectivity."[28]

Adorno's personal hostility toward Wagner is energized partly from what he saw as the continuity between the composer's art, his anti-Semitism, authoritarian personality, and identification with fascists and the ruling classes. He devotes the entire first chapter of *In Search of Wagner* to "Social Character," which draws connections between the musician's personal, political, and aesthetic. Adorno levels an overarching anti-authoritarian critique at Wagner, and by extension, the Wagnerian paradigm adopted by Hollywood studios, the oppressiveness and commodity function of classical cinema, and the culture industry at large. Adorno builds this argument with a musicological analysis of the leitmotif, the musical themes in an operatic or cinematic score that serve to represent the characters, locations, or situations in a narrative. In *Composing for the Films*, Adorno and Eisler do admit that leitmotifs aid in listeners' comprehension of narratives and help composers in the process of their work. Within Wagner's ideal and objective of constructing a complete artwork, the leitmotif also functions symbolically "to connote the sphere of sublimity, the cosmic will, and the primal principle." But leitmotifs operating in film scores are too rudimentary, repetitious, and use music in only a very superficial manner.[29] Hollywood cinema's use of melody is particularly guilty in this respect. Instead of lending "lyric-poetic" inspiration to the work, "all music in the motion picture is under the sign of utility, rather than lyric expressiveness."[30] Adorno adjudges light music manufactured by the culture industry in the same way. It can only transform music "into a conglomeration of irruptions which are impressed on the listeners by climax and repetition, while the organization of the whole makes no impression whatsoever."[31] Adorno argues that commerce clearly causes music's degradation in both instances, and Wagner's methods are not immune from this blight either. Of Wagner's exercise of leitmotifs, Adorno writes:

> Among the functions of the leitmotiv can be found, alongside the aesthetic one, a commodity function, rather like that of an advertisement: anticipating the universal practice of mass culture later on, the music is designed to be remembered, it is intended for the forgetful.[32]

Therefore, light music and film music's inexorable "advertising function" predisposes them to become "one of the departments of the culture industry."[33]

Commercial interests and fascist forces share a need for subjects who are defined not as autonomous individuals, but as slaves to external ideology. Adorno considers these economic and political cousins equally tyrannical. Just as film composers are stifled by the highly rationalized nature of the film industry and the commercial demand for standardized, unchallenging works, patrons of cinema and music experience parallel forms of sinister oppression. For instance, the authoritarian impulse residing in the core of Wagner's *gesamtkunstwerk* seeks to destroy the individual's power of perception. It accomplishes this by projecting a deceptive wholeness—a false unity that smoothes over social contradictions and the work's conditions of production.

> In the dubious quid pro quo of gestural, expressive and structural elements on which Wagnerian form feeds, what is supposed to emerge is something like an epic totality, a rounded and complete whole of inner and outer. Wagner's music simulates this unity of the internal and external, of subject and object, instead of giving shape to the rupture between them.[34]

Jay also compares these claims to those voiced by other critical theorists such as Herbert Marcuse and Leo Lowenthal, who liken such realism to the deception employed by authoritarianism as well.[35] Wagner's music thus foreshadows the culture industry. Jay explains in Adorno's biography: "Instead of expressing classical bourgeois man's triumphant struggle to assert himself, Wagner's operas betrayed late bourgeois man's capitulation to reified forces outside his control."[36] In the twentieth century, popular music and film scores, whose very form serves to atomize audiences and turn them inward, exercise capital's commodifying powers. For Adorno, leitmotifs are not "genuinely constructed," but blandly serve in "a kind of associative procedure." Their simplicity and repetitiveness cater to the "forgetful" and take away the necessity for listeners to conceive of that whole.[37] Correspondingly, the "Regression of Listening" that afflicts consumers of light music serves as a metaphor for fading subjectivity, and their diminishing ability to critically regard the world as a totality:

> The delight in the moment and the gay façade becomes an excuse for absolving the listener from the thought of the whole, whose claim is comprised in proper listening. The listener is converted, along his line of least resistance, into the acquiescent purchaser. No longer do the partial moments serve as a critique of that whole; instead, they suspend the critique which the successful esthetic totality exerts against the flawed one of society.[38]

At the same time, the culture industry reifies subjects' autonomy, packaging their individuality into commodities. From Adorno and Max Horkheimer's *Dialectic of Enlightenment*:

> Pseudo-individuality is rife: from the standardized jazz improvisation to the exceptional film star whose hair curls over her eye to demonstrate her originality. What is individual is no more than the generality's power to stamp the accidental detail so firmly that it is accepted as such . . . The peculiarity of self is a monopoly commodity determined by society; it is falsely represented as natural.[39]

In sum, Adorno's high regards for the negational subject's autonomy and the necessity for that individual to resist reification is plain enough to see. As a consequence, his remarkable change of heart in the later reconsideration of the cinema, "Transparencies on Film," becomes exponentially more noteworthy.

There, he willingly entertains the notion of more dynamic forms of reception, and of more nuanced and less monolithic views of the culture industry. To those who scoff that Adorno's condescending bourgeois elitism was behind his perception of passive spectators as deluded subjects of manipulation, "Transparencies in Film" reveals a kinder stance and more complex perspective, where interpellation does not lead "automatically" to false consciousness.[40]

> If . . . film accommodates various layers of behavioral response patterns, this would imply that the ideology provided by the industry, its officially intended models, may by no means automatically correspond to those that affect the spectators . . . In its attempts to manipulate the masses the ideology of the culture industry itself becomes as internally antagonistic as the very society which it aims to control. The ideology of the culture industry contains the antidote to its own lie. No other plea could be made for its defense.[41]

Evidently rethinking the hard line he adopted before, Adorno's generosity can sanction claims like this popular citation from Jameson's essay, "Reification and Utopia in Mass Culture":

> [All] contemporary works of art—whether those of high culture and modernism or of mass culture and commercial culture—have as their underlying impulse— albeit in what is often distorted and repressed unconscious form—our deepest fantasies about the nature of social life, both as we live it now, and as we feel in our bones it ought rather to be lived . . . [It] is surely an indispensable precondition for any meaningful Marxist intervention in contemporary culture.[42]

Jameson's appellation as a Marxist critic can be supplemented by the fact that he picked up Adorno's intellectual torch. Much of Jameson's writing so resonates with Adorno's—intellectually, politically, and stylistically. Take say, Jameson's idea of postmodern pastiche. It is uncanny to consider its similarity to Adorno's description—cited first below—of the regressed listener/subject's use of quotations as both "authoritarian and a parody," using a metaphor of the child imitating the teacher:

> No less characteristic of the regressive musical language is the quotation. Its use ranges from the conscious quotation of folk and children's songs, by way of ambiguous and half accidental allusions, to completely latent similarities and

associations. The tendency triumphs in the adaptation of whole pieces from the classical stick or the operatic repertoire. The practice of quotation mirrors the ambivalence of the infantile listener's consciousness.[43]

Pastiche is, like parody, the imitation of a peculiar or unique style, the wearing of a stylistic mask, speech in a dead language: but it is a neutral practice of such mimicry, without parody's ulterior motive, without the satirical impulse, without laughter, without that still latent feeling that there exists something normal compared to which what is being imitated is rather comic. Pastiche is blank parody, parody that has lost its sense of humor.[44]

Jameson's thoughts on "pastiche" extend from Adorno's on regressed subjects and their degraded "quotations." Highlighting the extent of this continuity between Adorno and Jameson is necessary because as the inheritor of the Adorno's thinking, Jameson apparently proceeds to re-shut the door on the subject, a door that Adorno had left ajar ever so slightly during his revaluation of cinema. Between these two closely linked authors, we arrive once again at what looks on the surface like an impossible tension between contradictory opinions on the subject's current status. But, suppose we do not comprehend Adorno and Jameson's positions on the matter simply from the content of their arguments. What if we account for their form?

Presume for the moment to take Jameson at face value, that the bourgeois subject has disappeared. With it goes the source of "ulterior motive" and "satirical impulse" that makes parody possible, along with the abilities to conceive and organize a totality, and to produce a "personal style." As such, Jameson appears to depart from Adorno, who holds on fiercely to the viability of the subject, just possibly in the spectator but certainly within the theorist or critic. In another late essay "Resignation," Adorno allows that the theorist need not be responsible for linking thought to praxis. At a time when meaningful action is less possible than ever before, when it often only replicates or reinforces existing means of production, Adorno rationalizes the detachment of critical critique from praxis.

The universal tendency of oppression is opposed to thought as such. Thought is happiness, even where it defines unhappiness by enunciating it. By this alone happiness reaches into the universal unhappiness. Whoever does not let it atrophy has not resigned.[45]

Such an argument rests entirely on the strength, let alone the viability of the subject, who is in this case a theorist such as himself. By instating the importance of thought, he must rely on the critic's possession of both originality and autonomy. We will hence discover the attitude regarding this most vital ability, to access Utopia via pessimism—of which Gramsci's pessimism of intellect and optimism of the will is a famous reiteration—embodied within Jameson's prose.

Jameson seems like he is literally sounding the death knell for the subject, but at the same time, it is difficult to also argue that his conscientious advancement of Adorno's thinking really represents an example of blank pastiche. One both identifies and senses within the outer discourse of Jameson's oeuvre, and the inner workings of his labyrinthine prose, connected by creative punctuation, and self-powered by an irrepressible dialecticism, the presence of subjectivity—both his own and Adorno's—within a parody of Adorno's own idiosyncratic writing style. In that context, it is poignant that Jameson chooses to highlight the Faulknerian long sentence to illustrate parody.[46] Therefore, while Adorno's dialecticism is articulated in content, between claims that often contradicted each other, Jameson proffers his Marxist approach within the opposition between what he says and how he says it. For this reason, contrary to what Jameson literally claims, the subject is very much alive, still powerful enough to reference Adorno and to continue the elder's project.

Jameson's perspective on popular culture, however, is actually different from Adorno's. Jameson is less dismissive and more sympathetic. In mass culture, he discovers ideological construction and economic reification, but a Utopian dimension too where class consciousness can aestheticize the commodity. It thus explains Jameson's greater analytical attention to popular culture and quotidian analysis. In contrast, Adorno's infamously absolutist point of view sees mass culture not as commodified culture as such, but pure commodity, imposed from above by the economic elite that controls the culture industry. But ultimately, at a time where postmodern intertextuality and its obliteration of high and low effectively transform all culture into mass culture, both Adorno and Jameson remind us of the prerequisite behind all criticism. The ability to recognize reification hinges on the existence of the subject, and draws from our resolve to cling on to its continued viability. Against the reifying clutches of capitalist culture, Adorno finds it paramount to protect the creative impulses of artists and the critical, active subjectivities of critics and consuming audiences. This main concern on his part is a tenet of his cultural and social criticism, revealed by charting the trajectory of his film criticism back toward the appraisal of Wagner. I might venture even further, and argue that the autonomous negational subject could well be his most primary concern, a position that is substantiated by the meditation on his work that follows.

The subject of Adorno's contradictions

Composing for the Films devotes substantial time to gathering recommendations for an alternative practice. In many ways, they can be gleaned easily from Adorno's general critique of popular culture. Those familiar with Adorno will not be surprised that his basic admonition calls for more dialecticism—a healthy mixture of affirmation and negation—to dispel the illusion of direct unity and immediacy that mass culture conjures. The autonomous artwork should consist of parts that highlight differences between what is real and that which is fantasy, and thus call forth a dialectical clash between itself and social reality.[47] It must alienate but not deceive. It should provide and ensure critical distance. It should be spontaneous rather than automated, programmed, or otherwise telegraphed. To defy classical convention, film music should provide spatial, emotional, and intellectual depth to cinema. Adorno and Eisler offer a variety of avenues to describe this added dimension; at one point terming it "momentum, muscular energy, a sense of corporeity, as it were."[48]

They prescribe a form of critical subjectivity that can be achieved with disunity. In music, he and Eisler recommend the use of irony.[49] Musical tone might contrast with the emotional mood of the narrative, where a happy scene is scored with somber music, or if we hear an up-tempo melody over a mournful moment in the story. The result is a dialectic moment where the end effect does not redundantly emphasize the image, but serves an abstract ideal of the work as a whole. "The use of music in motion pictures should be inspired by objective considerations, by the intrinsic requirements of the work."[50] For Adorno, what the work demands may transcend the romantic notion of the creative artist, composer, or auteur. That work possesses autonomy that should aim to reach a collective and not fixate on individual achievement. He concedes however, that there are drawbacks to the general principle of musical irony. Counterpoints can also regress into mere formula. If it were entirely a blind directive, if the means were simply the ends, it risks degenerating into a matter of automatism and fetishized style. Adorno and Eisler identify this very tendency in the work of *Les Six*, a sextet of French film composers—including Maurice Jaubert, Eric Satie, and Darius Milhaud.[51] The group had originally resolved to create an alternative paradigm to classical practice that eventually ossified into formulae. Regarding critical race film criticism in the context of this riposte, one could predict that Adorno would have easily condemned the corrective images advocated by stereotype studies.

Adorno and Eisler also advocate the judicious application of vagueness. They maintain a partiality toward significatory indistinctness over clarity, and for perceptual unity over illusionism. Like montage, they argue that hermeneutic indeterminacy is a mark of Brechtian self-consciousness, a means to jolt audiences out of complacency, and that it would emancipate "motion-picture music from its commercial oppression."[52] The resultant commitment to aesthetic autonomy inverts the process of deception, so to speak, prioritizing authenticity as a concern over the authoritarian need to predict and control audience response. However, although Adorno and Eisler affirm proper commitment to "the work," they also assert the legitimacy of public desires to have music "'motivate' the events on the screen," before reiterating the complaint about how the culture industry misuses that desire.[53] This impossibly contradictory bundle of prescriptive recommendations emphasize the uneasy rhetorical balance that *Composing for the Films* tries to achieve, and is what some might consider his argument's undoing.

In light of Adorno's absolutism regarding popular culture, just what is the utility in raising the prospects of autonomous work within the culture industry? *Composing for the Films* purports to take on the Hollywood studio production, where if we already believe Adorno himself, the possibilities of authenticity are slim at best. Even if Adorno is initially led into a discussion on cinema by his intellectual and emotional investments in music (the pre-capitalist art form whose authenticity counters the automatism of industrial film production), music remains just one element of cinema's aesthetic schema. How viable is a musical or aural solution for what is an admittedly visual medium that he has effectively condemned? Why does he bother? And how do we subsequently make sense of the sympathy that he later generated for avant-garde cinema? Indeed, the relative strength of the image compared to sound or music has been testified to by film sound theorist Michel Chion's description of "synchresis"— the forging of an immediate and necessary relationship between what one hears and what one sees at the same time.[54] Synchresis threatens to subsume aural or musical counterpoint into the unified dominion of the image. Contradictions abound in Adorno.

My feeling on this differs from, on the one hand, Jay and Huyssen who chart his perspective according to the progression or so-called shift of a hard-line stance into a more pliable one; and on the other from Hansen, who contends that the contradictions warrant a large-scale retroactive rereading of Adorno's work. I propose a triangulation of the two positions, an explanation that refrains from an impulse to categorize him, retains his pessimistic insistences with regard to the culture industry, and most important, integrates his unmistakable contradictions. Adorno's work on cinema is not the crude and confused proclamations of a filmic dilettante. Nor did his musical idealism cause him to overreach with his prognostications about film. But just as likely, the incongruities were implanted by overall design. At times, he recognizes them, but makes no effort at resolution: "Whither this contradiction will lead we cannot predict at the present stage of development, when it has not even been visualized by normal production."[55] Therefore, rather than seeking to connect or resolve the dots between these internal disagreements, it might be more crucial to remember his call for continual dialecticism (particularly in his debates with Benjamin); referring in other words, to his preference for a critical mix of affirmation and negation. It is if nothing else, his only unchanging characteristic. Perhaps the most important question is not what he really thought of film, music, or film music, nor is it whether his proposals for an intervention in film music are tenable, particularly if he was only secondarily concerned about how art forms can be transformed. Primarily, Adorno was ultimately occupied with how people's minds changed, how their rationality was appropriated, how their consent was manufactured, and how their listening regressed.

Now that we have enough to identify the Neo-Marxian subject, what is its import for critical race film studies? First and foremost, critical or authorial subjectivity must remain alive in some form and acknowledged in some fashion. It should be postured at the ready to perform negation and dialecticism. The text is not unimportant, for it has a part to play in protecting and stimulating those powers. Generally speaking, films should therefore refrain from illusionism or protecting the spectacle, and should instead promote ambiguity, irony, and historicism.

Consider how those principles would be called up for action in the following examples. The summer film *A Knight's Tale* (2001) was a commercial product for the teen market starring the then budding heartthrob Heath Ledger. The soundtrack scores a romantic comedy narrative in the Middle Ages with pop songs. At one memorable jousting match, the scene opens on a musical joke: a medieval crowd of apparent fans of the rock group Queen chanting "We will, we will Rock You!" The film exploits pop music, overexposed teen idols, and a bastardized version of history, but it also performs an act of utter self-consciousness that plainly revels in its own artifice. *Les Six* would balk, yet I suggest that an Adornoan treatment of this text would de-emphasize

Figure 3.1 Why does Mookie throw the trashcan at the end of *Do the Right Thing* (1989)? The answer is not as important as the enduring question.

the necessity to read or make a film according to some fixed standard of radicalness, in favor of valorizing its provocations of irony. In a sense, it matters less that a film checks all the prerequisites of a culture industry product, if it can somehow ignite within individual subjects their capacities for autonomy and alienation. I suspect that Adorno would appreciate the alienating effects and narrative ambiguity employed by Spike Lee in *Do the Right Thing* for the same reasons. The film's color palette is saturated, its soundtrack steps over dialogue, and it uses direct address to confront and invade viewers' headspace. In addition, a quarter of a century after its release the film continues to prompt an enduring debate about why the character Mookie threw a trash can through the front window of Sal's Pizzeria.[56] Lee's claim that the only people who have ever sought him out for an answer are white, even more acutely shows that moment to be the film's most politically effective (Figure 3.1). It matters less what Mookie's reasons are, if the film can lead people to keep asking questions. Witness Adorno's chronic reluctance to perform detailed specific analyses of mass culture. Dialectics occur in the mind, not on reified products of culture. If sufficiently profound, negational gestures challenge and incite the audience's imagination. I therefore feel that neither Adorno nor Jameson for that matter, ever loses faith in the public's potential for autonomy. It is therefore less crucial as to what film is or what Adorno thought it is, but how we all watch, listen, and think vigilantly about them; less about how an analysis would fit with his, and more about the fact that we must remain autonomously critical and materialistically conscious, whether as artists, critics, or audiences.

As it happens, we thus return to the exact sort of individual subjectivity assumed and implicitly constructed by critical race film theory, the kind perhaps abdicated by the likes of Althusser, Lacan, and the many film critics operating under their auspices on the issue of race. Moreover, it is noteworthy that this overlap occurs with a Neo-Marxian thinker as uncompromising as Adorno. Far from breaking away from Marxism, second-generation criticism on race and ethnicity is in fact still within its orbit. The approaches examined so far, from Stam, Spence, Bhabha, Manthia Diawara, Jacqueline Stewart, and others, might still maintain that the text is an unstable entity: discursively dependent, epistemologically unstable, interpretively fluid, and innately ambivalent. But all their theories depend ineluctably on the centrality and unity of the autonomous and dialectical subject. Even if their contradiction does not yet pry open a gap wide enough in critical race film studies for Marxism to rush in, it still establishes a basic precondition for its re-entry.

Racial subjects and the problem of biological essentialism

Prosecuting a case on behalf of the subject creates a conundrum that must be solved. If the subject is an historical being, conscious, autonomous, and able to transcend ideology, it is then by those accounts, an essential being. Within racial debates, however, essentialism is taboo. Biological essentialism partly infers genetic determinism and supports racist ideologies that draw direct correlations between ethnicity and anthropological or sociological phenomena. For example, it attributes elevated crime or reproductive rates in minority communities, to genetic predisposition or collective sub-humanity. "Common sense" like this consolidates ideas about the Other in the public imagination by referring to their all-important core racial identity. It encourages disregard for social conditions that confer disadvantage on those groups, and makes it easy to justify public policy or laws such as segregation, or categorical practices premised on the one-drop rule. Essentialism is therefore a very problematic concept.

We have already seen second-generation critical race film theory encounter the inverse difficulty when it tries to undermine racial ideology by disavowing essentialism and unified subjectivity, with tenets maintaining that both race and the subject are social ideological constructions. In spite of their efforts, the subject still lingers. Keep in mind that the eschewal of stereotype analysis is effectively a rejection of the subject too, since it sprouts from questions about whether reality is observable or whether it can even be objectively comprehended, by a unified subject that some presume to no longer exist. These doubts and wariness are motivated by more than antiracism. They also originate from an array of projects lined up against Western hegemony in all its intellectual, military, and political forms: the Enlightenment, colonialism, and capitalism. These parties broadly believe that the subject is an oppressive Eurocentric construction. But do they have to be tethered? Will the Eurocentrism linger? Is the subject necessarily racist? Can we advocate for critical subjectivity without getting tangled up in racial ideology?

For second-generation criticism at least, even the task of expelling both the subject and racial essentialism is thornier than it seems. The contradiction in identity politics already evinces that. Let us now follow the logic of another critical race analysis, Gary Edgerton's "'A Breed Apart': Hollywood, Racial Stereotyping, and the Promise of Revisionism in *The Last of the Mohicans*," a study of Michael Mann's 1992 update of James Fenimore Cooper's famous novel. Edgerton measures the film by the director's avowed intent to create a compelling adventure with an enlightened view of Native American peoples and culture. He contends that Mann ultimately fails in that quest, because the film continues to use Native American images "to present the viewpoint of the historically privileged rather than the oppressed."[57] Edgerton proceeds well aware of critical race film theory's methodological history. He cites Stam and Spence's landmark essay about subjective positioning as a methodological base for his analysis: he sets out to avoid merely branding images as "good" or "bad" and to consider other cinematic codes that involve plot structure, point-of-view, image composition, and editing strategies. I was struck by how he breaks down the opening scene, where the characters Hawkeye, Chingachgook, and Uncas participate in a spectacularly staged deer hunt.

Edgerton breaks down the sequence into its constituent shots and categorizes them into those that capture each of the characters. He records shot totals, screen time, and lines of dialogue, and concludes that the drama of the scene is animated from a "white, patriarchal viewpoint." He bases the claim on the observation that the action is shot primarily from Hawkeye's point of view. For example, the stag that the trio is stalking is seen only in reverse shots linked with Hawkeye's eyeline.[58] Edgerton takes Hawkeye plainly as a white patriarch. His premise can seem obvious because the production banks heavily on Irish actor Daniel Day-Lewis's masculine sex appeal as an action hero. Nevertheless, it is also intriguing because by all cultural and social accounts, Hawkeye's character is decidedly Native American. He dresses like one, speaks the language fluently, shares a kinship with Chingachgook and Uncas, is attuned to Mohican cultural mores, and participates in their rituals.

Edgerton then assumes a multiculturalist position and also charges that Mann's attempts to glorify Native American culture is undermined by putting forth a segregationist cultural view that makes assimilation morally unwise and narratively impossible. This is because the film indicts European colonialism in terms so absolute that any assimilation would constitute total corruption. Regarding the film's romantic couplings, Edgerton also argues that interracial relationships are either fatally punished in the case of Uncas and Alice, or expelled from both white and Native cultures, as with Hawkeye and Cora.[59] In fact, he rues the film's inexorable departure from the ideal of cultural coexistence depicted in the ritualism of the deer hunt.

> Now all of a sudden, Hawkeye is supposedly no longer Mohican but has become more Anglo as he falls further in love with Cora. The complexity raised by this evident dissonance in the text is, of course, whether Hawkeye's ethnicity is the product of his cultural experience or his biology. Although the complicated issue is never directly addressed in the movie, the characters behave as though genes are all that count in determining one's breeding.[60]

This antiessentialist position is confusing. The film does not actually clear up the ambiguity surrounding Hawkeye's ethnic standing at narrative's end. What is more crucial, Edgerton himself had made a definitive connection earlier between Hawkeye's ethnicity and genetic lineage during an analysis of the deer hunt sequence. He had assumed that Hawkeye's rearing is subordinate to his breeding, as it were. Edgerton overlooks the plethora of cultural indicators on the thoroughly assimilated protagonist with whom the film completely identifies, and implicates Day-Lewis's character with white, colonial patriarchy solely because he is marked as such in complexion and physiognomy. Edgerton goes so far as to attribute Lewis's locks to a masculine "rock star" aesthetic, as opposed to an equally plausible reason, Mohican cultural practice. Michael Mann in fact assiduously ties Hawkeye to the Mohicans. In addition to costuming, make-up, and dialogue, various shot compositions continually build the visual affiliation between Hawkeye, Uncas, and Chingachgook (Figure 3.2 and 3.3). It is Edgerton and not

(a)

(b)

Figure 3.2 Michael Mann's graphical symmetries identify Hawkeye as Mohican. (*The Last of the Mohicans*, 1992).

Figure 3.3 Mann's social blocking further separate him from the Europeans. (*The Last of the Mohicans*, 1992).

Mann who employs biological essentialism, and for whom genes are all that count.[61]

A similar tendency of reverting to essentialism and a definition of race based on descent, while operating in the name of race as consensual cultural practice, was previously identified by Walter Benn Michaels's study of 1920s American literature.[62] In *Our America*, Michaels identifies a thematic constant in those works that he calls "nativist modernism," which represented a paradigmatic change from defining race in terms of cultural hierarchies and away from the idea that identity is innately hereditary. That thinking from the Progressive Era was replaced by the rise of pluralism that conferred equal value to all cultures and an increased acceptance that one's racial identity is determined by what one "does" (consent) as opposed to what one "is" (descent). Nativist modernism however, signifies the contradiction of that position, and represents a problem for anybody who seeks antiessentialist alternatives to discuss race and culture.

> [P]luralism's programmatic hostility to universalism—its hostility to the idea that cultural practices be justified by appeals to what seems universally good or true—requires that such practices be justified instead by appeals to what seems locally good or true, which is to say, it invokes the identity of the group as the grounds for the justification of the group's practices.[63]

In other words, our cultural practices are predefined. If they were not, then whatever we do would constitute our culture, Michaels explains. A person's culture is thus not simply what one does, but more accurately described as what one should do, and those rules are in the end still defined by biology.

The notion of racial antiessentialism is therefore a paradox, a theoretical short-circuit caused by simultaneously competing and overlapping perspectives on the subject, essentialism, and poststructuralism. But these contradictions can be resolved by expunging race and ethnicity from the subject's defining identity. Identity politics' practice of framing critical subjectivity in terms of racially exclusive experiences is thus untenable. Adorno formulates his critical subject as one with the capacity for dialecticism, a unified consciousness able to discern the false unity projected by the culture industry, and able to access the irrational as an antidote to capitalist rationality. Although it can be constituted by its relationship to capital and defined most basically by capital's presence or absence, race and ethnicity are at best secondary in this view. To wit, we find in Adorno a way to think about the critical subject's relationship to racial identity. We also have the means to illustrate it in the films of Todd Solondz.

Palindromes (2004) is Solondz's black comedy about a maladjusted, white 13-year-old lead character, Aviva Victor. The most distinguishing element of the film is Solondz's decision to borrow from Luis Buñuel's *That Obscure Object of Desire* (1977), and portray the protagonist with eight different actors who vary in race, gender, size, and age. *Palindromes* follows the awkward, timid, and innocent Aviva as she tries to fulfill her childhood wish of having a child. She first conceives by seducing the young son of a family friend, a pregnancy that her suburban parents force her to abort. She runs away and begins a series of misadventures that begin with a rape by a pedophilic truck driver that she misrecognizes as a love affair. She is eventually taken in by a devoutly Christian family that is also plotting the murder of an abortion doctor. Through all of these experiences, Aviva's character remains unchanged, with the same motivations, emotions, and perspectives from beginning to end. Every actor playing the character does so with identical performances (Figure 3.4). Overall, the device produces the effect of forcing the audience to relate to Aviva's character while remaining unaffected by differences in her appearance due to race, gender, size, and age. In interviews, Solondz proclaims that the film attempts to reach humanity's inner core, a part that exists in a form of "stasis."[64]

Adorno and Jameson would appreciate how *Palindromes* compels us to comprehend a person's inner being, Aviva's subjectivity, and to differentiate between it and the discursive interference brought on by the various ideologies governing race, gender, and other identity markers. The most extraordinary form that Aviva takes in the film is that of an obese African American girl. It presents an infamous form of black womanhood, a socially vilified symbol of excess, gluttony, and sloth—the reactionary bête noire of the black single welfare mother—as inconsequential to understanding Aviva's humanity (Figure 3.4c). Solondz separates race and gender from her essence and neutralizes this racial and gendered stereotype. Perhaps more significant, Solondz cast Jennifer Jason Leigh as Aviva for the penultimate scene (Figure 3.4d). Leigh's star status as a relatively well-known actress in the 1980s and 1990s is purposefully at play in the narrative, not least because all the other actresses in the role are unknowns, but the advertising and marketing also foreground her presence. Leigh's performance therefore is not merely a function of her physical appearance, which Solondz describes as one of age and experience.[65] Rather, I argue that the film proposes more profoundly to equate star discourse with race and gender. I recall Adorno

(a)

(b)

(c)

(d)

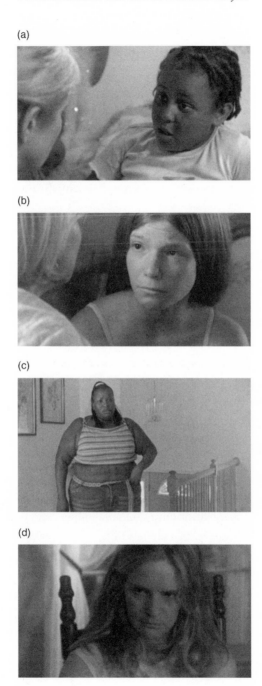

Figure 3.4 Four of Aviva's incarnations in *Palindromes* (2004).

on stars, referring in this case to musicians: "The star principle has become totalitarian. The reactions of the listeners appear to have no relation to the playing of the music."[66] He makes the point as part of a wider description of the culture industry, which utilizes the star system as a means of product differentiation. Stars operate as recognizable clichés, contrived advertising icons within the system of cultural mass production, and illusory subjects that project false unities. In this layered context, *Palindromes* suggests that unlike inner humanist subjectivities, race and gender are unsubstantial image ideas that exist solely in the service of capital. Essentially then (pun intended), the subject is not raced or gendered.

The film's companion theme is stasis, a less optimistic thread that might sit closer to Solondz's overall intentions. The director explains that his palindrome metaphor refers to the quality of something "folding in on itself," with a beginning and end that mirror each other. Translated to the human condition, it signifies the atomistic tendency to resist change. Without the expectation of growing out of one's failings and limitations, people would in a sense be liberated from the illusion that those weaknesses can be defeated through personal transformation.[67] Solondz's stasis does not refer to anything but the emotional aspects of personality, however, for he sees intellectual change as inevitable.

Even if that is true, he can appear to take up Jameson's fatalistic posture with regards to social change. The characters in his oeuvre—*Welcome to the Dollhouse* (1995), *Happiness* (1998), *Storytelling* (2001), and *Palindromes*—are distinguished by stasis, by their absolute incapability of change, of personal, and thus of social transformation. In *Storytelling* the protagonist, Generation X slacker Scooby Livingston is revealed in the final moments to be as self-absorbed as the automatons he rebels against. Solondz's films carry out an unrelenting critique of bourgeois and petit-bourgeois life. He drains the mise-en-scène of its color except in cases where pastels are used for irony, and directs the action with an intensity generated by the films' distinct lack of dynamic movement. The sterility of suburban landscapes in his works is rendered permanent by characters' inward atomism. In this light, the palindrome can also be read as an entity without temporal orientation, and to paraphrase Solondz, folding in not only on an individual but into an eternal present.

Still, like Jameson, Solondz enforces a critical distance among his spectators by alienating them. All his distinctive characters, especially the sympathetic protagonists such as *Happiness's* unassuming but homicidal and pedophilic Bill Maplewood, are invariably flawed and often in horrific ways. In Adornoan terms, Solondz arguably generates a dialectic in his dark comedy, counterposing lovable iconography with grotesquery. The genre thus prevents his audience from passive immersion in the narrative, and encourages it to regard the world in its totality; his films make an unambiguous link between its characters, their atomism and psychological crises, with the weariness of rationalized bourgeois culture and social institutions.

Again à la Jameson, Solondz's point of view seeks to capture a global dimension while rejecting the hope for genuine or totalizing politics.[68] His subject is hence constituted thus, a combination of Aviva's resistant human core and both the author and spectator's capacity to conceive of totalities. It is a formulation where identity is strikingly absent and which follows through smoothly on Jameson's claim about political action. Movements based on difference induce a political fragmentation that precludes substantive action and systemic change, but adopting class as a political paradigm then requires a proletarian alliance that now appears impossible. Jameson writes in *The Political Unconscious*:

> The privileged form in which the American Left can develop today must therefore necessarily be that of an *alliance politics* . . . the strict practical equivalent of the concept of totalization on the theoretical level. In practice, then, the attack on the concept of 'totality' in the American framework means the undermining and repudiation of the only realistic perspective in which a genuine Left could come into being in this country.[69]

That is to say, Jameson considers class politics to be a necessary precondition for both the planning and achievement of systemic change. The reason for that is because class runs as a "conceptual" category underneath all notions of difference. It is an "abstraction," capable of both articulating itself in terms of, say, race and gender, and transcending those categories.[70] All politics are class politics, and only class politics are meaningful.

One wonders if Tommy L. Lott's definition of the political corresponds with a declaration as uncompromising as that. What his essay on "A No-theory Theory of Contemporary Black Cinema" does recognize is that the messiness caused by racial essentialism can be cleared up by a critical subject. Contemplating "black cinema," Lott focuses on two questions: what black cinema is, and what it should do. He is unable to define blackness in films, struggling predictably with biological essentialism. Blackness can exist in multiple forms—the author, the film's aesthetic, or the text's content, to name a few—that are at the same time impossibly fluid. So to those who might maintain that blacks hold a monopoly over the power to articulate a black perspective, Lott points out that "from a cultural standpoint," a white director can be very suitably empowered in that regard. Depending on one's perspective, Lott either capitulates or solves his dilemma with an equally malleable "no-theory" due to his wish "to avoid any commitment to an essentialized notion by not giving a definition of black cinema."[71] The "no-theory" of what constitutes black cinema is guided only by films' advocacy of the appropriate "politics" and "social change." It is difficult to discern anything more specific in Lott's conceptualization of those terms, but it is clear that he counts on a critic's ability to know what those politics are, if or when he or she sees them.

In conclusion, Gayatri Chakravorty Spivak's idea of "strategic essentialism" offers a transition from this chapter's meditation on the humanist subject to the following study of postcolonial critic Edward Said. For her part, Spivak echoes Michaels in arguing that an absolutely antiessentialist position is impossible. Yet her deconstructionism obviously prevents her from accepting essentialism in and of itself, of a subject or otherwise.[72] But alas, to take a stand against essentialism necessitates a positivist assumption that "essentialism" itself has a stable meaning. "Strategic essentialism" recommends provisionally adopting humanist essentialism to allow the subaltern consciousness to establish a base of critical or political operations. It is in a way, a temporary and only "partially unwitting" betrayal of antiessentialism.[73]

The critique of this position recalls an earlier response to the aforementioned deconstructionist methodology of Bhabha as well as Lott's. In contemplating Spivak's "strategic use of positivist essentialism in a scrupulously visible political interest," one might inquire as to the source of that strategy, those scruples themselves, and the capacity to visualize politics.[74] Under her proposal to first stabilize an essential meaning followed by a formulation of "strategy"—to wage a Gramscian "war of position" if you will—that revolts against an essentialist ideology, requires no less than a critical subject. Spivak's explicit suggestion to lean on humanism in order to help the subaltern merely appears to be a less latent parallel of how poststructuralist film criticism covertly finds recourse in essentialism via the subject, as its means to begin charting a political dimension.

Therein lies the significance of the autonomous subject, and the disavowed but undeniable state that it finds itself in second-generation critical race film theory. The uncanny resemblance of its manifestation in that corpus of theory with the one in its Neo-Marxian brethren points to a continued existence. But when mobilized in debates on race however, the notion of biological essentialism appears and threatens to compromise its usefulness, being ironically both a tool in racist ideology as well as a justification and rationale for identity politics. Assuming that we believe in the eminence of the subject and some notion of its essence, we arrive thus at a political and theoretical juncture. We can lean on a subject, but not a racialized one. And if you reject the unified subject, can you then radically fashion a racialized, strategic, or contingent one? This appears to be a choice between class and identity politics, both underpinned by essentialism in some form. The next chapter continues to recover class and materialism as a paradigm, in much the same way that I retrieved the subject.

Notes

1   Robert Sklar, "*Oh! Althusser!*: Historiography and the Rise of Cinema Studies," *Resisting Images: Essays on Cinema and History*, ed. Robert Sklar and Charles Musser (Philadelphia, PA: Temple University Press, 1990): 14.

2   Sean Homer, *Fredric Jameson Marxism, Hermeneutics, Postmodernism* (New York: Routledge, 1998): 54.

3   Stephen Heath, "Film and System: Terms of Analysis 2," *Screen* 16, 2 (1975): 91–113.

4   Homi K. Bhabha, *The Location of Culture* (London and New York: Routledge, 1994): 189, 190.

5   Ibid., 76–77.

6   Fredric Jameson, *Postmodernism, or, The Cultural Logic of Late Capitalism* (Durham, NC: Duke University Press, 1991): 16.

7   Ibid., 77.

8   In *The Essential Frankfurt School Reader*, ed. Andrew Arato and Eike Gebhardt (New York: Continuum, 1982): 275–76.

9   See Martin Jay, *Adorno* (Cambridge, MA: Harvard University Press, 1984): 38.

10 Ibid., 25.

11 Theodor W. Adorno and Hanns Eisler, *Composing for the Films* (London/Atlantic Highlands, NJ: The Althone Press, 1994).

12 "On the Social Situation of Music" trans. Wes Blomster in *Telos* 35 (1978): 128–64.

13 Jay, *Adorno*, 27.

14 Andreas Huyssen, "Introduction to Adorno," *New German Critique* 6 (Fall 1975): 5.

15 Miriam B. Hansen, "Introduction to Adorno, 'Transparencies on Film' (1966)," *New German Critique* 24–25 (Fall/Winter 1981–82): 197.

16   Siegfried Kracauer, *Theory of Film* (New York: Oxford University Press, 1960).

17   Walter Benjamin, "The Work of Art in the Age of Mechanical Reproduction," trans. Harry Zohn, *Illuminations: Essays and Reflections* (New York: Schocken, 1968): 217–52.

18   Theodor W. Adorno, "Transparencies on Film," trans. Thomas Y. Levin, *New German Critique* 24–25 (Fall/Winter 1981–82): 200.

19   Adorno and Eisler, *Composing for the Films*, 12.

20   Theodor W. Adorno and Max Horkheimer, *Dialectic of Enlightenment*, trans. John Cumming (New York: Continuum, 1999): 124–26.

21   Adorno and Eisler, *Composing for the Films*, 20.

22   Ibid., 91.

23   Ibid., 111.

24   Adorno and Eisler, *Composing for the Films*, 22, 101; Jay, *Adorno*, 131–32, 136. See Max Weber, *The Rational and Social Foundations of Music*, trans. Don Martindal, Johannes Riedel, and Gertrude Neuwirth (Illinois: Southern Illinois University Press, 1958).

25   Adorno and Eisler, *Composing for the Films*, lii.

26   Ibid., 5.

27   Theodor Adorno, *In Search of Wagner*, trans. Rodney Livingstone (London: NLB, 1981): 153–54.

28   Jay, *Adorno*, 147

29   Adorno and Eisler, *Composing for the Films*, 4–5.

30   Ibid., 8.

31   Adorno, "Fetish Character," 281.

32   Adorno, *In Search of Wagner*, 31.

33   Adorno, "Fetish Character," 278; Adorno and Eisler, *Composing for the Films*, 52–53, 60–61.

34   Adorno, *In Search of Wagner*, 38. See also 85–87.

35   Martin Jay, *The Dialectical Imagination: A History of the Frankfurt School and the Institute of Social Research, 1923–1950* (Boston, MA: Little, Brown and Company, 1973): 194.

36   Jay, *Adorno*, 147.

37   Ibid., 31.

38   Adorno, "Fetish Character," 273.

39   Adorno and Horkheimer, *Dialectic of Enlightenment*, 154.

40   See Hansen, "Introduction to Adorno," 190–91.

41   Adorno, "Transparencies on Film," 201–02.

42   In *Signatures of the Visible* (London: Routledge, 1990): 34.

43   Adorno, "Fetish Character," 291. For more of Adorno's prescient identification of postmodern pastiche, see also his praise for "great music" as the kind

that possessed "musical synthesis" which preserves unity and prevents its disintegration into "diffuse culinary moments" (273), and his analysis of contemporary musical arrangement that "reifies bits and pieces out of . . . context," destroying "the multilevel unity of the whole work" (281).

44　Fredric Jameson, "Postmodernism and Consumer Society," *The Anti-Aesthetic: Essays in Postmodern Culture*, ed. Hal Foster (Port Townsend, WA: Bay Press, 1983): 111–25. Definition is on page 114.

45　Theodor W. Adorno, "Resignation," *Critical Models*, trans. Henry W. Pickford (New York: Columbia University Press, 1998): 293.

46　Jameson, *Postmodernism*, 16.

47　Adorno and Eisler, *Composing for the Films*, 70–71.

48　Ibid., 76, 78.

49　Ibid., 27.

50　Ibid., 120.

51　Ibid., 85.

52　Ibid., 88.

53　Ibid., 121–22.

54　Michel Chion, *Audio-Vision*, ed. and trans. Claudia Gorbman (New York: Columbia University Press, 1994): 63–64.

55　Adorno and Eisler, *Composing for the Films*, 85.

56　Tambay A. Obenson, "Why Do You Think Mookie Threw a Trash Can into Sal's Pizzeria Window in 'Do the Right Thing?'" *Indiewire* (February 26, 2003) <http://blogs.indiewire.com/shadowandact/why-do-you-think-mookie-threw-a-trash-can-into-sals-pizzeria-window-in-do-the-right-thing> Accessed December 19, 2013.

57　Gary Edgerton, "'A Breed Apart': Hollywood, Racial Stereotyping, and the Promise of Revisionism in *The Last of the Mohicans*," *Journal of American Culture* 17, 2 (Summer 1994): 16.

58　Ibid., 9.

59　Ibid., 11–12.

60　Ibid., 14.

61　While he also declares indifference toward judging images to be good or bad, he still conducts a lengthy discussion on their accuracy. He adopts Stam and Spence's position wholeheartedly, but repeats what they and Neale criticize.

62　Walter Benn Michaels, *Our America: Nativism, Modernism and Pluralism* (Durham, NC: Duke University Press, 1995).

63　Ibid., 14.

64　Cindy Widner, "This is a Love Story," *The Austin Chronicle Online* (March 11, 2005) <http://www.austinchronicle.com/issues/dispatch/2005-03-11/screens_feature6.html> Accessed August 17, 2005.

65 Quoted in the film's press kit.

66 Adorno, "Fetish Character," 276.

67 Widner, "This is a Love Story."

68 Jameson, *Postmodernism*, 330.

69 Fredric Jameson, *The Political Unconscious: Narrative as a Socially Symbolic Act* (Ithaca, NY: Cornell University Press, 1981): 54.

70 Jameson, *Postmodernism*, 331; and "Actually Existing Marxism," *Polygraph* 6–7 (1993): 170–95.

71 In *The Invention of Race: Black Culture and the Politics of Representation* (Oxford: Blackwell Publishers, 1999): 141.

72 Gayatri Chakravorty Spivak, *In Other Worlds: Essays in Cultural Politics* (New York and London: Methuen, 1987): 202–27.

73 Ibid., 207.

74 Ibid., 205.

4

Postcolonial Hazards:
Edward Said and Film Studies

In a 1978 essay, "The Problem of Textuality: Two Exemplary Positions," Edward Said makes some unambiguous declarations regarding the work of the literary critic. Critiquing the poststructuralists Michel Foucault and Jacques Derrida as writers whose "critical work is a cognitive activity," Said posits that their common penchant for "textuality" fails to meet the basic obligations of the contemporary critic to be more politically and radically engaged. "In our present circumstances," he argues, "criticism is an adversary, or oppositional, activity."[1] Highlighting his own "sense of the contemporary critical consciousness," Said advocates muscularly for "something more than contemplative effort or an appreciative technical reading method for texts as undecidable objects."[2] In particular, he alludes to a notion familiar to Neo-Marxian thinkers that critics should adopt dialectical and alienated positions in order to rebel against texts' ideological operations and repressions. Outlining the critic's responsibilities, he writes:

> Criticism cannot assume that its province is merely the text, nor even the great literary text. It must see itself, as well as other discourse, inhabiting a much contested cultural space in which what has counted in the continuity and transmission of knowledge has been the signifier as an event that has left lasting traces upon the human subject. Once we take that view, then literature as an isolated paddock in the broad cultural field disappears, and with it too the harmless rhetoric of self-delighting humanism. Instead we will be able, I think, to read and write with a sense of the greater stake in historical and political effectiveness that literary, as well as all other texts have had.[3]

The symbiosis of Said's intellectual and political commitments as he himself avers should be notable for several reasons. The most obvious is that it allows, or even compels us to view Said as a critic who, with as staunch a belief as any in the critical consciousness of the humanist subject, continues to voice the commitments raised in the previous chapter by Theodor Adorno and Fredric Jameson. In this way, Said himself provides the antidote to continuing misrepresentations of *Orientalism*'s thesis within a sizable portion of critical race film criticism.[4] What is more, the clarity of his worldview reflected here appeared in the same year that *Orientalism* was originally published.

In film and media criticism's long-standing and ongoing examination of racial ideology, Edward Said's *Orientalism,* published in 1978, is a frequently cited and foundational text. Critical theorist Robert J. C. Young credits it with founding the discipline of postcolonial studies because it redefined colonialization as the enactment of not just military and economic power, but also of political and epistemic violence. It was also Said who first connected anticolonial political movements and ideological critiques with structuralist and poststructuralist theory. Whereas by the 1970s radical intellectuals had successfully challenged the "language politics of colonialism," Said extended their theoretical articulations into questions of discourse.[5] Not surprisingly, film and media studies generally engage with the book as a theoretical buttress for poststructuralist analyses of Eurocentric representations of cultural or ethnic Others. However, many of them appropriate Said's work narrowly and incorrectly because they highlight *Orientalism*'s poststructuralist articulations over its materialist and humanist character. This selective reading makes assumptions that blur *Orientalism*'s Marxist affinities. Decades after first contributing mightily to the field's analysis of race, the book must be reconceived and repositioned in film—and perhaps media studies too—so that, more importantly, it may serve to renew the field's existing approaches to questions of race.

Orientalism attends most immediately to literature, where Said finds a perception of the Near East (or Middle-East) as a roughly monolithic set of ethnicities and cultures standing in diametric opposition to those of Western Europe.

> On the one hand there are Westerners, and on the other there are Arab-Orientals; the former are (in no particular order) rational, peaceful, liberal, logical, capable of holding real values, without natural suspicion; the latter are none of these things.[6]

Said traces this paradigmatic view back to the Classical period and argues that it is sustained by imaginative pressures, institutions, traditions, and cultural forces that are ideologically repeated and inherited. Orientalism was powerfully normalized through its incorporation into scientific disciplines, by way of the scientists, geographers, and philosophers who were present on colonial expeditions. Thus, Said also connects Orientalism within the arts and sciences to Western domination of the Orient. His book links an intertextual examination of ideological discourses to their political-economic cause, European colonial and imperial power. Said singles out Britain, France, and the United States for their political economic influence and makes straightforward references to those nations' "brute" political, economic, and military authority. When he speaks of "power" in the book, he does not merely refer to an imbalance of cultural or social capital tilting in their favor; instead, power comes specifically from material expressions of imperialism. If Said were merely talking about discursive representation, I venture that he would not have become a lightning rod for criticism. "The *strength* of Western cultural discourse" that he describes is not something ephemeral, intangible, or figurative, but instead is the part of colonialism that materially and physically oppresses.[7] Responding to his critical adversary, the reactionary Orientalist Bernard Lewis, Said termed it effrontery "to disassociate Orientalism from its 200-year old partnership with European imperialism and associate it instead with modern classical philology and the study of ancient Greek and Roman culture."[8]

Contrary to Said's distinctly drawn nexus between culture and imperialism, film scholarship on race and Otherness often elides the connection with startling frequency. The field often misunderstands *Orientalism* and those interpretations come to configure its study of race and cinema. I analyze a sample of works ranging from those who pull up *Orientalism* for a quick but important reference to those that engage substantively with it, including canonical work such as Homi Bhabha's essay "The Other Question. . ." and an anthology predicated on Said's analysis titled, *Visions of the East: Orientalism in Film*. Many works, such as *Visions of the East* and *Unspeakable Images: Ethnicity and the American Cinema*, are popular anthologies assigned in university courses about race and media. Therefore, the issue exceeds one of mere misinterpretation. Its implications affect how a much larger audience thinks about race.

The most egregious misreadings disregard Said's materialist grounding. Their analyses consequently fail to connect Orientalist discourse to political-economic reality, becoming ahistorical and overly preoccupied with cultural difference. Above all, they define Orientalism as cultural hegemony by the West over the Other. While that power is occasionally and vaguely located in an imperialist project, a poststructuralist tendency in film studies frequently treats the problem as a discursive one. Analytically, race is thus constructed as an issue whose impact is largely limited to the text and Othering is taken to be a process of socially constructed discourse.[9] A second misperception takes *Orientalism* to be antihumanist. This inclination originates in psychoanalytic screen theory, which reads Othering discourses as an index to the unconscious. In these instances critics look beyond the film text, and many follow the example set by Bhabha, who deconstructs the racial stereotype as a function of Freudian fetishism within a Lacanian schema of the Imaginary.[10] In other words, Orientalist imagery and discourse are seen as manifestations of the European unconscious, generated out of Western identity's need to posit a constitutive Other.[11] Summarily, these views place emphasis on the imaginative and discursive construction of the Orient, including its inhabitants and its culture, with diminished regard for its real, concrete existence.[12] They reflect an antiracist strategy of redefining race as a social construct. But these philosophical positions run counter to Said's. It is a disjuncture that makes Bhabha's critiques of Said's humanism seem misplaced.

By the time *Orientalism* was published, Said was already on record criticizing Bhabha and Michel Foucault specifically for their brand of theory's retreat from political or radical engagement in favor of criticism as a cognitive, contemplative, and technical endeavor.[13] For Said scholar Stephen Howe, the political aspirations that Said harbored for theory and criticism ally him much more strongly with Theodor Adorno than Foucault, with whom Said is commonly associated.[14] Said's stated positions are incompatible with the view of *Orientalism* as a poststructuralist if not postmodernist work and of himself as an exponent of those traditions. Said expert Andrew Rubin attributes the interpretive slant to French theory, poststructuralism, and Foucault's popularity during the 1980s, which is especially significant because of their influence in shaping film studies about race.[15] From the initial foray into image studies to canonical contributions such as Robert Stam and Louise Spence's essay about racial subjectivity and oppositional readings to Bhabha's deconstructionist take, film studies about race have indeed been structured by a fixation on signification, discourse, and interpretation.[16]

Said felt strongly that the prominent continental approach was too apolitical.[17] He thought that some of the work that was inspired by even the

Frankfurt School showed a "comparative absence of a continuous native Marxist theoretical tradition or culture to back it up and its relative isolation from any concrete political struggle." But readers who are introduced to *Orientalism* through film studies would easily misidentify it as a work that relies on Foucault's ideas about discourse and Antonio Gramsci's definition of hegemony. Howe demonstrates on the contrary that much of Said's work is "at one with the best parts of the Marxist intellectual tradition."[18] And as Rubin and Timothy Brennan observe separately, the perception of Said's affinity with Foucault overlooks Said's debt to the Romantic tradition of British Marxism and Raymond Williams's *The Country and the City,* for which the invisibility of subordinate classes, rural workers, peasants, guest laborers, and immigrant workers who come from British colonies created a "contested social relationship over the geographical, territorial, and property divisions that are part of the development of novels and other aesthetic forms from Virgil's *Georgics* onward."[19]

Howe, Brennan, and Rubin are not alone. In the last decade, a spate of scholarship occurring beyond the disciplinary boundaries and attentions of film studies has sought to clarify Said's warm relationship to Marxism. The authors of that scholarship collectively see him as an interlocutor between Gramsci, Foucault, the Frankfurt School, and British cultural studies, and have posited that while Said's reputation as an exponent of Foucauldian thought is understandable, the Marxian and humanist strains in his writing are more urgent. Other authors sought to clarify the specific influences, overlaps, and conceptual relationships that constitute Said's Marxist voice. In addition to Howe, Asha Varadharajan, Fred Dallmayr, and Abdirahman A. Hussein for example, liken Said's method to Adorno's negative dialectics, and E. San Juan examines Said's specific debts to Gramsci.[20] All of them evaluate Said's oeuvre produced over a prolific period of about three decades. In comparison, film and media scholars investigating issues of race and culture have only reached for *Orientalism*. While this is logical, it alerts us at the same time to apparent elisions of the book's materialist and humanist impulses that might have tempered the inclination to fashion Said as a poststructuralist. And although writers addressing Said's Marxism do not restrict their analysis to one book, many of their conclusions can be supported by *Orientalism* alone. To clarify, I am not holding film studies accountable for Said's writings beyond *Orientalism*. Nonetheless, the reconsiderations of Said's critical philosophy conducted outside the discipline compound that oversight and lend urgency to the corrective offered here in part.

Consequently, I too emphasize *Orientalism* at the expense of other works because I am more concerned with the state of film studies over that of Saidian scholarship. This is about more than repairing one author's legacy, or rectifying one field's grasp of a single text that has attracted justified criticism on several fronts. To wit, I contemplate what film studies' appropriation of *Orientalism* says about its scholarship on race. The implications are theoretical and political. Poststructuralist emphases on signification, social constructivism, and ideological discourse tend to lead film studies to distance or decouple race and gender from economics and class. Reconstructing Said in the tradition of the Frankfurt School as others have done while reminding film studies of his materialist and humanist commitments should reverberate powerfully enough for us to consequently think of race in the way that Mike Cole, Robert M. Young, and those in the materialist wing of critical race theory most prominently do, as an issue that necessarily involves the material base. The plight of poor whites and noncolor-coded racism against migrants are two examples of why we should perceive race in an economic dimension.[21] That, I believe, is the greater imperative. What then are the lessons for film studies? What might Said have advocated? He wrote surprisingly little about mass media, and the few pages of *Orientalism* touching on media hardly strain the limits of stereotype analysis–a mode of criticism that film scholars had sought to transcend even before Said published *Orientalism*. Left to extrapolate, I explore what it means to pursue a more Saidian methodology for race in film studies. It is a proposition, I find, that, despite the immediate need to fully come to terms with what he wrote, transcends the task of adhering to the letter of his text, and is fraught with an aporia ironically brought on by Said himself.

Film studies' poststructuralist readings of *Orientalism*

Contrary to Hussein's claims that debates over *Orientalism* have been "strangely indifferent to the contentious *present* realities of the Middle East," film scholars have always realized its importance for analyzing contemporary media.[22] *Orientalism* specifically addresses how today's postmodern media have reinforced and standardized Orientalist discourse. While conducting a stereotype analysis of Rudolph Valentino's Sheik characters, Said describes American mass media as the present's cultural vehicle for Orientalist hegemony within the Arab world. Media scholars concerned about ideological manifestations gravitated so strongly toward *Orientalism* that, as these examples show, mere mention of either the book or its author serves up an immediate reference.[23]

Specifically, they have come to serve as rhetorical shorthand for an essentially epistemological argument. Film scholarship uses *Orientalism* as a seminal theory on racial (and even sexual) representation and discourse. It is true that *Orientalism* is an indisputably important work, greatly concerned with characterizations of the Other. In his analysis of the Jerry Lewis film *The Geisha Boy* (1958), David Desser observes how the Orient functions to feminize the comedian's Jewish masculinity against Hollywood's long tradition of representing Eastern cultures and peoples.

> The concept of Orientalism in which the Orient (the Middle East, Asia) is exoticized and feminized is too well known to be repeated here. But it is worth noting that both before the Second World War and after, American associations with Asia followed a particularly masculinist tack that did not require the brilliant insights of Edward Said to reveal. For instance, American ideology, scripted into the Hollywood cinema, always allowed a certain white, male privilege in which "Other" women were available to white men (though obviously not the reverse).[24]

Desser reads the film as an indicator of how postwar American culture defined and negotiated gender and examines how masculinity and femininity were represented. *Orientalism* is evoked as an authoritative text on the issue of racial representation, and its contents are swiftly assumed to likewise refer to all cultural discourse. The book is in fact neither named explicitly nor cited. In limiting his reference to Orientalism only as a "concept," Desser's statements symptomize a larger habit to equate Said with the book and to assume that its content is obvious. Similarly, Charles Musser's essay "Divorce, DeMille and the Comedy of Remarriage" predigests *Orientalism* into familiar nuggets. He describes how "much of DeMille's spice box entails a rampant orientalism that has been discussed by Edward Said."[25] Musser places Cecil B. DeMille within the literary tradition that *Orientalism* decries and specifically compares the filmmaker with Flaubert, who depicts the Orient as a repository of exotic sexuality and unknown desire. In his study of 1930s "comedies of remarriage," Musser considers Orientalism purely as a phenomenon that confers referential value on the Orient in the Western imagination.

Desser, Musser, and others seem to ignore *Orientalism*'s more complex thesis. On one hand, Said does address images and their existence within discourse when he argues that "Orientalism is a style of thought based upon an ontological and epistemological distinction made between 'the Orient' and (most of the time) 'the Occident.'"[26] Hence, certainly *Orientalism* contains an essentially epistemological argument because it is on one level an intertextual discursive analysis that owes a substantial debt to Foucault. But Said does not end there:

> [*Orientalism*] proposes itself as a step towards an understanding not so much of Western politics and of the non-Western world in those politics as of the *strength* of Western cultural discourse, a strength too often mistaken as merely decorative or "superstructural."[27]

It seems that race-related film studies failed to receive this explicit warning to root Orientalism in the economic base. Poststructuralist film studies concentrate on cultural analysis and cling onto *Orientalism*'s Foucauldian elements at the expense of substructural considerations that are ostensibly not "merely decorative." Said's very words highlight the disjuncture.

There are few film scholars who demonstrate command of Said's full thesis.[28] Most conform in various degrees to the interpretation adopted in the following instances by Gina Marchetti. Her essay "Ethnicity, the Cinema and Cultural Studies" appears in the film studies anthology *Unspeakable Images*, whose editor Lester D. Friedman defines race and ethnicity in discursive terms. The collection never strays far from the stated intent to concentrate on matters of textual interpretation. In a maneuver similar to Desser's cited earlier, Friedman condenses *Orientalism* to relate primarily if not exclusively to the circulation of representations within racial and cultural discourse:

> When majority group members evaluate the work of minority group members, the results are at best simplistic misreadings and at worst cynical misappropriations. Edward Said forcefully demonstrates this position in *Orientalism* (1978), an analysis of Western discourse on the third world.[29]

Friedman proceeds with the assumption that ethnicity does more than just provide boundaries between nations and social groups; it determines how people perceive, interpret, and live their lives. "[A]ll categories of classification represent a cultural construction . . . all modes of interpretation are, in and of themselves, ideological positions that seek to order our interpretations of experiences."[30] To that end, *Orientalism* becomes a monolithic authority on how "misreadings" and "misappropriations" occur in "discourse."

Assuming Friedman's social constructivist position, Marchetti avers that ethnic and racial otherness is a polysemic, even dialectical interplay of conflicting discourses. She discusses "white America's power to define identity, to set racial and ethnic boundaries, to describe the foreign and, through this monopoly on knowledge, to control it."[31] Marchetti's use of the words "power" and "knowledge" is not coincidental. Her clear allusion to Foucault via the ideas he expressed in *Power/Knowledge* gathers significance in another example that reveals a continual commitment to discursive analysis.

In the collection *Classic Hollywood Classic Whiteness*, Marchetti's careful and detailed textual analysis argues that the film *Son of the Gods* (1930) displaces class issues onto racial, ethnic, and cultural ones.[32] Lead character Sam Lee is the son of a wealthy Chinese merchant who falls for a white socialite. The plot is driven by the need to overcome the social barriers to the interracial relationship in order to unite the couple. Set during the Great Depression, *Son of the Gods* depicts a milieu inevitably permeated by class conflicts that bubble to the surface at many points, only to be conveniently replaced by ethnic and sexual discourse. In a key plot point, Sam learns that he is actually the white adoptee of Chinese parents, paving the way for his unproblematic bourgeois union with a white woman, which enables the film to forward a progressive message of tolerance while simultaneously reinforcing the socioeconomic status quo. Marchetti gives minimal attention to an account of economic history, without which class would seem discursive. She relies only on a brief one-page survey of Asian American labor and migration during the Depression to provide the film's historical context.

Marchetti's use of *Orientalism* is revealing and once again sublates Said's materialism, an ironic move considering the author's claims about a film that, as she argues, sustains bourgeois domination by replacing class conflict with a deliberation on race and ethnicity. For the discussion about class, she notably defers instead to Sumiko Higashi, whose work on DeMille links commodified Orientalia "to the pleasures and potential dangers of consumerism and the construction of a new middle class in America."[33] As for *Orientalism*, Marchetti cites it as a psychoanalytic study:

> Edward Said points out that the Orient functions as "a sort of surrogate or even underground self" in European (and by implication, Euro-American) discourses about Asia and Asians. Desires for upward mobility [among film audiences of the 1930s] and the ambivalence created by those desires find their expression in Orientalist discourses and in Orientalist imagery.[34]

In an earlier work on miscegenation in Hollywood narratives, *Romance and the "Yellow Peril,"* Marchetti highlights the psychic aspect of Orientalism in much the same way. She accepts Said's material definition of European authority and domination but undermines it in a later passage:

> In *Orientalism*, Edward W. Said notes that although it would be wrong to look at the Orient as an idea without any material foundation, European ideas about Asia have more to do with Europe's definition of itself than with any genuine attempt to understand any other culture. Said states, "European culture gained in strength and identity by setting itself off against the Orient as a sort of surrogate or even underground self." Logically, Said's argument can be extended to include America, which has also used the "Orient" as a convenient gauge for a contested and divided self-identity.[35]

The American psyche, Marchetti argues, is divided between the liberal ideology of a melting pot and the need for a homogenous white Anglo-Saxon identity. In this context, Oriental culture functions almost psychoanalytically as a Jungian shadow of the white American mainstream. Marchetti is in fact rather moderate, since others have swerved away even more radically from Said's stated philosophy by supposing that European or European American discourse refers exclusively back to itself, thus representing *Orientalism* as a rather solipsistic theory.[36]

Within *Classic Hollywood Classic Whiteness*, Marchetti claims that under the unique pressures of Depression-era economic fears, chiefly racist xenophobia and materialistic consumerism, the dark side of the European American psyche had been roused and was consonant with Orientalist imagery and discourse. The link that Marchetti draws here between 1930s white racist discourse and the sociopolitical/socioeconomic concerns of the nation's bourgeoisie is in line with *Orientalism*'s perspective, although a more materialist understanding of Said would draw a stronger link between the two. Marchetti's connection is loosely formed by comparison. She reads *Son of the Gods* on a more or less discursive level to see how the film's narrative and style articulate the equivalent issues of class, race, and gender. Marchetti provides the overview of early twentieth-century sociopolitical/socioeconomic history to act as a historical context but through a seemingly self-evident reflectionism between society and cinema.

Although Said does consider Orientalist discourses to be manifestations of the European unconscious, he takes great pain to connect them to material causes and maintains a place in reality for the non-Western world. I also note that the fragment of *Orientalism* that Marchetti quotes above regarding European culture's "surrogate and even underground self" comes from the sentence in a paragraph where Said also writes:

> My contention is that without examining Orientalism as a discourse one cannot possibly understand the enormously systematic discipline by which European culture was able to manage—and even produce—the Orient politically, sociologically, militarily, ideologically, scientifically, and imaginatively during the post-Enlightenment period. . . . [I]t is the whole network of interests inevitably brought to bear on (and therefore always involved in) any occasion when that peculiar entity "the Orient" is in question.[37]

Such egregious examples of interpretive cherry-picking are noteworthy, especially when Said elaborates on the point of Orientalism's direct connection to imperial power two pages later.

> In the first place, it would be wrong to conclude that the Orient was *essentially* an idea, or a creation with no corresponding reality . . . There were—and are— cultures and nations whose location is in the East, and their lives, histories, and customs have a brute reality obviously greater than anything that could be said about them in the West. About that fact this study of Orientalism has very little to contribute, except to acknowledge it tacitly.[38]

Said concludes that initial thought with a tone that is subtle, but he very soon displays his materialism more forcefully:

> [I]deas, cultures, and histories cannot seriously be understood or studied without their force, or more precisely their configurations of power, also being studied. To believe that the Orient was created—or, as I call it, "Orientalized"—and to believe that such things happen simply as a necessity of the imagination, is to be disingenuous. The relationship between Occident and Orient is a relationship of power, of domination, of varying degrees of a complex hegemony. . . . One ought never to assume that the structure of Orientalism is nothing more than a structure of lies or of myths which, were the truth about them to be told, would simply blow away. I myself believe that Orientalism is more particularly valuable as a sign of European-Atlantic power over the Orient than it is as a veridic discourse about the Orient.[39]

Said unmistakably argues that the Orient has a material basis. He beats back any venture to wander away from it and associates "power" with an existence in the physical realm as opposed to the imagined or discursive.

I do not claim that *Orientalism* does not deal with aspects of the European unconscious and imagination, because it quite clearly does. In a section analyzing Barthélemy d'Herbelot's Orientalist reference text *Bibliothèque orientale,* for example, Said defines the "Orient" most directly as the product of an Othering process within the European psyche that essentially equates the scrutiny of Orientalism with a study on the West. He writes that "cultures have always been inclined to impose complete transformations on other cultures.... To the Westerner, however, the Oriental was always *like* some aspect of the West."[40] Nevertheless, Said's sweeping generalizations here of psychic projections on the part of the West and the Westerner in this instance appear to be motivated more by rhetorical convenience than specific conviction. We can dismiss this simplification because he had introduced *Orientalism* not as a broad treatise on everything Western but instead an investigation restricted to British, French, and to a lesser degree American Orientalism precisely and fundamentally because they represent the "greatest colonial networks" just prior to and during the twentieth century.[41] That narrowed purview proves that he found it necessary for his analysis of culture to be rooted in a material base.

Orientalism would seem to advocate a methodology that challenges the cultural studies orientation of critical race film studies. By "cultural studies," I refer to a general emphasis on the experiential and superstructural over attention to the substructural circumstances of their production. The field also prefers to study class as an identity, part of a triumvirate with race and gender studies. Cultural studies' objection to the premise of materialist analysis facilitates the poststructural tenets demonstrated by film studies' treatment of *Orientalism,* where detaching culture from a determinist base is frequently a precondition of spectatorial or consumer autonomy. These are principles and tendencies to which Said's writing does not conform. Nevertheless, film studies continues to embrace *Orientalism* as an exposition of a system governing representation, or of the workings of the European psyche, separating Said's thoughts on those matters from the connection that he makes between cultural phenomena and imperial power. Orientalism does pertain to the European experience of the racial Other, but, to paraphrase Said, it is the political, sociological, military, ideological, and scientific encounter, in addition to the imaginative, that interests him more intensely. Therefore, the final question for Said is not one of race or difference but fundamentally of "European *material* civilization and culture."[42] The real and physical conditions for the exertion of power are for Said the central topic of inquiry and target for change. It would be odd to recognize that axiom but bypass it. The following examples, however, promise not to.

In *Classic Hollywood Classic Whiteness*, editor Daniel Bernardi announces that the collection attends to material elements of cinema practice. "Most of the articles in this volume address the machinations of the studio system. Several focus on the industry's racial policies and practices."[43] Yet despite this declaration—one that makes *Orientalism*'s materialist approach to discourse a perfectly suited reference—the essays in *Classic Hollywood Classic Whiteness*, namely by Marchetti and Roberta Pearson, continue to tap Said solely for his poststructuralist arguments. In *Visions of the East: Orientalism in Film*, editor Matthew Bernstein states that the volume adopts Said's definition of Orientalism and elaborates on the thesis thus:

> *Orientalism* describes a strand of colonialist discourse in the ideological arsenal of Western nations—most notably Great Britain, France, and the United States—for representing the colonies and cultures of North Africa and the "Middle East" (and eventually those of Asia). It is a way of perceiving these areas that has been supported, justified and reinforced by the West's colonialist and imperialist ventures. Most generally, Orientalism is a distinctive means of representing race, nationality and Otherness. . . . Orientalism was an example of what Said called "imaginative geography," a social construct that coincides in many ways with the colonialist ideologies that prevailed in the 1800s, the peak of the British and French empires.[44]

Bernstein does not neglect the connection between Western perception and colonial power and correctly avoids drawing that relationship with direct causality. It must be stated that Said does not, as vulgar or even Neo-Marxists are often wont to, believe in crude economic reductionism. Rather, for an interesting analysis, imperial domination should not be applied "mechanically and deterministically to such complex matters as culture and ideas."[45] Hence by casting the relationship between colonial discourse and imperialist power in the mold of support, justification, and reinforcement, Bernstein accurately reflects Said's proposition of a two-way street in that regard. However, Bernstein also says that Orientalism is "most generally" about race, nationality, and otherness. I posit that it is problematic to rearrange Said's priorities, which privilege materialist analysis as an essential critical method.

When film studies expects *Orientalism* to "have general applicability to all colonial situations" or to be less about a particular geographical area and more crucially about "the historical experience of confronting and representing the other," the issue is transformed from a material to racial one.[46] The book's materialist exploration of imperial projects is effectively de-emphasized in favor of an interrogation of racial or gender difference. Centering the issue on race sublates Marxism by foregrounding specificity in race and generalizing colonialism. With this move, writers arguably assume the posture of identity politics whereby race and cultural specificity are privileged over universal Marxist values such as class consciousness. Certainly, *Orientalism* demonstrates Eurocentric discourse's relentless consistency across nations and periods and can be reasonably extended for the purpose of inquiring about separate circumstances of racist discourse and other sociopolitical situations where powerful and disempowered parties exist. Nevertheless, it would be a mistake to apply the book's ideas without Said's materialism that originally limited his study to Franco–British–American imperialism, because doing so risks ahistorically extending invitations to political paradigms such as identity politics that are more associated with poststructuralism, which Said opposed. He cited the failure of Third World and anti-imperialist activists in responding to the abominations of the Khomeini regime in Iran to illustrate that knee-jerk "nativism" can be reactionary.[47] That unholy alliance is but a form of identity politics premised on the notion that progressive Orientals have more in common with other Orientals than they do with the West. The presumption within an Orient-versus-Occident binary of an inherent and essential racial identity reestablishes Orientalist dogma itself. On that count, Said unwaveringly maintains a clear stand against identity politics and racial or cultural essentialism. He affords no credence to notions of "some Oriental essence" and repeated the sentiment in a 1994 "Afterword," saying that *Orientalism* is "explicitly antiessentialist, radically skeptical about all categorical designations like Orient and Occident."[48] *Orientalism*'s methodological and political framework was meant to steer us clear of tribalism that arises in the absence of class consciousness.

Against the narrow Foucauldian interpretation of *Orientalism* typified by film studies' treatments of the work, contributions from history, comparative literature, and literary and political theory have also decisively challenged the Foucauldian emphasis long held by postcolonial and British cultural studies that *Orientalism* channels Foucault when relating discourse to knowledge and power.[49] Their intervention now makes it difficult to overlook the book's affiliations with Marxism, which immediately tilts *Orientalism* away from Foucault and toward Gramsci. Even more contrary to poststructuralist opinion, they locate Said's brand of Marxism beyond Gramsci, who facilitated cultural studies' drift away from economic determinism. Several have in fact convincingly aligned Said's humanism with Adorno's based on their common belief in critical consciousness and autonomous intellectuals.[50]

Whereas previous examples highlight where film scholarship favors *Orientalism*'s discursive analysis over its materialism, Bhabha's eminent essay on cinema and race, "The Other Question," demonstrates the poststructuralist inclination to decenter signs and subjectivity. Bhabha begins his deconstructionist critique of Said with requisite praise of the book's "inventive" and "pioneering" theory that revolts against a "regime of truth, that is structurally similar to Realism." Said's critiques of signifiers that project a stable totality and of false unities that emit an aura of objective empiricism overlap with Bhabha's own Derridean view of colonial discourse. However, when Bhabha takes Said to task for not adopting deconstruction wholeheartedly and for not viewing both the sign and the subject with poststructuralist suspicion, he remains blissfully unaware of Said's materialist and humanist principles. For Bhabha, *Orientalism* falters when Said refuses to engage with notions of "alterity and ambivalence . . . which threaten to split up the very object of Orientalist discourse as a knowledge and the subject positioned therein." Bhabha argues that the potential for undermining ideological discourse lies innately within its own instability. In his estimation, Said wrongly attributes colonial discourse to simply a "political-ideological *intention*" because it posits in part a unified colonial subject.[51]

Bhabha assumes that if Said avails himself of Foucault's thinking on the issue of knowledge, Said is then obligated to embrace poststructuralism completely. One cannot deny that *Orientalism* relies heavily on Foucault, but it rests just as certainly on ideas that are antithetical to his. Consider the following criticism from "The Other Question" where Bhabha faults Said for defining a unified subject as opposed to a split subject:

> There is always, in Said, the suggestion that colonial power and discourse is possessed entirely by the coloniser, which is a historical and theoretical simplification. The terms in which Said's Orientalism is unified—the intentionality and unidirectionality of colonial power—also unify the subject of colonial enunciation.[52]

Bhabha thus appears to charge Said with mobilizing Foucault too selectively, since Foucault rejects subjective unity, implicit or otherwise. On that count, Karlis Racevskis voices an explanatory riposte, stating that Said was intensely ambivalent toward Foucault for several reasons. Politically, Said judged Foucault for having abdicated his obligation as a critic in being insufficiently attuned to human suffering and revolutionary praxis, which the latter's Zionist sympathies did little to mediate. Philosophically,

> Said and Foucault approached the question of power from two different, one could even say diametrically opposite, perspectives. For Said, power is something someone possesses and there is always an intention or a will using, exploiting, abusing power relations. What Foucault strives to understand and bring to light are the impersonal, anonymous ways in which power networks function. Thus, when Said points out that Foucault "surely underestimates such motive forces in history as profit, ambition, ideas, the sheer love of power," his objection is still formulated in terms of a traditional Cartesian/Kantian model of human agency.[53]

As Racevskis describes, Said's humanism in the tradition of Descartes and Kant is at odds with Bhabha's rejection of unified subjectivity. The latter's failure to notice how *Orientalism* introduces Gramscian ideas about hegemony and consent in order to elucidate the process whereby the colonized himself contributes to the power that oppresses the other, blinds him to how it moves Said to describe a subject's critical response to hegemonic discourse.

> In the *Prison Notebooks* Gramsci says: "The starting-point of critical elaboration is the consciousness of what one really is, and in *"knowing* thyself" as a product of the historical process to date, which has deposited in you an infinity of traces, without leaving an inventory." . . . [Gramsci] concludes by adding, "therefore it is imperative at the outset to compile such an inventory." . . . In many ways my study of Orientalism has been an attempt to inventory the traces upon me, the Oriental subject, of the culture whose domination has been so powerful a factor in the life of all Orientals.[54]

Indeed, *Orientalism* frequently presents Said's personal experience as both motivation and basis for the project—seeking to explain, for example, the disjuncture between cultural and academic depictions of the Orient and his own knowledge and experience. Regarding this "personal dimension," Said writes that being confronted with Orientalism's "cultural reality" invested him innately with the "awareness of being an 'Oriental.'" By his account, for people living in the everyday world, Orientalism is mostly a hegemonic system of discourses acting in the service of imperialism. While it might impose a powerful "saturating" force, its "internal constraints upon writers and thinkers were *productive*, not unilaterally inhibiting." He thus does not see discourse to be constitutive of his critical consciousness but instead as a separate "constraint" that functions alongside "instruments of historical, humanistic, and cultural research."[55] In Bhabha's defense, I could point out that within *Orientalism*, Said is neither declarative nor distinct about his investments in unified critical subjectivity and humanist origins of textual meaning. In any event, Bhabha needs no defending. His deconstructionist appraisal of Said is embedded within an analysis that has undeniably contributed to our understanding of stereotypes. The validity of poststructuralist appropriations of *Orientalism*, not that of poststructuralist analysis itself, is at stake.

Yet as the next example shows, interpreting Said from an antihumanist position reintroduces the identity politics that Said abhors as easily as antimaterialism can. In "Displacing Limits of Difference: Gender, Race, and Colonialism in Edward Said and Homi Bhabha's Theoretical Models and Marguerite Duras's Experimental Films," Christine Holmlund recognizes Said's sensitivity to the colonial underpinnings of Orientalism and also sees that he is creating "a larger project involving what may be termed the creation of a practical political theory." But like Bhabha, Holmlund is critical. In discussing their theories, she hardly extends beyond epistemology and the boundaries of cinematic texts, dwelling instead on how Bhabha and Said are concerned with "dominant representations of racial and/or ethnic difference." Both he and Bhabha are taken to "view difference as constituted intersubjectively in discourse." While that is true for Bhabha, it is not true for Said, for whom superstructural elements including the text are merely preliminary nodes of analysis that lead inexorably to political economy of empire. More importantly, Holmlund confronts Said's beliefs in authenticity and humanist knowledge because they give him the convenience of both "ideological purity" and access to "a space of pure truth." She argues that Said is therefore mistaken in assuming that the West, the Orient, domination, texts, and their reception are coherent or monolithic, when they are in fact contradictory and fluid entities. She posits that *Orientalism* sidesteps gender and gives patriarchal issues short shrift. In executing this identitarian maneuver, Holmlund urges for a more valued consideration of filmmaker Marguerite Duras. Marginalized on several levels while growing up poor, white, and female in French Indochina, Duras thus has insight into how racial, gender, and colonial oppression intersect.[56] Those sensitivities interact with her antirealist experimental film aesthetics to extend the limits of Said's and Bhabha's theories.

> By speaking from marginal positions to gender, race, and colonialism, Said, Bhabha, and Duras all, on different registers, displace the limits of difference. When their voices are intermingled, the possible centers of identity and agency are widened indeed.[57]

Holmlund's conclusions avoid giving definitive answers "to the question of how identity and difference, text and context, power and knowledge relate to resistance" because she believes that they are "best conceived as dialectics."[58] Yet since she rejects Said's humanist definition of identity, the case for dialectics is contradictory, for what else except the critical subject houses the consciousness where dialectics take place? The multiple identities within Duras's authorial subjectivity require the same.

Bhabha and Holmlund's contradictions arise when they divorce *Orientalism* from its materialist focus on imperialist power and reject Said's humanist claims for the subject. While itself useful, poststructuralist analysis alone cannot impose its assumptions on *Orientalism* because the latter is inherently averse. If, as I expect, *Orientalism* remains important to the field's examination of race, then writers should embrace the fuller implications of the text. This would still ostensibly entail injections of textual, discursive, and psychoanalytical analysis, which are appropriate and necessary since Said's treatment of cinema was never more sophisticated than image analysis. But they should be used in addition to Said's foundational philosophies: materialism, humanism, and a commitment to Marxist praxis.

What is a Saidian methodology for race in film studies?

A more insightful account of *Orientalism* can be found in Jane Chi Hyun Park's *Yellow Future: Oriental Style in Hollywood Cinema*. Park applies Said's thesis by extending materialist concerns effectively to cultural analysis. Her textual analysis weaves through production histories, cultural phenomena, and sociological trends while maintaining a view of political economic exchanges between East Asia and the West. Park's adherence to Said's materialist and humanist principles is discernible by her concern "with how human agency—specifically creative agency—simultaneously shapes and is shaped by larger processes of globalization." Through an attempt to extend and update *Orientalism*, she explores how "the dynamics of Orientalism [change] in the early twenty-first century as the cybernetic 'global village' of transnational capitalism meets the print- and nation-based 'imagined community' of industrial capitalism." *Yellow Future* not only lives up to its mission, but with a primary focus on Hollywood cinema's "oriental style," the book exceeds the predominant preoccupation with narrative and character analysis (Figure 4.1). Moreover, by privileging causal connections between aesthetics and capitalist economics, Park operates within the tradition of Adorno as well as Said, despite the fact that she locates herself within the field of cultural studies.[59] Like Said, Park forwards an argument that is initially about difference, identity, textuality, and signification but is ultimately framed by something larger, more material. *Yellow Future* is exemplary as a work that counters the poststructuralist tendencies that govern much of film studies' engagement with race vis-à-vis Said.

However, I offer that appraisal while being careful not to hold up *Yellow Future* as a model per se, the presumption that one might be tempted to reach. Despite the efforts expended thus far to address those who have overlooked critical aspects of *Orientalism*, we should also be careful to assume that there exists a "correct" Saidian methodology to emulate. The reason lies ironically with Said himself. He held clear and firm convictions about the nature of history and the responsibility of critics—they perform political acts that are obligated to transcend textual boundaries and touch material conditions. Said reiterated these philosophical objectives time and again but never promulgated a discernible means to achieve them. This absence of method is a perspicacious refusal partly attributable to the sheer multiplicity of Said's influences and greatly motivated by awareness of how academic professionalism reifies theoretical

Figure 4.1 Jane Chi Hyun Park reflected on *Blade Runner* (1982) using *Orientalism* faithfully.

activity. Said himself would therefore be loath to discover his own method ossified "into the lapidary forms of static orthodoxies, theoretical dogmas, and provincial forms of professionalism."[60] One would assume that his sensibility on the issue was heightened by the Foucauldian observations in *Orientalism*, lest he be guilty of countenancing dominating or coercive forms of knowledge. To Said's mind, ritualized expertise inevitably depoliticizes criticism and renders it ahistorical.[61]

> *Orientalism* is theoretically inconsistent, and I designed it that way: I didn't want Foucault's method, or anybody's method, to override what I was trying to put forward. The notion of a kind of non-coercive knowledge, which I came to at the end of the book, was deliberately anti-Foucault.[62]

In place of an identifiable method, Said preferred the notion of critical consciousness, which is a more flexible form of dialectical inquiry. Critical consciousness places worldliness over the insular preoccupation with "textuality" that he opposed. It is an activity that is contrapuntal, mobile, mindful of political economy, and starkly reminiscent of Adorno's dialecticism and humanism.[63]

We can further understand Said's "critical consciousness" by using it to clarify the contradiction that seems to exist between his Marxism and the way that *Orientalism* faults Karl Marx. Said charged Marx with submerging his analysis of conditions in India under a "classically standard image" of the Orient, conceiving it "in large collective terms or in abstract generalities" and dehumanizing its inhabitants. Said attributes Marx's Orientalism to the "lexicographical and institutional" consolidation of "professional terminology" and implies that Marx's perception of the East was due to his privileged position as a writer in the dominant West.[64] These passages are frequent bones of contention in debates over Said's Marxism. Irfan Habib declares that they are unjustifiable readings of Marx, while Aijaz Ahmad accuses Said of associating Marxism with colonialism and thus undermining Marxist analysis altogether. Attacking the book from the left, Ahmad takes exception to its poststructuralism and broadsides Said with an allegation of antihumanism.[65]

But Said probably viewed Marx's Orientalism simply as a taint and not a fallacy that compromises the latter's sociological analysis. As Said elaborates, we detect the materialism of Marx's consciousness coursing through his verbiage. Said clarifies that Marx was an "individual mind" and laments the way that he was a "non-Orientalist [whose] human engagements were first dissolved, then usurped by Orientalist generalizations." Said further acknowledges that "Marx was concerned with vindicating his own theses on socio-economic revolution."[66] These sentiments also indicate how Said might read Marx's *Zur Judenfrage* (On the Jewish Question), that is, as a description of socioeconomic conditions and not as a self-hating anti-Semitic attack on Jews' insularity and loyalty to Judaism. Said would assume that Marx was only exploiting popular prejudice as a rhetorical device, and that the greater significance is Marx's elaboration on the difference between seeking political emancipation from the Christian state (which Jews sought) and wanting human emancipation from the bourgeois state (which they did not).[67] That Said would countenance Marx's writings in that fashion is supported by the idea that their worldviews were largely congruent. The supposition in turn emerges directly from a grasp of the principles and beliefs that structured Said's critical consciousness.

Orientalism ultimately stands as a manifesto, leaving its readers with a set of commitments without a method. Yet the implications that confront film studies remain weighty. We might all prefer that it was a tome charting a methodological blueprint, but still it is far from ambiguous or of mixed mind. The book continues to present unquestionable utility for the unfinished business on race, ethnicity, and culture. While most immediately focused on those issues, *Orientalism* is constitutionally a Marxist humanist view of how socioeconomic conditions inflict misery on people and is not an emblem for poststructuralist principles. I doubt that Said, who valued flexibility in method, would have aspired for his work to be so provincial that it could determine or restrict the work of others. At the same time, the lessons that it offers compel us to adjust our field of vision and recognize race as a superstructural formation deeply tied to economic substructure. That is how film studies' examination of race must change if it adopted an approach more in line with Said's. Perhaps Said would not compel anyone to voice it distinctly, but rather than take advantage of that freedom, our own critical consciousness should feel the obligation nonetheless. *Orientalism*'s strength and indeed our own rest precisely on a fulcrum of that subjectivity.

Notes

1   Edward Said, "The Problem of Textuality: Two Exemplary Positions," *Critical Inquiry* 4, 4 (Summer 1978): 673.

2   Ibid., 713.

3 Ibid., 713–14.

4 Edward Said, *Orientalism* (New York: Vintage Books, 1978).

5 Robert J. C. Young, *Postcolonialism: An Historical Introduction* (Malden, MA: Blackwell, 2001): 383–84.

6 Said, *Orientalism*, 49.

7 Ibid., 12, 25.

8 Edward Said, "Orientalism Reconsidered," *Race and Class* 27, 2 (1985): 8.

9 Examples of this tendency are seen in the following: Lester Friedman, introduction to *Unspeakable Images: Ethnicity and the American Cinema* (Urbana, IL: University of Illinois Press, 1991): 3; Ella Shohat, "Ethnicities in Relation: Toward a Multicultural Reading of American Cinema," in *Unspeakable Images* (1991): 217; Matthew Bernstein, introduction to *Visions of the East: Orientalism in Film*, ed. Matthew Bernstein and Gaylyn Studlar (New Brunswick, NJ: Rutgers University Press, 1997): 2; Christine List, *Chicano Images: Refiguring Ethnicity in Mainstream Film* (New York: Garland Publishing, 1996): 13–14. Brian Locke, *Racial Stigma on the Hollywood Screen from World War II to the Present: The Orientalist Buddy Film* (New York: Palgrave Macmillan, 2009): 8.

10 Homi Bhabha, "The Other Question. . .," *Screen* 24, 6 (1983): 26–29.

11 Examples of this interpretation are seen in Jun Xing, *Asian America through the Lens: History, Representation and Identity* (Walnut Creek, CA: AltaMira Press, 1998): 64; Adrienne McLean, "The Thousand Ways There Are to Move: Camp and Oriental Dance in the Hollywood Musicals of Jack Cole," in *Visions of the East* (1997): 133.

12 See Roberta E. Pearson "Indianism? Classical Hollywood's Representation of Native Americans," in *Classical Hollywood Classic Whiteness*, ed. Daniel Bernardi (Minneapolis, MN: University of Minnesota Press, 2001): 247; Xing, *Asian America through the Lens*, 1. Pearson describes reality as a "vexed term."

13 See also Edward Said, "Interview," *Diacritics* 6, 3 (1976): 30–47. He also reiterates this invective in *The World, the Text and the Critic* (Cambridge, MA: Harvard University Press 1983): 37, 41.

14 Stephen Howe, "Edward Said and Marxism: Anxieties of Influence," *Cultural Critique* 67 (Fall 2007): 67–68, 78.

15 Andrew Rubin, "Techniques of Trouble: Edward Said and the Dialectics of Cultural Philology," *The South Atlantic Quarterly* 102, 4 (2003): 864.

16 Robert Stam and Louise Spence, "Colonialism, Racism and Representation," *Screen* 24, 2 (1983): 2–20.

17 Said, *The World, the Text and the Critic*, 164, 166.

18 Howe, "Edward Said and Marxism," 81.

19 Rubin, "Techniques of Trouble," 864–65; Timothy Brennan, "Edward Said: American Theory and the Politics of Knowledge," *Atlantic Studies* 2, 1 (2005): 100.

20 Asha Varadharajan, *Exotic Parodies: Subjectivity in Adorno, Spivak, and Said* (Minneapolis, MN: University of Minnesota Press, 1995); Fred Dallmayr, "The Politics of Non-Identity: Adorno, Postmodernism—And Edward Said," *Political* Theory 25, 1 (1997): 33–56; Abdirahman A. Hussein, *Edward Said: Criticism and Society* (New York: Verso, 2002): 232; E. San Juan, "Edward Said's Affiliations: Secular Humanism and Marxism," *Atlantic Studies* 3, 1 (April 2006): 43–61.

21 Mike Cole, "'Racism' is about More than Colour," *Times Higher Education Supplement* (November 23, 2007) <http://www.timeshighereducation. co.uk/311222.article>; Robert Young, "Putting Materialism Back into Race Theory: Toward a Transformative Theory of Race," *Red Critique* 11 (2006) <http:// www.redcritique.org/WinterSpring2006/puttingmaterialismbackintoracetheory. htm> Both accessed March 30, 2013.

22 Hussein, *Edward Said*, 230.

23 Said, *Orientalism*, 26, 286–87, 325.

24 David Desser, "The Geisha Boy: Orientalizing the Jewish Man," in *Enfant Terrible! Jerry Lewis in American Film*, ed. Murray Pomerance (New York: New York University Press, 2002): 156.

25 Charles Musser, "Divorce, DeMille and the Comedy of Remarriage," in *Classical Hollywood Comedy*, ed. Kristine Brunovska Karnick and Henry Jenkins (London: Routledge, 1995): 301.

26 Said, *Orientalism*, 2.

27 Ibid., 25.

28 These include Ella Shohat, *Israeli Cinema: East/West and the Politics of Representation* (Austin, TX: University of Texas Press, 1989); Ella Shohat and Robert Stam, *Unthinking Eurocentrism: Multiculturism and the Media* (New York: Routledge, 1994); Marie Thorsten Morimoto, "The 'Peace Dividend' in Japanese Cinema: Metaphors of a Demilitarized Nation," in *Colonialism and Nationalism in Asian Cinema*, ed. Wimal Dissanayake (Bloomington, IN: Indiana University Press, 1994); Melani McAlister, *Epic Encounters: Culture, Media, and U.S. Interests in the Middle East since 1945* (Berkeley, CA: University of California Press, 2005).

29 Friedman, *Unspeakable Images*, 3.

30 Ibid., 6.

31 Gina Marchetti, "Ethnicity, the Cinema and Cultural Studies," in *Unspeakable Images*, 297–98.

32 Gina Marchetti, "They Worship Money and Prejudice: The Certainties of Class and the Uncertainties of Race in Son of the Gods," in *Classic Hollywood Classic Whiteness*, 72–91.

33 Marchetti, "They Worship Money and Prejudice," 76. See Sumiko Higashi, *Cecil B. DeMille and American Culture: The Silent Era* (Berkeley, CA: University of

California Press, 1994) and "Ethnicity, Class and Gender in Film: DeMille's The Cheat," in *Unspeakable Images*, 112–39.

34   Marchetti "They Worship Money and Prejudice," 76. The citation is from Said, *Orientalism*, 3.

35   Gina Marchetti, *Romance and the "Yellow Peril": Race, Sex and Discursive Strategies in Hollywood Fiction* (Berkeley, CA: University of California Press, 1993): 6, 118.

36   See McLean, "The Thousand Ways There Are to Move," 133.

37   Said, *Orientalism*, 3.

38   Ibid., 5. For a similar example, compare Xing, *Asian America through the Lens*, 64.

39   Said, *Orientalism*, 5–6.

40   Ibid., 67.

41   Ibid., 3–4, 16–17.

42   Ibid., 2–3, emphasis in original.

43   Daniel Bernardi, *Classic Hollywood Classic Whiteness* (Minneapolis, MN: University of Minnesota Press, 2001): xv.

44   Bernstein, *Visions of the East*, 2, 5.

45   Said, *Orientalism*, 12.

46   Pearson, "Indianism," 247; Xing, *Asian America through the Lens*, 64; see also Marchetti, "Ethnicity, the Cinema and Cultural Studies," 297.

47   Said, "Orientalism Reconsidered," 12.

48   Said, *Orientalism*, 5, 273; Edward W. Said, *Orientalism* (New York: Vintage Books, 1994): 331.

49   Brennan, "Edward Said," 100.

50   Hussein, *Edward* Said, 232; Rubin, "Techniques of Trouble," 869–71; Dallmayr, "The Politics of Non-Identity"; Moustafa Bayoumi, "Reconciliation without Duress: Said, Adorno, and the Autonomous Intellectual," *Alif: Journal of Comparative* Poetics 25 (2005): 49; Howe, "Edward Said and Marxism," 70, 78.

51   Bhabha, "The Other Question," 23–24.

52   Ibid., 24–25.

53   Karlis Racevskis, "Edward Said and Michel Foucault: Affinities and Dissonances," *Research in African Literatures* 36, 3 (2005): 84, 87, 92.

54   Said, *Orientalism*, 25–26.

55   Ibid. Said, we must remember, is on the record as a critic of theory that confines itself to textuality at the expense of politics.

56   Christine Holmlund, "Displacing Limits of Difference: Gender, Race, and Colonialism in Edward Said and Homi Bhabha's Theoretical Models and Marguerite Duras's Experimental Films," *Quarterly Review of Film and Video* 13, 1–3 (1991): 1, 4–5, 9.

57 Ibid., 17.

58 Ibid., 16–17.

59 Jane Chi Hyun Park, *Yellow Future: Oriental Style in Hollywood Cinema* (Minneapolis, MN: University of Minnesota Press, 2010): x, 6.

60 Rubin, "Techniques of Trouble," 862–63.

61 Edward Said, "Response to Stanley Fish," *Critical Inquiry* 10, 2 (1983): 371–73.

62 "Edward Said," *Criticism in Society: Interviews with Jacques Derrida, Northrop Frye, Harold Bloom, Geoffrey Hartman, Frank Kermode, Edward Said, Barbara Johnson, Frank Lentricchia, and J. Hills Miller,* ed. Imre Salusinzsky (New York: Methuen, 1987): 137.

63 Rubin, "Techniques of Trouble," 863, 871, 873n13; Said, "Response to Stanley Fish," 373.

64 Said, *Orientalism*, 154–56.

65 Irfan Habib, "Critical Notes on Edward Said," *International Socialism* 108 (2005) <http://www.isj.org.uk/index.php4?id=141&issue=108> Accessed March 25, 2011; Aijaz Ahmad, *In Theory: Classes, Nations, Literatures* (London: Verso, 1992).

66 Said, *Orientalism*, 155–56.

67 Karl Marx, *A World without Jews*, trans. Dagobert D. Runes (New York: Philosophical Library, 1959).

Postmodern Multiracial, Keanu Reeves

The advance of postmodern culture intensified critical race film theory's offensive against the subject while fortifying poststructuralist positions. As a subset of poststructuralism, postmodern theory shares a suspicion of the subject and of ideas from the Enlightenment that underpin it. It also acts on behalf of social groups marginalized by Western authority. Their antieurocentric and antipatriarchal movements however, are decidedly more anarchic and aggressive. Postcolonial theorist Homi Bhabha's unyielding sympathy for fluidity and instability typifies the attitude. In this view of default skepticism, the fragmented individual subject possesses no central core and exists in a constant state of dissolution. Technology and especially digital innovation gave empirical proof to postmodern thinking. They facilitated cultural symptoms of depthlessness, surface pleasures, absences of closure, and intertextuality. Against that backdrop, film culture witnessed the appearance of related symptoms such as stylistic excess, aesthetic recycling, time travel narratives, digitized images, and the antihumanist cyborg figure. Where prior chapters document attempts in critical and theoretical literature to efface the subject, we now shift attention to how cinema and culture have ostensibly satisfied those aspirations through the trenchant example of a prominent multiracial actor whose public persona is marked by the properties of both depthlessness and the cyborg, and whose oeuvre displays an ongoing penchant for postmodern content.

In a world where the individual is under siege and race retains only contingent value, Keanu Reeves is very much a visage of the moment who personifies the wish fulfillment of second-generation critical race film theory principles. Both his critical and popular reception recapitulate that discourse while reveling in the postmodern phenomena floating in adjacent cultural orbits as well. As a performer, Reeves is often disparaged because he does not emote enough to suit the traditions of naturalistic acting, making him seem distant and aloof. Critics frequently interpret that inscrutability using a mélange of racial terms and technological metaphors. His multiracial identity, blankness and inarticulate nature resonate with theorizations of postmodern subjectivity: shallow, fragmented, split, and unstable. They all reinforce his oeuvre's keen emphasis on postmodern narratives, digital technology, and cyborgs, forming a persona that audiences, critics, and scholars feel like they plainly comprehend. On the contrary, this chapter reexamines their accepted wisdom and finds that it overlooks a modernist and in fact Marxian impulse on his part to retain and project a critical subjectivity.

Reconsidering Reeves's reception vis-à-vis Marxism unearths social, cultural, and political stakes in contemporary debates about cinema and race. The resurrected subject must negotiate evolving postracial dilemmas that crisscross the borders of, for instance, feuds between modernists and postmodernists over the viability of the subject, and the divisions between Marxists and cultural identitarians over the relative importance of race and class. Postracialism offers both benefits and drawbacks to adherents in every theoretical and political camp. Postracialism and color-blindness, for which multiracial bodies such as Reeves provide an au courant platform, appeal to diverse segments of the political spectrum and young people in particular. Color-blindness deploys aspirational civil-rights era ideals to withdraw from race-based thinking and policies, while postracialism's more radical advocates presume that racial progress has been sufficiently significant to justify race-neutral class politics. Condensed into slogans and broad themes, they were exploited effectively by Barack Obama's presidential campaign. Many justifiably believe that these ideologies risk ahistoricism if they prematurely jettison race from the discussion. Both would be unwise to hasten retreats from race politics because if racism subtends continuing legacies, disavowing necessary race-based solutions would prolong injustice.[1] If the fraught nature of postracial politics offer any indication, it is clearly vital to think through how race and other social factors like class presently interrelate. Where film culture and theory are concerned, I posit that the multiracial is an important interlocutor in that process.

It would be difficult to see how visual culture's recent history with race can be written without highlighting the *Time* magazine cover from 1993 that featured a computer-generated virtual woman, a composite of 14 different races using the first morphing software targeted for mass use, Morph 2.0.[2] When the editors placed the construction they nicknamed "Eve" out front, they established strong discursive parameters with which the postracial era would be seen. Eve's racially unreadable smile was captioned, "The New Face of America," and fronted articles about immigration trends altering the demographic landscape of the country. *Time* correctly anticipated the image's visceral impact for it captivated readers with a physiognomic vision from their technological and multicultural future, and fascinated them by showing external ethnic signifiers dissolving in front of their very eyes. Evelynn M. Hammonds described it as "the drama of miscegenation in cyberspace," in a country where "race has always been dependent upon the visual."[3] Reeves cuts a very similar figure to Eve because his multiracial ambiguity also provides an intense source of fascination and subtends significant portions of his appeal. The science-fiction film, *A Scanner Darkly* (2006), reifies his racial spectacle. His character dons a "scramble suit" that hides his identity by outwardly projecting constantly cycling images of every human facial variant. The resultant visual animates the static ambiguity of Eve (Figure 5.1). Together with his status on Hollywood's A-list, these reasons make him a perfect vehicle with which to investigate this moment in racial and cultural history. Of cinema's multiracial faces, his comes closest to replicating Eve's extraordinary and iconic confluence of discourses concerning racial identity, subjectivity, and technology. Reeves is a prominent artifact of cinema whose multiraciality has been both theorized and politicized as a creation of our present epoch.

Tracking Reeves's star discourse, we discover a critical subjectivity that is but the latest in a procession where Adorno, Jameson, and Said precede him. Together they illuminate a path to what a materialist approach to critical race film theory might look like. To get there, this chapter first examines how Reeves has ironically been constructed by both popular criticism and serious scholarship as a postmodern hybrid, piecing together interviews, commentary, and film analyses. The utter clarity of the subjectivity that emerges is all the more remarkable given the diversity of his films, which include teen flicks, action films, romances, blockbusters, art films, and cult films. Bhabha acts as both transition and primer for this critical survey. His reflections on Vargas the racial and national hybrid in Orson Welles's noir film *Touch of Evil* (1958) in particular, set down a historical and theoretical marker for my analysis. The next part of the study layers the dominant postmodern impressions with an exploration of how they dovetail with the discourse of Reeves's multiraciality. I locate that inquiry within a social history that allows us to grasp the fantasies and anxieties that the multiracial body

(a)

(b)

(c)

Figure 5.1 The scramble suit in *A Scanner Darkly* (2006): Digital animation helps represent a fluid form of racial hybridity.

triggers. With an understanding of his postmodern multiraciality in place, the second half of this chapter addresses the approaches with which critical race film criticism has taken toward Reeves politically and theoretically. Film scholars and reception studies are often quick to make counter ideological claims that his hybridity offers audiences unique opportunities to enact alternative modes of spectatorship, or that it prompts us to challenge the "subject" as Western philosophical hegemony defines. This readiness to deem him postmodern does not comport with what I believe his discourse has to say about autonomy and critical distance. This sets up a conclusion where I conduct a reassessment of how cyborg theory has been applied to multiracial bodies like his. Collectively, Reeves scholarship has shed interesting light on overlooked segments of our culture, but I preach greater caution and cynicism lest it unwittingly sanctions the status quo. I certainly share their conviction, however, that Reeves holds the potential to be a transformative cultural figure.

Hybridity, postmodern subjectivity, and Keanu Reeves

Bhabha's postmodern antiessentialism flows most powerfully from his development of hybridity theory. We recall "The Other Question," later anthologized in *The Location of Culture*, where his combination of Derridean deconstruction and Lacanian psychoanalysis contends that what constitutes racial identity and by extension all identity is neither pure nor clearly delineated.[4] Whether in discourse or material practice, race is fluid and ambivalent. Any invocation of race thus involves a play of difference, which the authority of colonial power denies in order to project false unities. Hence the clarity of racial distinctions results from ideological force. Contradictions and ambivalences are suppressed and disavowed, producing stereotypes that seem fixed and reinforce the apparently stable opposition between Self and Other. Therefore discursive utterances of race such as a film's stereotype, for instance, are not signifiers of distinct types. Instead, they should be reconsidered to be a constant and dynamic production of racial difference. More important, within that inherent instability lies the potential for oppositional critique and subversion. Reaching for a film that lays bare what ideology normally suppresses, Bhabha cites Welles's *Touch of Evil*. He latches on to Stephen Heath's earlier analysis of the multifaceted duality in the lead character Ramon Miguel Vargas, a Mexican police detective investigating an international incident. For Bhabha, Heath draws salient attention to the textual expression of movement and helps to unravel the workings of colonial power. To wit, *Touch of Evil* expresses the dynamism of cultural production and of hybridity itself. The film opens with a close-up of a bomb planted in the trunk of a car on the Mexican side of its American border. The vehicle, carrying a prominent citizen and his companion, explodes when it crosses over to American soil. While at the border at the same time, Vargas and his new blonde American wife Susan, witness the murder. Welles stamps his authorial mark on the film with the famously mobile three-minute-long opening shot capturing the sequence. Within that directorial gesture, the flamboyance and virtuoso combination of tracking and crane work serve to highlight the fluid movement of people and objects over national and juridical boundaries.

Bhabha's take on *Touch of Evil* can be extended to analyze Reeves's star discourse. Vargas, played by Charlton Heston under a dark wig, moustache, and make-up, produces a perceptual clash. White actor and Mexican character present an indefinable figure, physically and narratively traversing races, national borders, and the law. As Bhabha observes, contradiction is also textually encoded in the lighting contrasts of the mise-en-scène's chiaroscuro patterns. Vargas is a hybrid—a cinematic expression of the quintessential figure championed by Bhabha. Along those lines, I argue that Reeves may be an even more vividly ambivalent subject. "The Other Question" misses the opportunity to fully elaborate on the significance of Vargas, but if we infer from Bhabha's other writing, we can see that *Touch of Evil* not only problematizes the notions of racial and cultural essentialism, it also reveals the processes of racial and cultural production to be fluid and ambivalent. In this way, the film helps to illustrate the dynamic discursive and psychoanalytic processes normally repressed by colonial power or racist hegemony.

In *The Location of Culture*, Bhabha defines politics, agency, race, and culture as contradictory and ambivalent. Hybridity is the default state of all discourse. It is a nonstatic state that destabilizes discourse and ultimately, the structure of colonialism.

> Hybridity is a problematic of colonial representation and individuation that reverses the effects of the colonialist disavowal, so that other 'denied' knowledges enter upon the dominant discourse and estrange the basis of its authority—its rules of recognition . . . it is not simply the *content* of disavowed knowledges—be they forms of cultural otherness or traditions of colonialist treachery—that return to be acknowledged as counter-authorities . . . What is irremediably estranging in the presence of the hybrid—in the revaluation of the symbol of

national authority as the sign of colonial difference—is that the difference of cultures can no longer be identified or evaluated as objects of epistemological or moral contemplation: cultural differences are not simply *there* to be seen or appropriated.[5]

Bhabha does not see hybridity as a mix of knowable or pure, entities. So needless to say, reversing Orientalism or utilizing positive images are moot points. More significant, dialectical synthesis and thus Marxism are impossible since coherent theses and antitheses do not exist in the first place. It is therefore important not to confuse dialectical synthesis with Bhabha's idea of the "Third Space," the ephemeral realm he defines as what makes ambivalence possible in the first place. It is an atemporal "cultural space . . . where the negotiation of incommensurable differences creates a tension peculiar to borderline existences."[6] A more concrete definition of "Third Space" might be useful, except that Bhabha already avers with certainty that his position is contrary to Marxism, humanism, or any Adornoan sense of authentic or transcendent subjectivity.

> [E]mphasis on the disjunctive present of utterance . . . allows the articulation of subaltern agency to emerge as relocation and reinscription. In the seizure of the sign, as I've argued, there is neither dialectical sublation nor the empty signifier: there is a contestation of the given symbols of authority that shift the terrains of antagonism.[7]

Hybrid agency is akin to a camouflage or a contesting, antagonistic subjectivity functioning in the time lag of sign/symbol—the period within the process of signification between when pedagogical history positions a subject and that subject's enunciation of its own status.[8] By definition, it only occurs in discourse at the moment of articulating race or performing cultural practices. It is a nonessentialist, splitting subjectivity for which self-reflection is a traditional but impossible fiction.

Therefore, Bhabha does not advocate a simple multiculturalist view because multiculturalism's particular conception of cultural diversity involves two anathemas: unified identities of members from each individual culture and normative stability. If Reeves is rarely associated with either unity or stability, does that make him a Bhabhan hybrid? The popular as well as academic discourse described below surrounding his racial identity seem geared to help answer that question when it grapples with how he challenges traditional racial categories and how that boundary crossing resonates with liberal multiculturalism. This chapter examines his discursive construction as a postmodern hybrid and considers the ideological epistemologies at stake. Does the star discourse sketch out an ideological stand, and if so, what does that look like? And since the correlated cyborg trope is an indelible part of Reeves's hermeneutic constellation, does it give shape to a model of racial and Marxian politics?

Over the first decade of his film career, Reeves developed a public reputation that seemed obvious and intelligible. His initial roles in teen films caught the eye of youth magazines and celebrity culture as an attractive star commodity tipped for future stardom. These early films include *Youngblood* (1986), a sports film about young hockey prospects trying to become professional athletes, *River's Edge* (1986), *Permanent Record* (1988), *The Prince of Pennsylvania* (1988), and *Bill and Ted's Excellent Adventure* (1989). The films he made in the 1990s vary in tone from dark and foreboding to light-hearted spoofs, but do not stray far from the idea of Reeves as a disaffected teenaged social misfit. These performances were positively reviewed, but significant attention was still being paid to his newfound status as teen sex symbol and in that context, he was complimented for being an actor who makes a serious commitment to his craft. Contrary to later evaluations of his acting, he was seen in fact to possess an excess of emotion.[9] The entertainment supplement in The Toronto Sun even suggested without a hint of irony that he was "the new DeNiro."[10] That flattery evaporated somewhat when he began to appear in thematically weightier films and more dramatic roles such as *Dangerous Liaisons* (1988), the adaptation of Choderlos de Laclos's 1782 novel *Les Liaisons Dangereuses* about sexual decadence among aristocrats in pre-Revolution France, *Point Break* (1991), Kathryn Bigelow's esteemed Hollywood action blockbuster about a band of surfers who moonlight as bank robbers, *My Own Private Idaho* (1991), an independent contemporary adaptation of Shakespeare's *Henry V* by "indie" director Gus Van Sant, and Bernardo Bertolucci's *Little Buddha* (1993), a quasi-religious meditation on faith and reincarnation. As the items on Reeves's filmography grew more artistic and highly regarded, critics found greater reason to evaluate and analyze his acting, and within that discussion arose a consistent set of themes that still persist.

The general perception of Reeves became one of a movie star who lacked the acting chops of a traditional method actor. The following reviews of his work in more serious roles show that even compliments arrived backhandedly:

> The picture is overripe, and with few exceptions, so are the performances . . . As for Reeves, such lines as "Come, come let us thither" do not fall trippingly off this surfer dude's tongue.[11]

As Don John, Don Pedro's other half-brother (and archenemy), Keanu Reeves is a surly brat with a chip on his shoulder. Reeves plays him as if his face were frozen into a perpetual sulk.[12]

Not so Keanu Reeves, who, as estate agent Jonathan Harker, seems to have wandered in from the set of Bill and Ted's Transylvanian Adventure, his face registering a perpetually glazed look of befuddlement.[13]

Bertolucci's audaciously campy casting coup succeeds, and not just because Reeves's presence will lure Sassy readers and curiosity-seekers. He survives the heavy makeup and handles the accent, and his surfer-dude vacuity here makes him appear radiantly serene.[14]

From the manner in which he was judged during this period, two obvious reasons may explain the critics' overall view. Perhaps he was typecast as a listless and unaffected star from the over-commercialized teen movie genre. Or maybe the negative reviews from this period were the ironic product of his very convincing portrayal of the innocent but simple-minded "surfer dude" teenager Ted Logan in *Bill and Ted's Excellent Adventure*. The frequent invocation of that particular character's persona and trademark lingo in numerous profiles would appear to support both claims.

Therefore, the irony with which *The New Yorker* reported in the spring of 1994 the existence of a college class on "The Films of Keanu Reeves" should not be unexpected. Although the article concedes that Art Center College of Design (Pasadena) Professor Stephen Prina harbored serious intent in relating Reeves's films to writers such as Roland Barthes, Michel Foucault, and Matei Calinescu, its author liberally sprinkles the piece with surfer-speak from the *Bill and Ted* movies that were now inextricable from Reeves's public image. The magazine reacts to the idea of a university-level course on the subject with the words "gnarly," "righteous," and of course, "excellent"—the character Ted Logan's favorite exclamation.[15] The report's bemusement illustrates Reeves's enigmatic nature. A host of postmodern tropes circulates within that hermeneutic field, such as fragmentation and loss of affect alongside an innate awareness of his racial ambiguity and hybridity. His racial identity is also often overlaid with digital technological discourses of postmodernity. A multiply inflected figure, he is as Guy Debord describes, a spectacle that "brings together and explains a wide range of apparently disparate phenomena."[16]

Reeves's star persona is imbued strongly with a handful of basic ideas, among them his stupidity and peripety reinforced by a seemingly expressionless face and wooden acting style that dissociates his performances from popularly held notions of artistic work or production. Critiques again disguise themselves as compliments. *The Washington Post* reviewed his work in *Point Break* thus:

> Reeves is a perfect choice for the youthfully malleable Utah; as an actor, he seems perpetually on the verge of a thought that can't quite work its way to the surface. He's charismatically puppy-brained and, watching him, we get caught up in the slow-motion meshing of his mental gears.[17]

The incredulity that *The New Yorker* expresses toward the possibility that he could be an academic subject to be studied relates to the very notion that he simply is not a subject in the traditional sense of an individual with depth and a central core. As a critic describes in a review of *A Scanner Darkly*, "the Buddha is perhaps the best-suited to his own personal iconography as an actor. Like the self in Buddhist philosophy, Keanu is less a person than an empty place-holder."[18] Reeves only reinforces that public image when he maintains an inaccessible air about him by inhabiting a bubble of irony during interviews and in interactions with the media. He plays no small part in depicting himself as someone whom fans can never understand.

This may prompt us to separate him from his star discourse, media representations and audience. We can also start to discern a conscious reaction to the postmodern moment. When art critic Timothy Martin describes Reeves's presence as "a foot of Robert Bressonian space around him," he hints unmistakably at a mobile emanation, perhaps what Walter Benjamin might call an aura.[19] On the surface, Reeves appears to most gazers as a perfectly postmodern star. But is there within him and the discourse circulating around him, the possibility of an authenticity, of critical subjectivity? The "Bressonian space" buffering Reeves from his surroundings as much as it isolates those who look at him manifests itself in media characterizations of him as "blank," "detached," or "empty." His face is said to be incapable of the emotional shifts and twitches seen in traditional (or as is often the implication, better) method-actors.[20] Some have diagnosed such a symptom as an effect of postmodernity. For example, Fredric Jameson considers William Hurt an actor who epitomizes a postmodern depthlessness that spills over into his films as anonymity.[21] Reeves's face does the same, but it also reflects a much wider discourse concerning the present moment overdetermined by digital technology. Although Reeves carries in his teen genre movies a tinge of what Jameson terms the "rebellion and nonconformism" (in, for example Marlon Brando, Steve McQueen, and Jack Nicholson), others like film critic Lisa Schwarzbaum view his look as one that more closely resembles a kind of oblivious displacement or "serene blankness," almost a refusal to invite spectators to identify with him in the same way that they do with traditional method actors.[22] Consistently, it is a countenance around which all his films can be tacitly organized.

The most profound cinematic faces, it seems, are ambivalent. Roland Barthes famously lionized Greta Garbo's face for simultaneously carrying no meaning and all meaning.[23] To Barthes, Garbo's face presents a modernist opportunity "to draw an existential from an essential beauty." But the optimism that Barthes derives from Garbo flies in the face of postmodernity's assault on our senses and experiences. To Walter Benjamin, the social and experiential effects of the twentieth century were recorded on faces by the media of the same era, photography, and cinema. In "A Short History of Photography," Benjamin charts a progression of facial expressions in portraiture, from a time when people still possessed an aura—what he defines as a connection to history, authority, and heritage, or a hope for unity in the midst of an assault at the hands of modernity—to a period when the aura, and subsequently the hope associated with it, is slowly lost. He writes that there was a time "when people did not yet look out into a world as isolated and godforsaken."[24] The redemption that Barthes found on Garbo is thus further in question when we speak of Reeves, who arrives at a time when postmodernity is in full swing.

In addition to Barthes's essay on Garbo, an analysis of Reeves will be reminiscent also of Miriam Hansen's focus on Rudolph Valentino.[25] Like Barthes's earlier work, what Hansen describes in *Babel and Babylon* feels similarly dated in the sense that the postmodern subjectivity Reeves embodies belongs to a rather unique present. Hansen describes Valentino as a cult figure and exoticized film star, whose multivalent place within a patriarchal cinematic institution created an alternative public sphere for female spectators. For Reeves's audiences, however, it is a public sphere that has collapsed and been invaded by multinational capital.[26] What arguably existed as a public sphere in the 1920s—if we assume that film-going was not already an intensely intimate and private act of consumption—is now occupied by multinational corporations. Valentino might have provided women access, via the cinematic institution, to an alternative public sphere, but that is now greatly diminished. The conglomeration and vertical integration that took place in the film industry during the last 25 years have seen to that. Our very experience of cinema is being continually transformed. Theaters have relocated into multiplexes and malls, transferring spectators into spaces that are public in name, but which are built and sustained by private capital interests and predicated on private property exchange. Free expression only occurs within a consumer economy and under the aegis of the culture industry. The growth of the video market and digital media technologies such as mobile devices that make possible personal exhibition, also transform spectatorship into a profoundly private activity. These cultural developments are very much implicated in Reeves's films and star discourse.

The exposition of Reeves's public persona as specifically postmodern must begin with *Bill and Ted's Excellent Adventure*. It is a film most would dismiss as an inconsequential teen flick embodying the brain-dead mentality of its two anti-intellectual title characters. In reality, it is an unexpected but utterly lucid treatment of Jamesonian theory. The light-hearted science-fiction comedy tells the story of two heavy-metal loving teenagers who are cultural descendents of the iconic pot-smoking surfer Jeff Spicoli from Amy Heckerling's contribution to the genre's canon, *Fast Times at Ridgemont High* (1982). Bill and Ted inherit Spicoli's wardrobe and surfer affectations. They are also about to fail an important history test and not graduate high school. The film then flashes forward to the future, which we discover is a utopia where all existence is founded on the music of Bill and Ted's band, The Wyld Stallyns. Failing the history test would eventually disband The Wyld Stallyns, and change the course of history. So an emissary from the future named Rufus (comedian George Carlin), is sent to the present in a time machine to ensure that the duo passes their history test. For that purpose, Rufus instructs the teenagers to retrieve various historical figures for a final history presentation that will decide the fate of the world.

With canny precision, the film illustrates Jameson's exposition of the postmodern condition. The time machine in which Bill and Ted swerve through time is a telephone booth that travels literally like telecommunicatory data through "the Circuits of History," to retrieve the historical figures who all arrive back in the late 1980s, only to lose themselves in the consumerist utopia of a suburban San Dimas mall (Figure 5.2). We see Beethoven on electronic keyboards, Joan of Arc leading an aerobics demonstration, and Napoleon Bonaparte running wild in a water park named Waterloo. The scenes thus realize what Jameson calls the eternal present, a theme revisited in the time-travel romance *The Lake House* (2006) (Figures 5.3 and 5.4). An architect (Reeves) romances a doctor living two years in the future after they meet and correspond through a magical mailbox that transports its contents through time. Anchored

Figure 5.2 "They are the Circuits of History, gentlemen. They'll take us to any point in time we wish." (*Bill and Ted's Excellent Adventure*, 1989).

Figure 5.3 Historical figures at the eternal present of a San Dimas Mall, in *Bill and Ted's Excellent Adventure* (1989).

firmly within the romance and magical realist genres, the characters do not spend much time wondering about the mailbox beyond how it facilitates their relationship. *The Lake House* defies logic even more than time-travel narratives inevitably do, but distinctively, it has no pretensions about its own absurdity. One long shot for example, presents the couple sitting in a park, conversing contemporaneously in voice-over as they read their letters. A split-screen is used to show that they are two years apart in the same space. The visible suture highlights the temporal distance between their emotional closeness. Most importantly, the effect expresses the film's willingness to disregard plausibility, undermining the notion of temporal progression and once again representing the eternal present. Almost two decades after Bill and Ted's numbed and blissful

Figure 5.4 The eternal present in *The Lake House* (2006). Time travel across a split-screen.

detachment appeared in their eponymous film, audiences were asked to adopt the same attitude toward *The Lake House*'s preposterous premise.

This postmodern sensibility embodied by "Ted" resonates at a juncture that, as a number of writers have described, thwarts all attempts at unity or ambition. Jean-Francois Lyotard, for instance, equates postmodernism with the loss of all faith in a Marxist futurology. There is a suspicion of master narratives, authority, the feasibility of universal values, moral clarity, and of commitment to the long term, to the point where we content ourselves with fragments of information, where we make sense only of what we are allowed. Unlike Reeves's characters in *River's Edge* and *The Matrix*, Ted never breaks out of his interpellated trance. It is thus significant that of all of Reeves's characters, especially the acclaimed performances where he is deemed professionally or dramatically credible as the dependable "lost boy," the one that seizes and inhabits his public persona is the politically and socially passive "Ted."[27] While the principals portrayed by Reeves are frequently active subjects whose heroics hinge on ethics and consciousness, Ted on the contrary, submits to postmodern logic and in fact thrives on it. The question therefore becomes: Why is it Ted who becomes "Keanu Reeves?"

In addition to the allusions cited earlier, Ted's lingo constantly punctuates Reeves's star discourse. The character and his favorite exclamation, "excellent," peppers the titles of the actor's profiles, such as "Keanu's Excellent Adventure," "A Most Excellent Enigma," and "Goodbye, Airhead."[28] Another commentator felt that "there was some genuine essence of Keanu in his performance as the dim-witted Valley boy Ted."[29] Reviews consistently evaluate his performances by using "Ted" as some form of behavioral benchmark. In *Bram Stoker's*

Dracula (1992), Reeves's Jonathan Harker is called "a perfectly innocent, 19th century goofball."[30] Critics also conflate the two personas, like when they hailed the casting decision that placed Reeves in the title role of *Johnny Mnemonic*, reinforcing the unproblematic equation of Johnny's literally empty brain with the actor's shallow acting style and real-life stupidity.[31] And when *The Matrix* was released, late night talk shows parodied Reeves by replaying a two-second clip in the film where the character is awestruck and exclaims a line often uttered by Ted, "Whoa!" The campy joke relies on the strong connection between the actor and a specific character, and is a direct jab at his poor acting skills. Frequent mention is also made of his awkward physicality, slightly uncoordinated limbs and de-centered movements, akin to Ted as well as another similar Reeves character, Rupert of *The Prince of Pennsylvania*.[32]

Reeves only reinforced preexisting perceptions by continuing to select roles in postmodern allegories and cyborg parables. These range from the post-apocalyptic forecasts of technological domination in *Johnny Mnemonic* (1995) and *The Matrix* (1999), to the less likely but just as poignantly Baudrillardian *Bill and Ted* comedies (1989, 1991), and Generation X films like *River's Edge*. *Johnny Mnemonic* was postmodern artist Robert Longo's first directorial feature film effort from cyberpunk author William Gibson's script from his own short story of the same name. Within the writer's dark and cacophonous cyberpunk milieu, the eponymous cyborg courier (Reeves) has sold the long-term memory space in his own neural network to corporate clients who use his cybernetic memory space to transport information. The postmodern genre's speedy narratives and relatively shallow characterizations uncannily fit the dominant understanding of Reeves as a bad actor. Joshua Clover explains that the actor is perfect for *The Matrix* because his character's virtual existence makes him a depthless "man without qualities." Reeves's personified blankness fits the role's need for him to "appear as appearance itself."[33] Popular film reviewers describe him similarly.

> Even if Reeves could act, his character as written would be flatter than a floppy disk.[34]

> It's tough selling bloody heroism on a Homeric scale to a younger crowd raised on Luke Skywalker and Rambo. These days, the machinery of spectacle has gotten so sophisticated and so stunt-driven that emotional depth only slows a guy down. (The apotheosis of hero-dude blankness: Keanu Reeves' Neo in *The Matrix*.)[35]

In *The Matrix*, Reeves's character Neo is the last hope for rescuing the human race, whose unconscious bodies rest in pods where they are farmed for energy that fuels a supercomputer. The humans' brains are connected by plugs to the machine, and managed by a program called the Matrix. The computer controls their consciousness by substituting a virtual reality for the actual one, which the film represents as a post-apocalyptic dystopia. The film therefore fashions the Matrix after a sort of Debordian spectacle, or perhaps more like a Baudrillardian simulacra. With a famous intertextual reference, Neo retrieves contraband disks from inside a hollowed-out edition of Jean Baudrillard's *Simulacra and Simulation* in an early scene. Neo's mission as action-hero is as Debord asserted: to overthrow the spectacle and the apparatus that subtends it. The machinery oppressing humans stand in as allegories of omnipotent multinational forces that exploit technology to control social relations and suppress social agency.

In that narrative context, while contrary to the preponderant percentage of his star discourse, we note that the messianic Neo adopts a faith in the modernist ethos. He rejects the simulated life in the Matrix where postmodernism is reified—the eternal present, lacking both history and future. The film's expository drive and function throughout most of its duration, untangling the *syuzhet* to reveal the master-narrative of the *fabula*, parallels Neo's need to make up for the forward-looking vision of modernism that is missing. Neo's choice here is one of an authentic subject. It privileges active consciousness and critical distance over passivity. Among the tales from postmodernity that dominate his oeuvre, Reeves is consistently the character that possesses those capacities. *The Matrix* valorizes Neo's choice by contrasting it with the easy pleasures that come from being an interpellated subject. Neo is first introduced to the joy of illusionist fantasies during a training sequence where virtual martial arts skills are simply uploaded from a disk. Reeves delivers an important punchline in a close-up when he wakes up startled and deadpans an absurdist joke that plays on his discourse of stupidity, "I know kung-fu!" Who would not want to "know kung-fu?" Yet Neo recognizes that the Matrix is still a lesser existence than that of social reality, even when the latter is a dark, obliterated dystopia. To paraphrase a line uttered by an antagonist who betrays Neo and chooses to live in the digital simulacra, Neo's choice recognizes that "ignorance is" in fact not "bliss." The apocalypse stands as a dialectical reminder of technology's triumph and as a constant awareness of history. The film would appear to argue that enlightenment entails a movement away from postmodernism, toward modernism and its critical subject. Deliverance comes with the modernist belief in a more authentic existence.

The Bressonian aura that Timothy Martin sensed is real, and Reeves carries it from film to film, rendering him noncomplicit with postmodernity or even resistant to its effects. Where the science-fiction films depict their characters' lack of social and political autonomy, the social realist *River's Edge* depicts how Generation X suffers the ethical consequences of that deficiency. Director Tim Hunter's contribution to the teenage coming-of-age genre historicizes the alienation of contemporary youth. Based quite faithfully on the true story of teenage killer Anthony Jacques Broussard, the film is about a murderer who then boasts about the crime at school and leads a group of friends to view his victim's dead body. Hunter's film posits a cause and effect. Consumerist excesses have begotten suburban culture and a prior generation's hippie idealism has degenerated into the figure of the kids' didactically impotent high school teacher, a parody of new-age psychotherapy. As a consequence, the characters lose the moral bearings required to deal with even mortality itself, the material repercussions of which are suffered most devastatingly by the working-class existence of the lead characters. Matt (Reeves) is the one character that manages to float above the moral morass. Among the clique of teens who discovers that one of its own has killed his girlfriend and left her naked corpse on the local river's edge, only Matt manages to remember that murder is indeed a crime. He reports the homicide and suffers the social consequences of violating his friends' perverted idea of solidarity. The character that almost punishes him for that transgression is his younger brother Tim, who confronts Matt with a gun. At the climactic moment, Matt rescues himself from a physical death and his brother from a spiritual one by appealing to Tim's decency and persuading him to lower the weapon.

Interviewing Reeves for *Vanity Fair*, writer Michael Shnayerson hints that the actor is indeed trying to alienate himself from postmodernity. Shnayerson suggests that he plays "Keanu-as-Ted offscreen [as] a smart way to keep the world at bay."[36] According to that estimation, we can rethink Ted's passive acceptance of the postmodern condition as a brand of ironic detachment and coping mechanism. The world in this case is one where its citizens face the reality of their mortality, their impotence in the face of late capitalism, and their loss of coherent identity.[37] It is no coincidence then that *Time* magazine once dubbed Reeves's cohort of actors "Generation X-cellent."[38] Douglas Coupland's seminal 1991 book, *Generation X*, applies another interpretive layer. Although the term "Generation X" was appropriated as a corporate marketing strategy and a means to brand a consumer demographic, what both Coupland and the advertising industry shared was the knowledge that postmodernity's children lack political impetus and social consciousness.[39]

Generation X describes young characters who turn away from Reaganism and the corporate creed, but have no other viable political paradigm to turn to. The resultant existence that Coupland depicts is reified in the book: a pastel-covered screed divided into ultra-comfortable bite-size chapters, standing alone as independently as the manner that Reeves's limbs swing from his body. The narrative of *Generation X* internalizes fragmentation, constructing pockets of vignettes each of which is liberally appended on the book's spacious margins with occasionally explanatory but frequently tangential illustrations. Integration of word and image result in a text that while of a length extremely readable in a single burst, is nevertheless perfectly designed to be consumed one chapter at a time. The protagonists Andy, Claire, and Dag inhabit a superficial state of endless irony. While affluent and technologically literate, they unmistakably abhor the detritus of mass culture in which people are forced to live. They cynically and often accurately critique the conditions of late-stage consumerism such as "historical slumming," "legislated nostalgia," and "ultra short term nostalgia."[40] Yet they remain simultaneously very able to draw upon a massive vocabulary of pop-culture references, and inject a vast amount of mass-produced commodities into their vernacular. It ultimately confirms the substructure's infiltration of the symbolic. The characters try to escape, driving out west in an attempt to discover an alternative society by way of the mythology of the American road. The journey is inevitably futile, and as a result of that despair they simply cannot help but replicate the look, speak, and mannerism of a Keanu/Ted-like persona. To the degree that Coupland's *Generation X* did express a side of the postmodern human condition, it explains why audiences respond to Keanu Reeves the movie star who can "speak in doggerel," who is lovable because he cannot finish a sentence.[41] Doggerel might be the only language that makes sense in a recycled culture of pastiche.

When postmodernity at large spins a cultural fabric so inextricable with Reeves's star discourse, it becomes unsurprising that its fragmentation in the cultural, social, and political realms also informs the racial component of his persona. The actor's multiracial heritage is continually mentioned and used to explain two noted characteristics: his peripety, and the indiscernible and multivalent collection of ethnic markers on his face. Reeves's multiracialness is therefore not understood as a static mixture. It is rather imbued with components of dynamism, movement, if not fluidity. He is thus a racial hybrid in Bhabha's sense of the word, with a face where all those discourses meet. To fully comprehend the scope of how they all interact and relate, we require a cultural–theoretical understanding of postmodernity along with a social and political history of multiraciality.

Multiracials and postmodern ahistoricism

The 1967 Supreme Court ruling in Loving v. State of Virginia that struck down anti-miscegenation laws was handed down shortly before the Paris évènements of 1968, where general strikes were on the verge of claiming its first industrialized casualty before the movement was halted by the capitulations of the French Communist Party and labor unions. It marked a definitive turning point for Jean-François Lyotard, and harbinger of the end for Marxist metanarratives. Other events were also taking place internationally. In the United States, radicals were active but eventually faced comparable trauma, marking 1968 as a key turning point in their history as well. Protests over civil rights and the Vietnam War were ongoing, assassins claimed the lives of Martin Luther King, Jr and Robert Kennedy, President Lyndon B. Johnson withdrew from the election, and the violent crackdown on protests at the Democratic National Convention was captured live by television cameras. In that historical environment, it becomes tempting to think of the *Loving v. Virginia* decision as a Lyotardian event in that it places multiracial history squarely in the so-called postmodern period when Marxism ebbed as a political and theoretical paradigm. *Loving v. Virginia* is one of the last progressive developments that the Johnson administration oversaw. The case began when Perry Loving, a white man, married Mildred Jeter, a black-Native American woman in 1958. Trial judge Leon Bazile sentenced them to one year in prison for violating Virginia's anti-miscegenation laws. The case was adjudicated for years all the way to the highest court where on June 12, 1967, Chief Justice Earl Warren handed down a decision that overturned laws in the last 16 states that still banned interracial marriage. Sociologist Maria Root identifies a "multiracial baby boom" that followed *Loving v. Virginia*.[42] US Census figures show that the rate of interracial marriage has doubled for each decade since 1970.[43] The ruling might have struck down all the legal opposition to miscegenation, but it is probably not the sole reason for that baby boom. The heightened levels of liberal racial views as well as a culture of defiance among young couples during the 1960s probably contributed as well.

Loving v. Virginia layers the period when postmodernity conquers culture, with a time when a new body, a racially fragmented body, emerged into greater presence and visibility. The circumstances arguably endow the multiracial body with a postmodern worldview that inflects multiracial politics and identity as well. With miscegenation decriminalized and socially sanctioned, the multiracial body becomes one of evidence, but of what? Does it prove that race as postmodernists would have it, is merely a social construct? Should we go on to celebrate the multiracial body as a pluralist utopia? Perhaps clues can be found in Reeves's star discourse, constructed in racial, gender, and sexual terms, if we read the components of his star discourse at the conjunction of postmodernism with contemporary modes of ethnicity and identity formation. The discourse constructs him as a fragmented racial subject, one whose identity dissolves before our very eyes. Immediately, we can recognize and diagnose postmodern symptoms in that racial discourse. Often, the cyborg's specter creeps beyond the boundaries of his films' narratives and reaches his persona. The resultant convergence of technology, ethnicity, and identity can then enable us to weigh the merits of infinite fragmentation and decenteredness, especially since he also evinces nostalgia for unified subjectivity.

Talk of Reeves contains multiple references to his unquestioned but indefinable appeal. The size of his box-office numbers and résumé, the range of important and respected directors who have cast him, and his general popularity attest to that attraction. It is particularly true among women who flocked from around the world to his January 1995 performance of Hamlet in Winnipeg, attend his gigs with the rock band Dogstar, and sweep men's magazines off newsstands when he adorns the cover.[44] According to consensus, the source of his attractiveness lies in the manner that Reeves deviates from traditional definitions of white masculinity; he is not rugged, erudite, or articulate. It is an "interesting . . . unthreatening sexuality," one that is "soft-looking rather than controlling and macho," "like a lost puppy who needs caring."[45] This softer masculinity is, I suspect, intertwined with the specter of his ethnic otherness, where the usual threats of sexual aggression are mitigated by discourses of Asian emasculation.

Reeves's racial otherness shape-shifts in public consciousness. Knowledge of his ethnicity mostly appears with a tone that mixes exoticism with pluralist celebration. For example, published articles often remark on how his mixed

Chinese–Hawaiian–English heritage shapes his physiognomy: "his dark, Eurasian, sleepy-eyed sexuality," "the angular face with its ethnic and sexual ambiguities" or "that subtly Asian beauty—the dark, intense eyes, the prominent cheekbones, the golden skin."[46] Almost as many display awareness of his ethnicity by pausing to explain and pronounce his Hawaiian first name. The actor even elicits specific comments on his "exotic eyes."[47] Nevertheless, some spectators may still express surprise that he is not just white. LeiLani Nishime claims that he is "the most visible, or conversely the most invisible, hapa star, since he is undoubtedly the most famous and least acknowledged."[48] Ethnicity is rarely a component of his films' narrative economy and for that reason too, many plead ignorance about his ethnicity, but his multiraciality is demonstrably present. There is no reason to doubt the truthfulness of those who deny knowledge of his race, even if claims like Nishime's remain anecdotal. Yet, ethnicity remains implicitly part of the overall aesthetic. There is the remarkable example of a 2005 article in *Vanity Fair*'s "Theater" section regarding the role of Shakespeare's Hamlet and how playing the title character provides a rite of passage for actors. The piece leads off with a review of Reeves's 1995 stint onstage in Winnipeg as the Danish prince. While the text itself makes no allusion to race, the accompanying illustration reifies the specter of Reeves's ethnicity. It depicts an astoundingly Orientalized drawing of Reeves with high cheekbones and narrow, slanted eyelines, in contrast to an Anglicized sketch of English actor Ralph Fiennes.[49]

Implicitly or explicitly, Reeves's visual otherness imbues his overall reception. This occurs despite the fact that all of his films place him in roles of white men. One exception is Bertolucci's *Little Buddha*, in which two monks invite a young Seattle boy named Jesse to Bhutan because he might be the reincarnation of an important Lama. Bertolucci narrates Jesse's story in parallel with that of Prince Siddhartha (Reeves), who will grow up to be Buddha. Bertolucci chose to cast Reeves on the basis of the actor's face. The director developed an interest after learning of his mixed heritage, which triggered an expectation for what Reeves looks like—a look that he eventually got for Siddhartha. To Bertolucci, the multiracial face held a universal aesthetic: an innocence that made him look like he walked on air. In essence, he equated racial ambiguity with social dislocation and spiritual detachment.[50]

Little Buddha looks optimistically at how spirituality can serve as a possible antidote to postmodernity's onslaught. Little Jesse is accompanied to India by his father, Dean, played with little emotion by pop singer Chris Isaak. The film's encouraging perspective promises spiritual transcendence to those currently devoid of history and affect. Dean, for example, struggles to cry even in the face of tragedy. His proclamation that his friend "Evan's bankrupt" is a clear and direct statement on his own spiritual vacuum. For both Siddhartha and Dean (an architect who builds unoccupied structures in Seattle, home of Microsoft, Starbucks, and Amazon), detachment inspires them to embark on their journeys. Bertolucci and famed cinematographer Vittorio Storaro bathe their two locales with luminous hues, contrasting the cold bluish–green of Seattle with the warm orange–red of India. The family's South Asian pilgrimage helps them to eventually reconcile with postmodernity.

Bertolucci's interpretation of Reeves's multiethnic physiognomy recapitulates the popular tendency for writers to consider his demeanor emblematic of Generation X and symbolic of the postmodern condition. On that score, we find film critic Carrie Rickey going even further. Her review of *Little Buddha* layers the triumvirate discourses of race, gender, and sexuality with the idea of digital (postmodern) technology:

> "He has a beauty," marveled his *Little Buddha* director Bernardo Bertolucci, "that's not Eastern or Western," a product of Reeves's Chinese-Hawaiian and English ancestry. The actor's enigmatic face suggests a computer-generated composite of every known race and gender. His effect is pansexual and so is his appeal. At the trill of his name—say key-AH-noo—fans female and male heave libidinal sighs.[51]

Poignantly, a computer did indeed generate a famous racial composite that very year, "Eve." The significance of *Time*'s cover image to its postmodern moment is threefold. First, by generating this face from a collection of photographs, its creators reified the multiracial body from a play of surface signs. Under multiculturalist axioms, "The New Face of America" is a utopian signal for racelessness. Although it relies nonetheless on the notion that races are identifiable by facial features, the image's production through a process of computer-aided physiognomic mapping then defines race by visual markers that are freely reproducible and thus inconsequential, rendering these very differences politically passé. Second, the visceral impact of the *Time* cover was premised on the indecipherability of the cover model's racial features, which de-emphasizes the social and cultural histories at play. This includes the magazine's coverage of political economic circumstances that drive immigration trends and migrational flux. But the main preoccupation remains with the integrity of external ethnic signifiers. In a way then, we might find race standing in for material history. And if race is an indeterminable fiction, the latter inevitably slips away.

Finally, the image fetishizes multiracial bodies with postmodern technology. At a time when digital imaging had just begun to reveal its creative potential for film and video, the most visible if not most significant experiments in these visual effects concentrated on the element of race, as it was two years prior in Michael Jackson's music video for the song "Black or White," where different ethnic faces took turns morphing into each other. The computer—whose basic unit, the "bit," fetishizes fragmentation—is central to the narrative and production of *The Matrix*. The technology that gives Neo/Reeves the power of flight is the very thing that houses the characters' consciousness. Schwartzbaum's review of the film summarized the system of meanings orbiting the actor with the term, "handsome cyber-Buddha."[52] Technology is indeed the instrument whose workings *Vanity Fair* had earlier invoked to illustrate Reeves's disjointed enunciation.

> "Now, you haven't said yet that [*A Walk in the Clouds* is] a romance." Keanu laughs. *Hee-hee*! "When I first read it I didn't like it at all. I found it very harsh.. . . I've given it to a couple of people and they've . . ." Word search; search fail. "But then when they read it again they see it."[53]

In totality, the postmodern tropes circulating in Reeves's star discourse—social dislocation, fragmentation, digital technology, and the loss of affect, historicity, and subjectivity—are attributed or connected at least in part and often substantially to his multiracial hybridity. How then is this interpretation of hybridity mobilized politically in specific regard to the substructural causes of those dislocations and losses? Does it attain liberty from colonial power, or is the result a little more regressive?

In Norma Field's analysis of contemporary Japan, *In the Realm of a Dying Emperor*, the historian all too briefly alludes to the possibility of interpreting multiracial physiognomies in a way that is politically useful for the oppressed. She describes half-Okinawan offspring fathered by American soldiers stationed on the island's base as the "embodiment of sex."[54] In this case, sex is a tool of domination under colonizing regimes that carry out both physical and cultural rape. Recalling Bhabha, colonial power is the ability to arrest fluid meanings and hybrids are the instrument to destabilize those imperial holds. What Field appears to describe—a hybrid body and physiognomy that prompt reminders and current awareness of an unwelcome occupation—evokes Bhabha's definition of ideology and presents itself as a subversive response to that power. The multiracial body does not just arrest history in this case, it *is* history.

But Claudia Castañeda fears the threat of postmodern ahistoricism. Her analysis of Eve suggests that the connection between hybrid bodies and history—of migrational flows or of the global economics and power imbalances that cause them—might be fading. Writing in the context of transnational adoption, Castañeda interprets Eve as a symptom of how racial categories are "evacuated of the histories and politics of culture, geography, and nation that they might otherwise signify."[55] The superficiality of creating Eve with reproducible visual signifiers of race is, she argues, the image's act of racism.

> Its violence—its racism—consists . . . in the evacuation of histories of domination and resistance (and of all the events and ways of living that cannot be captured in those two terms).[56]

The process of historical "evacuation" occurring with Eve's electronic-racial fetishization also takes place in the star discourse of Reeves, whose hybridity operates similarly. The Generation X label attached to Reeves already demonstrates that it is far easier to celebrate dislocation, peripety, and loss of affect, as positive but shallow signs of liberty and anti-establishment rebellion. In the analogous manner that *Time*'s computer-generated photograph pushed socio-political history backward into afterthoughts, Reeves's modernist subjectivity is sublated. And in *Johnny Mnemonic* and *The Matrix,* the digital technology that is so notably part of Reeves's persona literally destroys his characters' historical memories.

Castañeda is far from alone. Many others share her unease that technology and multiracial bodies will lead us to forget history. Hammonds contends that *Time*'s technophilia sublimates miscegenation anxieties and violent histories to reinstate white patriarchy.[57] In the anthology *Mixed Race Hollywood,* Jane Park and Nishime independently aver that Reeves's multiraciality deflects attention from "social, historical, and political contexts," or alternatively, "the weighty legacy of racial history."[58] Regarding postracialism, Sumi Cho argues that discrepancies between rhetoric and reality should be addressed by always situating racial critiques in material conditions.[59] The point might actually be best encapsulated by comedian Stephen Colbert's satirical declarations that "I don't see race, people tell me I'm white." The joke mocks the way in which color-blindness reinstates white privilege. So in these various contexts,

Clover's statement on the actor's function in the narrative of *The Matrix* is ominous.

> With his unassignable looks (often attributed to his genetic heritage of Chinese, Caucasian and Hawaiian) already seeming digitally smoothed, and his immediate proffering of pure surface without depth, he's closer to the dream of a next generation—a post-national, post-modern poster boy. In both appearance and manner, his quality is that of the actor without qualities—the New Star, destined not to distract from the digital *mise-en-scène* but to integrate with it seamlessly.[60]

To wit, multiraciality becomes a metaphor of the digital age, where speed and the play of surfaces are left to compensate for the losses inflicted by postmodern depthlessness. Clover's description of his features as being "digitally smoothed" performs a double reference, first implicitly to the effacement of racial boundaries that multiracial faces are seen to embody. Second, enabled by technology, multiraciality itself—contrary to Field's analysis—seems to smooth over the historical substances of colonial violence, imperial domination, suffering, and so on.

Technology obliterates history spectacularly in the 1995 romantic melodrama *A Walk in the Clouds*. The film is a remake of Alessandro Blasetti's 1942 proto-neorealist *Quattro Passi fra le Nuvole* (Four Steps in the Clouds) scripted by Cesare Zavatinni. Reeves plays Paul Sutton, a returning war veteran who meets and romances a young Mexican woman, Victoria, who is returning home from college. The antifascist social critique of urban life in Blasetti's original, of claustrophobic domestic relations, bureaucracy, and the petit bourgeois lifestyle, is lost in director Alfonso Arau's contemporary remake. And in place of the Bazinian landscape aesthetic, stands a cinematography produced with an ethereal quality and magical realism made possible by digital special effects. In Arau's (re)creation of the Napa Valley, we find mystical landscapes in red and gold that are what Umberto Eco would call "the Absolute Fake," where imitations do not merely attempt to reproduce reality but to "improve" on it.[61] *A Walk in the Clouds* represents the first film that overtly attempted to construct a mainstream heterosexual romantic fantasy around Reeves. His character is an orphan and a traveling salesman, placing Reeves once again in the role of a dislocated nomad, which is in turn a metaphor for the stereotypical in-between social existence of multiracial misfits. Sutton is at one point derided by Victoria's father who remarks, "Not only do you not have a future, you have no past!" The moment elicits sympathy for its male romantic lead and prompts audience identification with Sutton/Reeves through the multiracial metaphor. Sutton eventually enlightens the father and persuades him to loosen his control of Victoria by expressing his lifelong yearning for family and belonging. The inevitable acceptance of Sutton into the clan calls for a colorful celebration of his admission into the family and of the enlightenment that he introduces to the patriarch's rigid bourgeois perspective.

In a sense, when these revelations occur under the digitally enhanced hues of the Napa Valley sky, the film presents the very kind of idealism that Rey Chow warns of in *Ethics after Idealism*. When the postmodern is presented as an alternative to nativist centrism and purity, she argues that it is accompanied by an inevitable suppression. Calling these postmodern advocates "hybridites," she states:

> [M]any recently popularized concepts such as "hybridity," "diversity" and "pluralism," which are usually invoked as a liberatory alternative to cultural phenomena that are held up as monolithically dominant and prohibitive . . . (One can add to this list . . . "heteroglossia," "dialogism," "heterogeneity," "multiplicity," etc.[62]) . . . typically obliterate significant portions of the reality of a colonized culture . . . postmodern hybridites tend to downplay the legacy of colonialism *understood from the viewpoint of the colonized* and ignore the experiences of poverty, dependency, and subalternity that persist well beyond the achievement of national independence.[63]

Chow in fact cites Edward Said in reminding us of how both the postmodern mood and spectacle can hide our eyes from material oppression.[64] She is also joined by Donna Haraway, who extends the critique of how *Time* and Eve facilitate an "evacuation of history" in the essay, "Universal Donors in a Vampire Culture":

> The denials and evasions in this liberal, antiracist, technophilic exercise are . . . thick . . . All the bloody history caught by the ugly word *miscegenation* is missing in the sanitized term *morphing*. Multiculturalism and racial mixing in *Time* magazine are less achievements against the odds of so much pain than a recipe for being innocently raptured out of mundane into redeemed time. It is the resolute absence of history, of the fleshy body that bleeds, that scares me. It is the reconfirmation of the Sacred Image of the Same, once again under the sign of difference, that threatens natural rebirth. I want something much messier, more dangerous, thicker, and more satisfying from the hope for multiculturalism.[65]

Despite these warnings, the discourse related to Reeves will also show that multiculturalism retains a powerful influence. In what critical race film studies has said about these phenomena, there is abundant multicultural optimism about Reeves's hybridity and its import for reception and star studies.

Hybrid politics in film studies

Critical race film studies of Reeves predominantly tend to associate his multiraciality with what they perceive as an unstable identity. Coupled with his sexual ambiguity, these qualities make his body and persona utopian, transgressive, if not ultimately subversive of traditional subjectivity. He is believed to be a star that transcends his films, and maintains a unique relationship to his fans. Many value his multiple subjectivities because they provide fans an unusually diverse set of avenues for identification. I concur on these observations to a degree but would resist the tide of conclusions that rush in after, particularly the more political claims. In addition, as my earlier readings of his characters Neo (*The Matrix*) and Matt (*River's Edge*) have begun to demonstrate, I believe as well that insufficient attention is paid to evidence that makes his subjectivity look more modernist than postmodernist.

In *Gay Fandom and Crossover Stardom* for example, Michael DeAngelis finds "a virtually unlimited range of possibilities of constructing the gender, sexuality, and ethnicity of Keanu Reeves—a range that conversely applies to the multiple positions of access that his indeterminate persona accommodates."[66] A youth culture that is progressively rife with bisexual gender identities provides an illuminating context for the star's "pansexuality."

> [A]t the current historical moment when, in a discourse of ambiguity that posits the absence of stable gender or sexual identities, terms such as "androgyny" and "bisexuality" are used overtly and strategically to designate states of liminality, boundary blurring, and sexual transgression that youth culture embraces, and that star figures are purported to address strategically.[67]

DeAngelis utilizes Reeves's pansexuality as a platform for "the heated debate between essentialist and social constructivist factions within 1990s queer theory and politics."[68] He argues that Reeves's ambiguous sexual identity is an act of resistance to stability and coherence. This argument arises frequently among scholarly and popular critics alike and is hardly challenged by the affinity between Reeves and postmodernism. Apart from Clover's description of Reeves's lack of depth as a progressive postnational quality, R. L. Rutsky states the impulse to redefine traditional identity and subjectivity perhaps most plainly.

> [H]is persona raises certain questions about the division between the intellectual and the physical on which Western notions of identity, of the thinking subject, are based . . . Keanu's films often seem to emphasize a kind of fluid kineticism over character depth, over any fixed notion of 'identity.'"[69]

The *Mixed Race Hollywood* collection joins this attitude by ruing films that miss the opportunity to shed racial essentialism. Its contributors lambast binary recapitulations of white supremacy and racial Othering. Bhabha would agree, given his position that stable identities, or racial and sexual boundaries, are ideologically enforced. He would look kindly on the hybrid Keanu's apparent aversion to fixity and ability to bring up those liminal states.

Some claims go further. Besides illuminating social boundaries, Reeves's hybridity is said to precipitate acts of transgression. For example, DeAngelis points out that Reeves does not recoil from rumors of his homosexuality, or object to the idea that he is attracting a gay audience.[70] The star thus advocates "an egalitarian politics" in the spirit of multiculturalism, "one that questions the efficacy of maintaining culturally established definitions of 'appropriate' roles of gender and sexuality."[71] By way of this inclusiveness, gay fans are allowed if not encouraged to empower themselves by writing Slash fiction—the genre of fan fiction whose narratives are based primarily on homosexual relationships. Facilitated by the creative liberty afforded by the internet, these "private and personal appropriations of the star persona" proliferate. Ultimately,

> Private fantasies become political statements demonstrating that the workings of the individual imagination are capable of exceeding whichever restrictions the Hollywood film industry may impose on the representations of its characters in film narratives in the contemporary period.[72]

When DeAngelis goes on to describe this virtual space as "a common place for sharing, debating, and negotiating their versions and perceptions of popular cultural icons," he implicitly considers it to be a new form of public sphere. He thus leads us to recall *Babel and Babylon*'s take on Rudolph Valentino's audiences at the cinema, which Miriam Hansen identifies as a similar sort of political arena. But in comparison, we can observe a significant change from Valentino's time when the public sphere is a physical space housing a common experience, to Reeves who is said to support a virtual realm that accommodates private fantasies.

Even if it is evoked spectrally, an idea as weighty as public sphere carries a specific set of connotations, such as community, participation, collective action, and social governance akin to an Aristotelian *polis*. To equate mass culture with that form of political culture requires a substantial leap, particularly during late-stage capitalism. It stretches credulity to believe that a gang of fans constructing sexual fantasies online is somehow engaging in civic agenda. But Reeves, the postmodern multiracial subject, seems to invite these hopes. DeAngelis is joined by Nishime's spectator study where, although she does not invoke political notions that are as lofty, her cultural discussion of the "pleasures of knowing" affirms a brand of transgression that is just as isolated. She argues that private and exclusive insider knowledge of multiracial actors' ethnic makeup unlocks transgressive pleasures and oppositional readings of textual narratives that otherwise treats these figures as racially unmarked.[73] But these pleasures are subversive in a limited way and do not challenge power structures. DeAngelis and Nishime both essentially admit that the politics here are limited. Nishime concedes that the pleasures of knowing when multiracial actors are closeting their ethnicity paradoxically depend on this knowledge's exclusion from the mainstream.[74] By likewise not connecting "spectatorial negotiation" to a material political program, DeAngelis makes it hard to see how what he calls "social resistance" translates to substantive change. His argument is not that these communities of knowledgeable readers are a holding stage for future action. Rather, they seem to be the ends themselves:

> That the spectatorial negotiation of star sexuality constitutes an act of social resistance is most clearly demonstrated in the contemporary historical period, in which members of a specific subculture have found ways to become more visible to one another, and also to mainstream culture, through the development and widespread circulation of their own publications and discourses, and through the still unregulated new media technologies of the Internet.[75]

To the socially marginalized suffering in isolation, cultural visibility and community are not unimportant even if partaken in silence. The intolerable frequency of gay teen suicide for one thing, makes that clear. Still, the Internet is unregulated no more. It ceased to exist once the culture industry was apprised of new media's fertility as a frontier of opportunity. Authentic autonomy from and within it is increasingly fleeting and difficult. Although DeAngelis demonstrates full awareness of capitalist appropriation with a chapter that tackles "The Marketing of Homosexuality in the 1990s," it might be overly optimistic to trumpet how "gay men have secured their efficacy as social 'agents.'"[76] It all comes down to whether one believes that agency can be authentic without independence from the culture industry.

The Frankfurt School represented by Adorno and Jameson makes its positions quite clear on this. They define authentic subjectivity as that which maintains critical distance from the culture industry and prevents ideological interpellation. Herbert Marcuse describes such a character as a "two-dimensional man" capable of "negation"—the ability to conceive of an established reality as well as an alternative one that is truer and more ideal.[77] Are DeAngelis and Nishime positing a comparable mode of fandom or spectatorship? The fans whom DeAngelis points out do not appropriate that ability in a manner where it can inform their own connection to mass culture and thus to Reeves himself. Rather, he speaks of fans whose relationship with Reeves's apparent rebellious persona—one that does not take fame too seriously—is predominantly one of identification. From that point of view, Reeves is thus a star who provides access into the culture industry, not one who cultivates a suspicion of mass culture and of star culture itself. The end result is not resistance, but interpellation.

The same can be said about the spectator-centered concept of appropriation. Take the "Society for Keanu Consciousness," for instance. Although it is now defunct, the fansite was one of Reeves's most active for several years. Its webmaster and author, "Lama Jahvah," extended the actor's role in *Little Buddha*, and moderated an online gathering of those who "believed" that Reeves occupies the "virtual temple" Keanumandu. Lama Jahvah interpreted quotes from both actor and characters to devoted "acolytes" who worship Buddhist-style values of enlightenment and spiritual harmony.[78] DeAngelis argues that the doctrine proposed by these acts of "textual poaching" evince Reeves's liminal position while challenging Western notions of stable identity. Yet, as ingenious as these appropriations may be, these audiences still maintain a subservient relationship to the star and thus the culture industry. As Adorno explains in "Culture Industry Reconsidered," the ironic effect of what the Society for Keanu Consciousness takes to be enlightenment might in actuality be dehumanizing.[79]

> [I]ndividuality itself serves to reinforce ideology, in so far as the illusion is conjured up that the completely reified and mediated is a sanctuary from

immediacy and life. Now, as ever, the culture industry exists in the 'service' of third persons, maintaining its affinity to the declining circulation process of capital, to the commerce from which it came into being. Its ideology above all makes use of the star system, borrowed from individualistic art and its commercial exploitation. The more dehumanized its methods of operation and content, the more diligently and successfully the culture industry propagates supposedly great personalities and operates with heartthrobs.[80]

DeAngelis and Nishime correctly identify instability within Reeves's identity and it is indeed a quality that the star actively fosters. Nevertheless, Reeves expresses ideas that align with Adorno. Consider the statement he gave to *A Walk in the Clouds* screenwriter Robert Kamen about how he deals with demanding fans:

Kamen: "How do you do it?"
Reeves: "I'm Mickey [Mouse]. They don't know who's inside the suit."
Kamen: "But you're a movie star."
Reeves: "[Laughs] So's Mickey."[81]

There thus appears within Reeves an alienated but conscious subject fully capable of negation and of holding the fragments of a postmodern subjectivity together. He encourages spectators to remain at a critical distance by separating himself from the public persona (Figure 5.5). To adopt that critical subjectivity essentially keeps the culture industry at bay.

Figure 5.5 "I'm Mickey [Mouse]. They don't know who's inside the suit." A close-up of Bob Arctor (Reeves) inside his scramble suit in *A Scanner Darkly* (2006).

The film texts themselves can once again supply added clarity. There is a scene from *Little Buddha* in which Prince Siddhartha decides to venture forth from the palace where his father protects him from reality, from old age, poverty, pain, and suffering. Before a royal procession, the king tries to shelter his son by ordering only the young and healthy to people his son's parade route through the city, showering the prince with cheers and petals. However, Siddhartha manages to spy two weak old men through the crowd. He breaks from his entourage and follows the men through an alleyway, where he discovers the unvarnished world that his father has tried to shield him from. The empathy that Siddhartha feels at that moment eventually sparks his journey toward enlightenment, a turning point that provides a metaphor for Reeves's spectators. Siddhartha's movement past the first few rows of excited devotees also reminds us that those who idolize are as much a part of the spectacle as the idols themselves. If we are invited onto Reeves's panethnic and pansexual body, the impetus he presents is to look past the distractions of the spectacle and break out of its seductive trance.

Members of The Society for Keanu Consciousness admire the actor because they find appeal in the enlightened persona constructed by his star discourse so pregnant with notions of hybridity, liminality, fluidity, and instability with specific regard to his race, sexuality, demeanor, physicality, and even his very presence. While these postmodern notions may resist racial categories or sexual mores, fetishizing those values may well reinforce neoliberal logics. Rutsky formulates a model of fandom for Reeves that is more complex and negotiational, but it remains undisruptive.

> To some degree, the very act of being a star involves a superficiality, a public mask, that inevitably stirs interest in the "real identity" behind it. Yet Keanu's star persona—in its superficiality—seems at once to exacerbate and confound this desire to know "just who he is."[82]

Rutsky finds that this desire of fans to find out who Reeves is, is thwarted by the actor's apparent insistence on being elusive, articulated through a combination of public statements, star discourse, and thematic threads in his films. But the message, Rutsky suggests, is that they should give in. He argues that Reeves's discourse of stupidity and fluidity must make us more willing to take "the risk of losing one's self in the stupidity of the motions and images that stream around us [a risk that] has perhaps always been inherent to cinema, and to popular culture more generally."[83]

This inclination to acquiesce to the culture industry's superficiality and stupidity runs counter to Frankfurt School sensibilities, and this interpretation of Reeves discounts the modernist subject that rises above the postmodern discourses and tropes within the actor's interviews and films. But if we learn anything from this particular elusive but critical subject, who does somewhat reject stardom in real life and whose characters find morality (*River's Edge*), reject interpellation (*The Matrix*), or resist postmodernity (*Little Buddha*), it is to maintain critical distance and an alienated state. It is not to passively mimic or identify with either star or spectacle for that only reinforces Marcuse's one-dimensionality. Certainly, it can neither be left up to chance in the way that Siddhartha's momentous revelation occurred, from his chance sighting of the old men.

The films themselves may again offer wisdom. His statement to *Vanity Fair* where he uses the analogy of an actor wearing a Mickey Mouse suit to illustrate the separateness of true self from star persona, encourages spectators to liberate themselves from interpellation. A major plot point in *My Own Private Idaho* hinges on such an alienation. The character Scott Favor (Reeves) begins the film as a rebellious teenaged son of a wealthy politician, who defies his father by experimenting with homosexuality and running with street hustlers and male prostitutes. Toward the end of the film, Scott does a much unenlightened thing. He inherits his father's fortune on his twenty-first birthday and abandons his friends and companions at the social margins. Looking out at them from behind the windows of a limousine, the "blankness" on Reeves's face magnifies the coldness of Scott's betrayal. It is a stunning reversal and depicted in the film as an unconscionable act. One might expect it to thwart the expectations of fans repulsed by this decidedly anti-Keanu character progression, and therefore alienate audiences in that respect. But as DeAngelis himself observes, metatextually attuned fans were all too willing to forgive and overlook the character's disloyalty because the actor's overall star discourse—as someone who is perfectly willing to play gay characters and work for openly gay directors—only gave them enough reason to disregard Scott's fictional actions as mere aberrations on Reeves's broader oeuvre.[84] Generally speaking, Reeves's immediate willingness to defy acting conventions, traverse identity boundaries, and destabilize traditional categories, are not in question. His willingness to allow and encourage ambiguity and multiplicity adds to those qualities. Collectively they lend him a rebellious air and make him more widely accessible. It is understandable that the fans will identify so strongly with Reeves's postmodern image on some level. Indeed, the habit of journalistic and academic writers (such as Rutsky) to presume familiarity and refer to him by his first name further demonstrates that phenomenon. But Scott's betrayal of his friends in *My Own Private Idaho* is the kind of artistic act that simultaneously counters that intimacy or familiarity with a distantiating counterpunch.

A comparable narrative operation occurs in *Bill and Ted's Excellent Adventure*. This film may seem like an aberration because unlike most of Reeves's characters, Ted remains blissfully satisfied with his interpellated trance in postmodernity. But film culture's persistence in conflating Reeves with Ted ideologically suppresses its modernist impulses. Confusing Reeves with Ted assumes that either he is the character, or that he identifies with the role. Yet in a way, the film actually forbids its audience to identify with the character and see the world through his perspective because its comedic narration necessarily holds the viewer at a distance. For Bill and Ted, the realization that Napoleon will be found at a water park named Waterloo is merely a logical deduction. But the irony of seeing Napoleon Bonaparte half-naked on a water slide can only be funny if the audience possesses enough historical awareness and critical distance to comprehend the absurdity. Regardless of how successful the jokes ultimately are, the film's genre institutes a critical distance by default, and a critical subjectivity by extension.

I approach Reeves in a way that is not all that different from DeAngelis and Nishime's. Fundamentally, we all extrapolate Reeves's star discourse to ascertain his admonition to transcend, liberate, and defy. But the privately practiced egalitarian politics highlighted in their reception studies give me pause. Mine are political misgivings, aroused by what appears to be a postmodern combination of multicultural celebration and private consumption. I read Reeves's ironic manner a little differently. For my money, he projects a subjectivity to his audience that is more traditionally knowing: alienated, distant, critical, authentic, and autonomous. We can all agree that "Keanu Reeves" and his multiple planes of racial and sexual identity make him a liminal figure that transgresses cultural boundaries. But freedom from racial or sexual categorical stricture can also be circumscribed. For Slavoj Žižek those liberties end where global structures and capital's reification begin. In "Multiculturalism, or, the Cultural Logic of Multinational Capitalism," he argues that multiculturalism is an ideology comparable to the popular ideas that fascism will re-appropriate as a means to continue social domination and exploitation. Late capitalism, for example, uses multiculturalism to politicize race in contrast to capital's supposed apoliticism. As a result, capital decouples from ideology and thus enjoys protection from political assault.[85] To Arif Dirlik, "multiculturalism does not point to a way out of existing structures of power, only to modifications within it."[86] Žižek and Dirlik have a point. The problem that they identify is seen in C. Richard King and David Leonard's analysis of *The Matrix*. They value multiculturalism but reject the film's aesthetic practice of it, criticizing its racial stereotyping for contravening the cast's racial diversity.[87] King and Leonard begin by listing Reeves among that list of multiracial players, but later, they curiously consider him white when trying to make the case that Morpheus (black actor Laurence Fishburne) is an "Uncle Tom" character that recapitulates racial "Huck Finn" narratives.[88] They contend that these stereotypes reinsert race as the primary discursive theme, and thus undermine the film's radical depiction of racial equality where "everyone [is] born into bondage." Paradoxically, they rely on Reeves's racial ambiguity—as someone who can be simultaneously read as white and multiethnic—to criticize the film for not being sufficiently multicultural. Just as important, they deploy it to nullify the text's Marxian metaphor for universal oppression.

If unchecked, capitalism reifies the multiracial hybrid. Keanu Reeves is an image from a postmodern era inflected with the discourse and forces of global capitalism and consumer society. It is not surprising if that economic order can and would commodify his racial multiplicity. Recall Eve, the computer-generated "New Face of America" on the cover of *Time* that digitally fetishizes multiraciality. Just a few years after, *Time* followed up with a report on a precise example of such a commodification. Asian advertisers searching for cosmopolitan, international looks that locals could still accept and identify with, began using Eurasian faces as "global marketing miens."[89] This is a perfect example, but most of the time, ideology does not work so clearly, neatly, and directly. Still, it is an excellent demonstration of what can happen if our politics eject economics and class. Race will be transcended, but not capital. If we take Reeves as a metaphor for the moment, we must thus look past his veneer of superficiality and movement, or otherwise fail to notice that beyond the multiracial physiognomy of pastiche lies an authentic critical subject. It is that individual within all of us who can meet the challenge to be materially historical in the postracial period, when we have to "see" race without seeing it, even when it is visible, especially when it is invisible. It is vital to hold on to autonomy, critical distance, and dialecticism.

Cyborg metaphors

Resistance to the idea of autonomous subjectivity also comes from cyborg theorists who employ the postmodern metaphor to claim the death of the subject. Let us reconsider this. Cybernetic organisms are strictly defined as beings with cybernetic and organic parts. Postmodernists feel partial to cyborgs because they help advance the antiessentialist notion that human identity is mutable. To critical race studies in particular, cyborgs demonstrate that race is a social construction. Namely, their part-human and part-machine constitution is analogous to racial hybridity. Cyborgs occupy a familiar presence in science fiction, and it is no coincidence that Reeves has a long history of roles as cyborgs. His star discourse conflates him with one as well. This chapter concludes with a look at how theories of the cyborg have been articulated in film studies with regard to multiracial issues. Through the textual and extratextual examples subtended by Reeves, I examine how Donna Haraway's touchstone, "Cyborg Manifesto," has been used by critical race film studies as a base for its two-pronged attack on antihumanist and antiracist positions. The critique of Western humanism takes dual aim at humanist philosophy and Eurocentrism. Recall Clover's case for Reeves as an exemplar on this score. That rhetoric can be felt throughout the commentary on the actor, but it crystallizes most clearly through the cyborg comparisons. However, that popular perception is challenged not just by Reeves's discourse but also by the cyborg itself, for it is not an ideologically neutral object. Haraway is in fact aware of this conceptual crinkle, and I take great interest in her attempt to smooth it out. I argue that she does so in a way that undermines the antihumanist–antiracist charge against individual subjectivity. As I continue to read "Keanu Reeves" alongside Haraway and critical race film studies' interpretations of the "Cyborg Manifesto," I will redeploy both to further a materialist approach to multiraciality.

Reeves's connection with the cyborg is forged on numerous levels. The most obvious are his roles in science fiction films, including the cyberpunk adaptation *Johnny Mnemonic*. Although that film is neither as acclaimed nor as profitable as the blockbuster *Matrix* series, Reeves's turn as the eponymous cyborg courier who transports information stored in his cybernetic "wet-wired brain" is commonly cited as an instance of perfect casting, and a notable precursor for his portrayal as Neo in the "tentpole" trilogy that came later. Clover's verdict that in "both appearance and manner, his quality is that of the actor without qualities—the New Star, destined not to distract from the digital mise-en-scène but to integrate with it seamlessly," epitomizes the widely held sentiment.[90] The association is in fact so strong that it pervades both the manner that he is reviewed in other films as well as how he is personally described. The discourse of his alleged stupidity or physical awkwardness is strewn with technological metaphors. When Reeves paused to think during the interview with *Vanity Fair*, writer Shnayerson conveys the moment with the following fragment: "Word search; search fail."[91] Indirectly, many also infer that his depthlessness, physicality, and movement comprise a corporeality that is incompatible with character depth and identity, in a performative, theatrical, and human sense. Without those presumably more human traits, all that remains is a shell of moving mechanical parts that in this case, are observed to be oddly uncoordinated.[92] And when Clover and the "New Face of America" independently refer to multiraciality as a quality that can be digitally created and "smoothed," the confluence between Reeves, technology, hybridity, and race is sealed.

Critics such as Clover and DeAngelis, for example, who feel that Reeves traverses ethnic, gender, and sexual categories, dovetail with Haraway's post-Marxist feminist theoretical perspective. Her valuation of the cyborg relies on the potential "for pleasure in the confusion of boundaries and for responsibility in their construction," and for "theory in a postmodernist, non-naturalist mode and in the utopian tradition of imagining a world without gender."[93] The cyborg does not just blur socially derived distinctions, it transcends them. Haraway lays down an important marker against the Enlightenment's subject when she explains, "the cyborg has no origin story in the Western sense." It bypassed the stage where traditional subjects would attain "original unity," develop coherent fullness, and become unique individuals. Haraway rejects outdated dualisms such as Self–Other and Man–Woman in favor of fluidity and "permanently partial identities and contradictory standpoints."[94] In this way, there is a dynamic quality to her view that corresponds with Bhabha's definition of unstable hybridity, especially when she detects "no drive in cyborgs to produce total theory, but there is an intimate experience of boundaries, of their construction and deconstruction."[95]

In theorizing "The Mulatto Cyborg: Imagining a Multiracial Future," it thus makes good sense for Nishime to proceed from Haraway in her analysis of cyborg films. Nishime then uses Jennifer González's essay, "Envisioning Cyborg Bodies," which finds that cyborgs' human-machine hybridity is often described in terms of racial mixing.[96] After laying that path from cyborg theory to race, Nishime transposes racial passing themes onto cyborg narratives, and argues that cyborg films where the hybrid being experiences nostalgia or melancholy for his or her humanity, express subtextual yearnings for unity, origins, and purity.[97] She considers this sentiment reactionary according to poststructuralist presumptions that the Enlightenment's unified subject should be rejected. Therefore, cinema's cyborgs that search for mythical origins support reactionary politics due to "Western culture's long history of equating human with white European." Furthermore, if that nostalgia is strong, it demonstrates "the staying power of biologically essentialist beliefs even in the most postmodern of films."[98] Nishime categorizes cinema cyborgs as "good," "bad," and "mulatto." She derides cyborg characters that are guilty of the regressive desire for unity and origins as "good" because they conform to tradition. "Bad cyborgs" are unruly ones exemplified in films such as *Terminator* (1984) whose "narrative logic is bent upon fulfilling the humanist fantasy of human mastery over the machine."[99] Nishime uses these "good" and "bad" cyborgs to set up "mulatto cyborgs," which she valorizes as progressively "posthuman" in that they confront and accept hybridity as an ideal state, thus rejecting "romantic ideals of transcendence and purity."[100] However, in light of the fact that Nishime published her work on "Guilty Pleasures" and Reeves in the same year, it is curious that her analysis of "mulatto cyborgs" neglects to mention probably the most famous multiracial cyborg of all. Needing an example of a "mulatto cyborg," she reaches instead for white title character Alex Murphy (Peter Weller) in *Robocop* (1987). The most interesting cyborg, therefore, is missing. Through that absence, Reeves manages to underline how the conventional wisdom about his multiracial discourse is perhaps askew.

Johnny Mnemonic and *The Matrix* most definitely showcase the "good cyborgs" that Nishime opposes. They are humanist films that mourn the loss of history and alienation from one's origins. Johnny spends literally the entire film trying to unify his humanity by regaining his childhood memories, which he lost by renting out his cybernetic brain as a mobile data storage unit. As the film begins, a one-night stand asks him, "so where is home, Johnny?" "Home?" he replies, "home . . . would you believe, I don't even know?" The conversation presages a similar line of questioning in Reeves's other 1995 release, *A Walk in the Clouds,* in which his love interest's father admonishes, "not only do you not have a future, you have no past!" The films are thus connected by its star and the connotation of alienation and dislocation that accompanies him. Johnny Mnemonic is hired by scientists from a corporation named "Pharmakom." They are corporate "whistleblowers" attempting to smuggle industrial secrets out to anticorporate underground guerillas called "LoTeks." It is easy to read the "low tech" rebellion allegorically as a pre-capitalist collective supporting the film's nostalgia for a bygone modernity, because a similar sentiment is expressed in *The Matrix* by the film's mixture of visual references to film noir and Neo-Classical production design. The LoTeks also parallel the human freedom fighters in *The Matrix*. And just as Neo (Reeves) chooses reality over hyperreal fantasies, Johnny wishes to extricate the machinery from his brain and retrieve the childhood memories of authentic experiences that it replaced. Those recollections are shot in over-exposed soft-focus jump cuts of Johnny's mother, his childhood home, and his seventh birthday party. The low-angle images of the boy's point of view are sentimentally scored, and capture scenes from a parochial house and garden. The images' unsullied innocence signifies a combination of origins, historicism, and temporality.

Nishime is likely to view these memories to be feeble counterpoints to cyberpunk postmodernity. Her critique of nostalgia contrasts with the more sentimental opinion of Fredric Jameson, whose take on postmodernism differs. Nishime does not mourn the loss of authority and authenticity. For her, the cyborg's subversive potential lies in its postmodernism. "It is the [posthumanist] mulatto cyborg, chaotic, ironic, without nostalgia or origin, that promises a future of mixed-race subjectivity."[101] Jameson indicates that nostalgia represents at least an attempt to recover historicity.[102] But Nishime considers these ideas essentialist, passé, grounded in Eurocentrism and ideological myths. In effect, the cyborg's nostalgia and melancholy is essentially a racist grief because they mourn white purity, represent a xenophobic rejection of Otherness, and reinstitute racial hierarchies.[103] In short, desire for humanity is by logic a desire for whiteness. If that is so, the unified subject becomes a racist proposition. Haraway seems to agree: "Marxian humanism, with its pre-eminently Western self, is the difficulty for me."[104]

However, if the unified subject is considered Eurocentric or to embody colonial ideologies, the cyborg may be implicated as well. Haraway emphasizes the cyborg's specific advantage of being independent from origins, but also admits that it does indeed owe its existence to the military industrial complex as well as the American and Western European capitalisms that it serves.[105] On that count, economic historian Philip Mirowski would add that capitalism did not just begat the cyborg, but has also been altered by it since. In *Machine Dreams: Economics becomes a Cyborg Science*, he argues that cyborg science has in actuality remade the economic orthodoxy in its own image. He explains how neoclassical economics merged economic theory with mid-nineteenth-century physics, and therefore dates the gradual birth of a cyborg form of economic agency.[106] Its maturation accelerated in the middle two decades of the twentieth century, when economics was increasingly understood as mechanical, scientifically causal, and rigidly deterministic. It ultimately transformed economic agency into a process merely of information processing unencumbered by the interference of free will.[107] Postwar economic crises and development relied upon, motivated, and financed cyborg technological innovation. In turn, the cyborg provided a significant paradigm in the formulation of economic models. Most important, this irreversible development "derives from the need to subject heterogeneous agglomerations of actors, machines, messages, and (let it not be forgotten) opponents to a hierarchical real-time regime of surveillance and control."[108] Where Haraway questions if "a cyborg world is about the final imposition of a grid of control on the planet, about the final abstraction embodied in a Star Wars apocalypse waged in the name of defence, about the final appropriation of women's bodies in a masculinist orgy of war," Mirowski elucidates that reality in painstaking detail.[109]

Why then, does the cyborg not carry the burden of that ideology when the unified subject is so encumbered by its Western roots? Haraway extricates the cyborg from its origins and herself from the contradiction thus:

> The main trouble with cyborgs, of course, is that they are the illegitimate offspring of militarism and patriarchal capitalism, not to mention state socialism. But illegitimate offspring are often exceedingly unfaithful to their origins. Their fathers, after all, are inessential.[110]

Now, if we can divorce the cyborg from its military, patriarchal, and industrial origins, would it be any different to decouple liberal humanism from Western Enlightenment with a similar gesture? If the cyborg is extricable from the material and ideological conditions of its conception, the liberal subject should be allowed to shed Eurocentrism as well. For that matter, the critical ability to be "exceedingly unfaithful" requires precisely the dialecticism and negational powers within that individual. We should not be forced to sacrifice them while appreciating the values of transcendence or enlightenment that hybrid states bring. Consequently, if we can take the "Cyborg Manifesto" to sanction retrieving humanism like this, it dismantles the equivalence that many make between the human-machine and white-Other binaries. In other words, the tautology of "if it is humanist then it is racist" crumbles.

Their logic would certainly not find support in *Johnny Mnemonic*. If humanity is linked to Westernism, then the machine is essentially Other within the metaphor. But the film marks humanity with ethnicity throughout. Johnny is aided by the LoTeks, whose name itself is an Asian modulation on the term "low tech." Its leader, J-Bone, is played by African American rap icon Ice-T. The evil yakuza characters engaged by Pharmakom do not serve to villainize otherness either. The yakuza leader Takahashi is portrayed by Takeshi Kitano, an eminent figure in Japanese media. But when he bares his torso to reveal what should be a massive and intricate tattoo (part of yakuza initiation rituals), the inkwork is a kitschy dragon, a mere pastiche of Japaneseness. Takahashi also admonishes a subordinate for his incomprehensible Japanese and instructs him to speak in English. The yakuza is thus a mercenary organization and no longer a meaningful signifier of the Other. The film simply refuses to allow its humanist nostalgia to be read as Eurocentric. When *The Matrix* privileges unified and modernist subjectivity, it does so without concern for subjects' race and ethnicity too. The multiethnic resistance movements in both films proffer a humanist ideal that transcends race. For Reeves, the ambivalences of his racial hybridity are peripheral phenomena that enrich but do not bear upon his subjective core around which fragmentation, fluidity, and kineticism swirl.

Haraway, though, might still differ. I doubt that she would countenance the humanist label for herself, but nevertheless, how does this reconceived understanding of humanism theoretically or politically repurpose her Manifesto? It would be difficult to persuade her that class, for instance, is not a contingent social formation like gender and race.

> Identities seem contradictory, partial, and strategic. With the hard-won recognition of their social and historical constitution, gender, race, and class cannot provide the basis for belief in "essential" unity. There is nothing about being "female" that naturally binds women. There is not even such a state as "being" female, itself a highly complex category constructed in contested sexual scientific discourses and other social practices. Gender, race, or class-consciousness is an achievement forced on us by the terrible historical experience of the contradictory social realities of patriarchy, colonialism, and capitalism.[111]

She considers gender-, racial-, and class-based categories to be nonessential social identities brought about by ideology. She also criticizes "totalizing" projects such as Marxism repeatedly in the Manifesto. And yet, I distinctly sense that Haraway construes a similar type of agency and subjectivity in her various formulations of the strategy she prefers, "affinity" politics, where collectives are formed "not by blood but by choice." She thus rejects identity politics for its essentialist assumptions.[112] Edward Said would have probably agreed. He too avoided totalizing theory for fear of ideological totalitarianism. He would have also keyed on her idea of "choice," to organize, to be "illegitimate," to be "unfaithful," to be critical, to be "building and destroying machines, identities, categories, relationships, space stories."[113] This is the work of a critical subject—that which is also implied by others described earlier such as Bhabha, Gayatri Spivak, and Tommy Lott.

When Haraway identifies affinity politics among "women of color" as an example of affinity politics, she cites Chela Sandoval's theorization of "oppositional consciousness"—"a self-consciously constructed space that cannot affirm the capacity to act on the basis of natural identification, but only on the basis of conscious coalition, of affinity, of political kinship." Far from rejecting "an epistemology based on the ontological structure of 'labour,'" she states that it is "the daily responsibility of real women to build unities, rather than to naturalize them."[114] Elsewhere, she adds:

> I am sick to death of bonding through kinship and "the family," and I long for models of solidarity and human unity and difference rooted in friendship, work, partially shared purposes, intractable collective pain, inescapable mortality and persistent hope.[115]

Conscious decisions and movements are involved here in the process of finding political affinities. They necessarily come from the agents and subjects who force historical change, and who are allegorized in *The Matrix* and *Johnny Mnemonic*. So although Haraway prefers postmodern political strategies to contest patriarchy, colonialism, and capitalism, she does so while refusing to succumb to postmodernism's debilitations such as the loss of affect and historical depth. "It is the resolute absence of history, of the fleshy body that bleeds, that scares me."[116] In the same breath, she desires "something much messier, more dangerous." Thus the feminism of "A Cyborg Manifesto" surfaces visibly in the author's abiding concern for women's working conditions, autonomy over their own labor, and physical suffering.

The Matrix and *Johnny Mnemonic* once again reflect this sensibility. Both begin with one view of the world, before bringing the viewer underneath where things certainly are in Haraway's words, "messier" and "more dangerous." When the referent is revealed, *The Matrix* depicts a dark post-apocalyptic world.

When Neo first awakes from induced hibernation, wide-angled shots reveal the cavernous space that houses the pods where humans are suspended and tapped quite literally for their biopower. The shot of multiple jacks popping out of the sockets along Neo's spine reverse technology's penetration. Haraway would appreciate this detail: the sockets disappear in virtual reality because it illustrates false human unity. Contrary to Reeves's stereotype as an actor with difficult access to his emotions, when those sockets are utilized again to place him back in virtual reality, the corporeal pain from the jacks entering his body registers on his clenched face. His crewmates are clothed in oversized, unwashed sweatshirts, pointing to the physical nature of their endeavor. In *Johnny Mnemonic*, Reeves's title character possesses an external socket too, not along his spine but at the back of his head, used to upload data into his "wet-wired brain." For that process, Johnny wears a mobile display monitor over his eyes and movement-sensitive gloves that he manipulates to navigate cyberspace. Although the imagery appears to fulfill fantasies of virtual reality technology, uploading is still a physically punishing process. Below the opaque display monitor, Reeves bares his teeth during the data transfer, and the overload causes a nosebleed. The transition from technological fetishism to physical pain is also mirrored in the plot. Johnny's pick-up location is in Beijing, depicted as a multisensory neon-filled city of billboards and multiethnic consumers. His arrival is met with a street protest, which he bypasses by climbing onto and walking over stationary cars. He proceeds up the elevator of a posh hotel and eventually finds out that he must deliver the information to Newark. The journey from Beijing to New Jersey is literally and figuratively a descent, through basements and sewer tunnels, to meet with the LoTeks, an impoverished underground resistance movement. Newark, portrayed only slightly less dystopically than *The Matrix's* "desert of the real," is filled with dilapidated buildings and broken bridges. The mise-en-scène at the LoTeks' base acts as counterpoint to the slick computer-animation that visually signifies cyberspace. Exposed wiring and television screens symbolize old media. In *The Matrix*, production design of the rebels' spaceship is similar. While the equipment runs advanced software, the hardware is dated from the late 1980s to early 1990s, emphasized by dense sound design consisting of intricate clicks.

These untidy settings connote corporeality, highlight physical pain, and combine to signify the scene of production and the processes of labor. The agent who shows us what the postmodern world hides is Reeves. His character Neo's conscious choice of reality over virtuality, to unjack himself from the

Matrix, matches Johnny's essential need to restore his memory and subjectivity by rejecting fragmentation. Both characters recover unity, historicism, and a critical perspective of the real. They remind us about the importance of affect and pain as indices of exploitation and oppression. That complement of senses ultimately constructs a materialist worldview. Haraway is correct to argue that gender, race, and class are not essential identities along which we should blindly form political unities. But I would demur from her suggestion that class identity is equally nonessential or discursively constructed, and rebuff her tautologically invalid critique of Marxian humanism where she dismisses it as a product of Eurocentric ideology. Nevertheless we are also of one mind that the concerns of material economic issues are vital and inescapable.

Notes

1 Sumi Cho, "Post-Racialism," *Iowa Law Review*, 94–95 (2009): 1594–99, 1648.

2 "Rebirth of a Nation: Computer Style," *Time*, Special Issue (Fall 1993): 66.

3 Evelynn M. Hammonds, "New Technologies of Race," in *Processed Lives: Gender and Technology in Everyday Life*, ed. Jennifer Terry and Melodie Calvert (New York: Routledge): 75, 83.

4 Homi Bhabha, *The Location of Culture* (London/New York: Routledge, 1994): 68. "The Other Question" was cited previously from the journal *Screen* in order to historicize developments in film theory. It is referenced here from the anthology because this chapter wishes to investigate his elaborations on hybridity, textuality, and agency as a whole, which are available in the 1994 volume.

5 Ibid., 114.

6 Ibid., 218.

7 Ibid., 193.

8 Ibid., 148.

9 Leonard Klady, "Faces. . . 'Like a Chinese Menu,'" *Los Angeles Times* (October 1, 1988): Part V, page 1.

10 George Anthony, "Is this Teen Scream the New DeNiro?" *Showcase (The Toronto Sun)* 5 July 1987. For other articles and interviews from this early period, see Tom Green, "Psst—This Snitch Is Going Places in 'River,'" *USA Today* (May 20, 1987): 6D.

11 Peter Travers, "*Much Ado about Nothing* (Review)," *Rolling Stone* (May 27, 1993): 56.

12 Hal Hinson, "Nothing Much about 'Ado,'" *The Washington Post* (May 21, 1993): B7.

13 Michael Savlov, "*Bram Stoker's Dracula* (Review)," *Austin Chronicle* (November 20, 1992) <http://www.austinchronicle.com/gbase/Calendar/Film?Film=oid%3A139352> Accessed September 24, 2006.

14 Joe Brown, "*Little Buddha* (Review)," *The Washington Post* (May 27, 1994).

15 Susan Orlean, "Keanu Reeves (In Theory)," *The New Yorker* (March 21, 1994): 58.

16 Guy Debord, *The Society of the Spectacle*, trans. Donald Nicholson-Smith (New York: Zone Books, 1995): 14.

17 Hal Hinson, "'Point Break': Wipeout!" *The Washington Post* (July 12, 1991): F6.

18 Dana Stevens, "The Blur: On the Enlightened Fuzziness of Keanu Reeves," *Slate* (July 14, 2006) <http://www.slate.com/id/2145690/> Accessed September 22, 2006.

19 Kristine McKenna, "Keanu's Eccentric Adventure," *The Los Angeles Times* (June 5, 1994): 35.

20 McKenna, "Keanu's Eccentric Adventure," 3; Carrie Rickey, "The Importance of Being Keanu," *The Chicago Tribune* (June 26, 1994): 16–18.

21 Fredric Jameson, *Postmodernism, or, the Cultural Logic of Late Capitalism* (Durham, NC: Duke University Press, 1991): 20.

22 Ibid.; Lisa Schwarzbaum, "Techno Prisoners," *Entertainment Weekly* (April 9, 1999): 45–46.

23 Roland Barthes, "The Face of Garbo," *Mythologies*, trans. Annette Lavers (New York: Hill & Wang, 1975): 56–57.

24 Walter Benjamin, "A Short History of Photography," trans. Phil Patton. *Artforum* 15, 6 (February, 1977): 48.

25 Miriam Hansen, *Babel and Babylon* (Cambridge, MA: Harvard University Press, 1991).

26 In his early response to Hansen's work on Valentino, Richard deCordova already highlights the need to consider "the broader system of star publicity and promotion within which Valentino and countless other stars were inscribed." See "Richard deCordova Responds to Miriam Hansen's 'Pleasure, Ambivalcence, Identification: Valentino and Female Spectatorship," *Cinema Journal* 26, 3 (1987): 55.

27 David Kamp, "The Importance of Being Hamlet," *Vanity Fair* (March 1995): 74.

28 Lyle Slack, "Keanu's Excellent Adventure," *MacLean's* (January 23, 1995): 52; Natasha Stoynoff, Karen Brailsford, and Kristina Johnson, "A Most Excellent Enigma," *People* (July 11, 1994): 49; David Ansen, "Goodbye, Airhead," *Newsweek* (June 13, 1994): 52.

29 Adam Sweeting, "Hunk on a Motorbike," *Mail and Guardian* (July 19, 1996): 7.

30 Desson Howe, "Bram Stoker's Dracula (Review)," *The Washington Post* (November 13, 1992): 44.

31 See Michael De Angelis, *Gay Fandom and Crossover Stardom: James Dean, Mel Gibson and Keanu Reeves* (Durham, NC: Duke University Press, 2001): 197, 261n56.

32 The most significant description that highlights his physicality is found in the early interview with Dennis Cooper. See "Keanu Reeves," *All Ears: Cultural Criticism, Essays and Obituaries* (New York: Soft Skull Press, 1999): 13.

33 Joshua Clover, *The Matrix* (London: BFI Publishing, 2004): 22–23.

34 Rita Kempley, "*Johnny Mnemonic* (Review)," *The Washington Post* (May 27, 1995): C3.

35 Lisa Schwarzbaum, "Fight Club," *Entertainment Weekly* (May 12, 2000): 47–48.

36 Michael Shnayerson, "The Wild One: Keanu Reeves on Sex, Hollywood and Life on the Run," *Vanity Fair* (August 1995): 96.

37 See Todd Gitlin, "Post-Modernism: The Stenography of Surfaces," *New Perspectives Quarterly* (Spring 1989): 56–59.

38 Ginia Bellafonte and Patrick E. Cole, "Generation X-cellent," *Time* (February 27, 1995): 62.

39 The difference lies in their divergent attitudes and how the same condition viewed differently by various camps. It was taken cynically by corporate marketers keen to capitalize on this consumer data. The executive who became the pre-eminent expert on this matter is Karen Ritchie. See her writings "Get Ready for 'Generation X,'" *Advertising Age* (November 9, 1992): 21. That article in her trade press was developed into a book, *Marketing to Generation X* (New York: Lexington Books, 1995). Douglas Coupland eventually rued the corporatization of his cultural critique in "Generation X'd," *Details* (June 1995): 72.

40 Douglas Coupland, *Generation X: Tales for an Accelerated Culture* (New York: St. Martin's Press, 1991): 11, 41, 96.

41 Shnayerson, "The Wild One," 96.

42 Maria P. P. Root, "Within, between, and beyond Race," *Racially Mixed People in America*, ed. Maria P. P. Root (Newbury Park, CA: Sage Publications, 1992): 3.

43 Maria P. P. Root, *The Multiracial Experience: Racial Borders as the New Frontie* (Thousand Oaks, CA: Sage, 1996): xvi.

44 According to men's magazine Details columnist Anka Radakovich, an analysis of newsstand sales revealed that 80 percent of those who bought that issue of the magazine were women; from Rickey, "The Importance of Being Keanu," 18.

45 Rickey, "The Importance of Being Keanu," 18.

46 Barbara Shulgasser, "Much Ado about Keanu Reeves," *San Francisco Examiner* (August 12, 1995): 1; Rickey, "The Importance of Being Keanu," 16; Shnayerson, "The Wild One," 96.

47 Schwarzbaum, "Techno Prisoners," 45; See also Sweeting, "Hunk on a Motorbike," 6.

48 Literally defined as "fragment" or "fraction," *hapa* is the Hawaiian word that has come to mean "mixed race." See LeiLani Nishime, "Guilty Pleasures: Keanu Reeves, Superman and Racial Outing," *East Main Street: Asian American Popular Culture*, ed. Shilpa Dave, LeiLani Nishime and Tasha G. Oren (New York: New York University Press, 2005): 273–91. Quoted from page 274.

49   Kamp, "The Importance of being Hamlet," 74.

50   McKenna, "Keanu's Eccentric Adventure," 36.

51   Rickey, "The Importance of Being Keanu," 16. Even more interestingly, Keanu is correctly pronounced "*kay*-ah-noo," suggesting that exoticized difference and not accuracy prompts the fascination with his name.

52   Schwartzbaum, "Techno Prisoners," 45.

53   Shnayerson, "The Wild One," 97.

54   Norma Field, *In the Realm of a Dying Emperor* (New York: Vintage, 1993): 37.

55   Claudia Castañeda, *Figurations: Child, Bodies, Worlds* (Durham, NC: Duke University Press, 2002): 95.

56   Ibid., 96.

57   Hammonds, "New Technologies of Race," 83.

58   Jane Park, "Virtual Race: The Racially Ambiguous Action Hero in *The Matrix* and *Pitch Black*," and LeiLani Nishime, "*The Matrix* Trilogy, Keanu Reeves, and Multiraciality at the End of Time," in *Mixed Race Hollywood*, ed. Mary Beltran and Camilla Fojas (New York: New York University Press, 2006): 183 and 297.

59   Cho, "Post-Racialism," 1648.

60   Clover, *The Matrix*, 21.

61   Umberto Eco, *Travels in Hyperreality*, trans. William Weaver (New York: Harcourt Brace, 1986): 8.

62   Chow here echoes the critique of Ella Shohat and Robert Stam's reliance of these Bakhtinian tropes from Chapter 1.

63   Rey Chow, *Ethics after Idealism: Theory, Culture, Ethnicity, Reading* (Bloomington, IN: Indiana University Press, 1998): 155.

64   Ibid., 227n12.

65   Donna J. Haraway, "Universal Donors in a Vampire Culture: It's All in the Family. Biological Kinship Categories in the Twentieth-Century United States," *Modest_Witness@Second_Millenium.FemaleMan©_Meets_OncoMouse* (New York and London: Routledge, 1997): 264.

66   Michael DeAngelis, *Gay Fandom and Crossover Stardom: James Dean, Mel Gibson and Keanu Reeves* (Durham, NC: Duke University Press, 2001): 201.

67   Ibid., 185.

68   Ibid., 205.

69   R. L. Rutsky, "Being Keanu," *The End of Cinema as We Know It: American Film in the Nineties*, ed. Jon Lewis (New York: New York University Press, 2001): 192.

70 DeAngelis, *Gay Fandom and Crossover Stardom*, 203–05. See also Cooper, *All Ears*, 17, and Shnayerson, "The Wild One," 146.

71 DeAngelis, *Gay Fandom and Crossover Stardom*, 203.

72 Ibid., 234.

73 Nishime, "Guilty Pleasures," 274, 288.

74 Ibid., 285.

75 DeAngelis, *Gay Fandom and Crossover Stardom*, 235.

76 Ibid.

77 Marcuse, *One-Dimensional Man: Studies in the Ideology of Advanced Industrial Society* (Boston, MA: Beacon Press, 1964): 125, 132.

78 DeAngelis, *Gay Fandom and Crossover Stardom*, 197.

79 Theodor Adorno, "Culture Industry Reconsidered," *The Culture Industry: Selected Essays on Mass Culture*, ed. J. M. Berstein (London: Routledge, 1991): 98–106. On "pseudo-individuality." See Theodor W. Adorno and Max Horkheimer, *Dialectic of Enlightenment*, trans. John Cumming (New York: Continuum, 1999): 154.

80 Adorno, "Culture Industry Reconsidered," 101.

81 Shnayerson, "The Wild One," 148.

82 Rutsky, "Being Keanu," 191.

83 Ibid., 193.

84 DeAngelis, *Gay Fandom and Crossover Stardom*, 225.

85 Slavoj Žižek, "Multiculturalism, or, the Cultural Logic of Multinational Capitalism," *New Left Review* 225 (September/October 1997): 30, 49.

86 Arif Dirlik, *The Postcolonial Aura* (Boulder, CO: Westview Press, 1997): 17.

87 C. Richard King and David Leonard, "Is Neo White? Reading Race, Watching the Trilogy," *Jacking in to the Matrix: Cultural Reception and Interpretation*, ed. Matthew Kapell and William G. Doty (New York: Continuum, 2004): 37.

88 Ibid., 43.

89 Hannah Beech, "Eurasian Invasion," *Time* (April 16, 2001) <http://www.time.com/time/world/article/0,8599,106427,00.html> Accessed November 23, 2006.

90 Clover, *The Matrix*, 20–21. See also DeAngelis, *Gay Fandom and Crossover Stardom*, 197, 261n56.

91 Shnayerson, "The Wild One," 97.

92 Cooper, *All Ears*, 13.

93 Donna Haraway, "A Cyborg Manifesto: Science, Technology, and Socialist-Feminism in the Late Twentieth Century," *Simians, Cyborgs and Women: The Reinvention of Nature* (New York: Routledge, 1991): 150.

94 Ibid., 151, 153, 154.

95 Ibid., 181.

96   Jennifer González, "Envisioning Cyborg Bodies, Notes from Current Research," *The Cyborg Handbook*, ed. Chris Hables Gray (London: Routledge, 1995): 275–78.

97   LeiLani Nishime, "The Mulatto Cyborg: Imagining a Multiracial Future," *Cinema Journal* 44, 2 (Winter 2005): 42.

98   Nishime, "The Mulatto Cyborg," 35–37.

99   Ibid., 39. She is quoting from Forest Pyle, "Making Cyborgs, Making Humans," *The Cybercultures Reader*, ed. David Bell and Barbara Kennedy (New York: Routledge, 2000): 128.

100   Nishime, "The Mulatto Cyborg," 37, 44–47.

101   Ibid., 47.

102   Jameson, *Postmodernism*, 19.

103   Nishime, "The Mulatto Cyborg," 35, 44.

104   Haraway, "Cyborg Manifesto," 158.

105   Ibid., 151.

106   Philip Mirowski, *Machine Dreams: Economics becomes a Cyborg Science* (Cambridge, MA: Cambridge University Press, 2002): 7.

107   Ibid., 9.

108   Ibid., 17.

109   Haraway, "Cyborg Manifesto," 154.

110   Ibid., 151. González, "Envisioning Cyborg Bodies, 275, points out that Haraway's use of the term 'illegitimate' poignantly inserts the specter of miscegenation and multiraciality into cyborg discourse, once again positioning multiracial subjects as privileged figures within the cyborg debates."

111   Haraway, "Cyborg Manifesto," 155.

112   Ibid.

113   Ibid., 151, 181.

114   Ibid., 156, 158.

115   Haraway, "Universal Donors," 265.

116   Ibid., 264.

Conclusion: A Materialist Method for Critical Race Film Studies

The subject lives! And it does not carry the mark of Eurocentrism from its birth in the Enlightenment. What then? These theoretical or epistemological points seem rather distant from *realpolitik*. Having perhaps funneled the discussion into relative esoterica, I will try to climb back out by first thinking briefly about one of the most frequent ways that cultural and class issues clash on the political stage. In the discourse about voter behavior, we often hear those in American leftish circles wonder about why people vote against their economic interests. The so-called duping hypothesis is popular among those like Thomas Frank who attribute conservatives' electoral success to their skill in fooling the working-class into feeling outrage at manufactured controversies over racially tinged cultural issues, but social psychologist Jonathan Haidt has for one tried to move the focus away and toward what he calls the Moral Foundations Theory (which lies beyond the scope of this inquiry).[1] The duping hypothesis is similar to the old Marxist concept of false consciousness, based on the idea that there exist obscured or unexposed truths. It predicts that people will stop being duped and gravitate leftward if only the ideological wool over their eyes is lifted and they see the true nature of social relations. The conceit of this position is that the underlying economic perspective will be both clear and self-evident to all when that happens. Liberal commentators assume this whenever they highlight the chasm between public opinion of where wealth inequality stands, and what that distribution really is. But what if the economic evidence is not so straightforward? In a 2004 television interview, Barack Obama explained the challenge of swaying rural voters in this way:

> They're not optimistic about the prospects for them to be able to attain the kinds of economic security that they had under the old system, so they've got insecurity in their economic life. They don't know where their health

care is coming from, they don't know what's happening with their pension. What they do know is that they can go out with their friends and hunt, and feel a sense of camaraderie, and there's a connection between hunting and them going out with their father to hunt, just as there's a connection maybe for their wives to go into church, and going with their grandmother to church. And if we don't have plausible answers on the economic front and we appear to be condescending towards those traditions that are giving their lives some stability then they're going to opt for that party that at least seems to be speaking to the things that still provide them something solid to stand on.[2]

Obama alludes here to a view of the substructure that is far from explicable, obvious or even "plausible." By this description, we should presume that available knowledge about it is neither plausible nor stable or solid.

Obama describes a symptom of the Late Capitalist present, a vexing period that continuously overwhelms our existing capacities to comprehend it, and thus frustrates cognition by being perpetually abstruse. Fredric Jameson and David Harvey's lucid attempts to track these historical shifts within the metanarrative make the task before us abundantly clear.[3] In what Jameson describes as a world system of capital networks as complex and confusing as to be unrepresentable, and what Harvey terms a compression of both time and space so severe that one can only recognize capitalism in abstractions, they consider it vital that our critical subjectivities keep pace. Just as important, neither man ultimately doubts the subject's ability to do so. Jameson believes that the unrepresentable is still eminently knowable, while Harvey retains a Marxian faith that "internalized dialectics of thought and knowledge production" along with materialist methods can grasp these historical shifts and resist them both culturally and politically.[4]

On the other hand, poststructuralist theory consigns the unified subject to the ranks of myth, constructed and propped up by the Enlightenment's forward-looking promises of truth and progress. Poststructuralism's antifoundational ethos disavowed the modern unified and critical subjectivity on the grounds that it is split and fragmented. Its suspicions extended to metanarratives such as those put forward by Marxism. This book has tried to forge a critical method by first of all pushing back against that antihumanist argument. I argue that the subject does not seem to have ever departed, having remained implicitly present in critical race film scholarship, namely in the form of author, active spectator, and critic.

A materialist method for critical race film studies

What does this all mean for how critical race film criticism can operate differently? How *should* it be carried out? What does a materialist approach for race in film studies look like? Let me begin by marshalling prior arguments to advance a set of suggestions. By way of a conclusion, I posit the following principles:

1   Theoretically, a Neo-Marxian method must constitutionally hold on to an avowed commitment and reliance on the unified subject. This critical subjectivity would be able to grasp capital's totality, especially as it relates to the culture industry, and construct a political project of equal measure. This recommendation merely takes its lead from a comparative reading of second-generation critical race film theory, where the critical subject present within casts a strikingly similar shadow to that of the Frankfurt School's Marxist humanism. So my advocacy on behalf of humanism bases itself on more than mere sympathy for Frankfurt School positions. The rationale would have looked very different if Bhabha, various reception studies, or (most outwardly) Edward Said, to name a few, had not harbored the critical subject within their models. As things stand, contrary to his own stated positions, Bhabha apparently relies on the very autonomy that Adorno prizes. And Said most definitely does, contrary to how the field has come to understand his. Collectively, this shared impulse represents the imperative to lean on Neo-Marxism.

2   A materialist film scholar would certainly not object to class-based film analysis—reading a film for how class issues function in the narrative—that would reverse any bias that favors the identities and interests of racial or gendered subalterns. But the point of that cannot be to just replace race-based criticism with class-based criticism however much one may believe that class is an intractable social category, for that would recapitulate the same identity-political dynamic that is short on radical value.

3   Therefore, critical race film criticism should be wary of identity politics, especially if it reproduces sectarianism in a political sense in the form of scholarly redundancy or methodological stagnation. It should be incumbent on critical race film research in one ethnic subset, for instance, to be cognizant of theoretical developments within other racial

interests, or to draft a historical narrative from a wider perspective. I would further urge ethnically defined projects to reconsider on principle if they have opted beforehand to assume poststructuralist definitions of race. If race is a contingent value, then how long can it serve to stabilize an identity, a set of films, or a discipline? The theorists discussed at the conclusion of Chapter 3 struggle with this aporia of essentialism, which led me to think that its resolution hinges on the strength of critical subjectivity. As a consequence, the individual's involvement leaves the approaches of structural Marxism diminishingly useful. In any event, my humanist rejection of identity politics leads me to even turn away from Robert M. Young's call for "a materialist theory of race," with which I basically agree.[5] I am on board with his idea that since "race encodes the totality of contemporary capitalist social relations . . . the eradication of race oppression also requires a totalizing political project," or otherwise a "revolutionary class politics." I also second his aversions to Bhabha's poststructuralist formalism and to identity politics.[6] However, he eschews humanism in the end, insofar as the humanist "philosophical-ideological commitment to the subject" refers to Afrocentrists whose black essentialism fetishizes a specific racial experience. In contrast to Young, the theory forwarded here jettisons racial essentialism but considers it vital to retain human essentialism and critical subjectivity.

4   Foregrounding the connection between base and superstructure is obligatory. This commitment most immediately entails sharper focus on cinema's mode of production: films' production histories, and empirical work into capital flows and labor relations. Sociologically or philosophically, it also means trying to find causality for racial phenomena in the substructure. Care is hence required, for more than anywhere else the rules loosen appreciably here, where the rubber of Neo-Marxian principles hits the road, so to speak. The analytical execution by the theorists whom I have cited at length is by and large problematic. The jeremiads by Adorno, Jameson, and Said set bad precedents. They do not offer ideal models for cinema study because they lack attention to detail, especially to the mode of production. Adorno's engagement with specific objects or historical contexts lacks sufficient descriptive specificity. His treatise on jazz is universally perceived to be recklessly narrow and uninformed. Similarly, Jameson's rapid, sweeping bird's-eye-views of

culture rarely pause long enough for historical verification. He too has been criticized for oversimplification. And despite Said's commitment on the page to the political-economic aspects of colonialism and imperialism, he can also be faulted for not drawing empirical connections between his cultural analysis and the West's colonial projects.[7] His attempts in *Orientalism* at film criticism rose no higher than stereotype analysis. In a way, it is better to emulate these writers' commitments rather than their methods.

I believe that these are a sufficiently malleable set of guidelines that can allay the reservations that many in fields like cultural studies harbor about old school Marxism's rigid insistence on reductionist models and economism.[8] Some readers however, may feel less than satisfied because I demur at providing a more concrete checklist at the end of it all. They might grumble that I have led them out into the desert without a canteen. But I do not wish to impel dogma—Adorno's, Jameson's or otherwise—even if I want these nodes to generate enough of a current with which many will decide to flow.

In the meantime, I see persuasive evidence that we should somewhat force the issue. Anecdotes have limited value, of course, but I find a compelling pattern in the following two. A few years ago on my campus at the time, I attended a discussion of Walter Benn Michaels's book, *The Trouble with Diversity*. A multidisciplinary program dedicated to ethnic studies organized the session and invited interested faculty and graduate students to take part. Criticizing how the politics of diversity are practiced, Michaels argues that identity politics' demand for tolerance and ending discrimination reduces American liberalism's mission on this matter to a battle for etiquette. Where class difference and economic inequality are concerned, he claims that diversity policies merely wish for the poor to receive respect, rather than adopt the goal to eliminate poverty.[9] The attendees overwhelmingly skewered the book. One accused the author of setting up liberal multiculturists as convenient straw persons. He dismissed the book's argument *tout court*, and denied that liberal academics could ever be insensitive to class issues, simply by virtue of *being* liberal. Another stated that Michaels's argument is undermined by his personal position as an economically privileged white member of the academic elite. A Latino faculty member was curious to know if Michaels is one of those old-fashioned Marxists or socialists bitter at being institutionally displaced by ethnic studies and scholars of color, while another complainant charged the author with appeasing neo-conservatism as part of a cynical publicity strategy to generate book sales. Most of the room roundly affirmed these opinions. I felt something akin to Henry Louis Gates's criticism of Warren Beatty's *Bulworth* and Spike Lee's hostility to Quentin Tarantino's *Django Unchained* reverberating in their opposition, in the sense that Michaels's whiteness and economic privilege served to confine what he can say about those who were not white and privileged. Moreover, several discussants articulated an antifoundationalist aversion to his universal or objective claims. The sentiment was enough for them to nullify two of Michaels's more Marxian contentions: first, he stresses that unlike race, gender and sexuality, class identity is an empirical property and therefore not cultural, performative, or discursive. Second, he thinks that the politics of difference are unsuitable for addressing economic inequality because the goal should be to eliminate class difference and not respect it. I vainly attempted to steer the discussion toward the author's central and thoroughly debatable contentions about class, only to be met with profound and irate resistance.

The experience provided motivation to attend a workshop some time later at the 2012 Society for Cinema and Media Studies conference titled, "Should Studying the Politics of Representation Be History?" The panel was in many ways ground zero for critical race film studies, and very well attended by any measure. Premised on whether some fairly outdated modes of stereotype and discourse analysis were still relevant or useful, those gathered affirmed the rhetorical question resoundingly. Actually I too wholeheartedly agree that discourse analysis must continue. Ideology grows in sophistication and criticism must likewise evolve to meet it. Nevertheless, although the crowd was united in its wariness of neoliberalism's tendency to celebrate difference and yet do so with condescension and little regard to social inequality, I found it both striking and somewhat disconcerting that many perceived neoliberal economic ideology as a new adversary. The field, to paraphrase a panelist, needs to figure out a method to deal with how racial stereotypes circulate in a neoliberal climate. I wondered if Marxism is such a method. Why was all this a surprise? The symptoms of divorcing materialism from cultural analysis seemed to flare up here.

These two anecdotes do not prove anything conclusive of course, but they hint at the difficulties involved with fostering a new approach for film studies toward race. It demands a rethinking of political conventions, disciplinary habits, and academic fault lines. The increased acceptance of materialism's importance during the more recent conference event however, is encouraging and noteworthy.

Perhaps the wake of the housing crisis softened some attitudes, especially since we are now only left to wait for the next financial catastrophe that will surely hit closer to home, the looming student loan bubble. If my submissions here are returned with the same indictments that greeted *The Trouble with Diversity*, if they are characterized as an paradoxical attempt to move critical race film studies forward by taking it back to retrograde Marxism, there is little else to do but point at these surrounding calamities from the past, present, and future. The question is not so much why we should move backward, but if we have let our eyes stray off the ball in the past, and why we should never let it happen.

As we reconceive critical race film theory and its relationship to politics, or the subject's relationship to the Enlightenment, it is easy to lose sight of the basic focus of these pages. This is ultimately about how we understand films. Thus I circle back to reflect further on *Django Unchained*, for what struck me about the film can help to explain what I hope will be the fundamental implication of this book.

With the bounty hunter King Shultz's (Christoph Waltz) help, the former slave Django (Jamie Foxx) tracks his wife Broomhilda (Kerry Washington) to the slave-owner Calvin Candie (Leonardo DiCaprio). Aware that Candie would greatly raise the price if he knew that it would reunite an ex-slave with his wife, Shultz and Django hatch the pretense to buy a Mandingo fighter from Candie for $12,000 before asking for Broomhilda as a $300 afterthought to the deal. They would then leave with Broomhilda and not return to finalize the main purchase. Unfortunately, Candie's cunning house slave Stephen (Samuel L. Jackson) sees through the ruse. He alerts his master, who angrily demands $12,000 for Broomhilda's freedom alone. At gunpoint, Shultz performs an instantaneous calculation and agrees to pay immediately. But Candie eventually insists on shaking hands with Shultz to close the transaction. Unwilling to do so with someone so vile, Shultz decides in the moment to shoot Candie, and is swiftly blasted by henchmen.

Waltz's performance as Shultz was the most critically recognized of the cast, and it is easy to see why. His was the most fully formed character in the film. He enjoyed the bulk of the screenplay's jokes and the amplest share of opportunities to exploit Quentin Tarantino's penchant for ironic dialogue with his idiosyncratic Germanic inflections. However, the character's prominence also comes about because of how out of place he is in the genre. As Jane Tompkins has mused so well, the standard Western hero's verbal economy is part of his contemptuous aversion to civilized society's corrupted reliance on language. "For the Western is at heart antilanguage."[10] Foxx's Django is a Western hero. But Shultz's mellifluous logorrhea, undulating syllable by syllable through his manicured beard and slowed by Waltz's Austrian accent and comedic affectation, decidedly is not. As someone so oddly juxtaposed and unbound to archetype, it makes sense that his character arcs so dramatically from amoral and merciless mercenary, to someone who offers the ultimate sacrifice for Django. Shultz begins as a self-interested businessman, living for currency notes and by the sanctity of written contracts. He is well aware that human beings are being traded as commodities, but for a time it does not move his conscience. Somehow, Shultz only learns about racism's physical cost from gazing at the network of whipping scars on Django's back (Figure C.1). His protégé humanizes American slavery for him. Over the narrative's course, Schultz sees enough through Django's eyes that the acts of racial injustice he witnesses morally overwhelm him, enough for him to make the suicidal decision to rectify them.

So although the film is about the quest of Django the reconstructed African American hero in a baroque Western, Shultz's perspective as external observer and his inner journey make the narrative equally his. On that character's trajectory hang key questions about race's relationship to class and capital. Does *Django Unchained's* narrative place capital as the structural base of racism, or vice versa? On the one hand, Candie's willingness to be condescended to by Stephen in exchange for the latter's reliable bookkeeping and devious counsel would suggest that capital takes precedence. Shultz too was perfectly willing to grab the short end of what is a financial deal with his life on the line. On the

Figure C.1 King Schultz (Christoph Waltz) catches the sight of Django's scars, when his capital interests first meet racial compassion in *Django Unchained* (2012).

other hand, Shultz chose shortly thereafter to risk certain death in order to kill the racist Candie. His mortal decision is utterly compelling, for it subsequently makes it impossible for us to ignore the moral, emotional, and indeed humanist implications of race and racism. I do not offer this reading of *Django Unchained* as a decisive one—not everyone will find Waltz as funny as I do for that matter—but it represents a choice to engage with cinema in a way that is more politically fitting and necessary for the present. What critics disparage as economic reductionism does hold great appeal, especially in comparison to the fairly common view that its white director possesses no moral standing to voice a historical perspective about slavery, even if it is a black Western and we still controversially end up talking about the white guy. The materialist proposals that this book offers, I should repeat, do not strictly mandate a singular approach for shifting the paradigm, but they do recommend a choice to participate in critical and theoretical discourse more politically and collectively.

Notes

1   Jonathan Haidt, *The Righteous Mind: Why Good People Are Divided by Politics and Religion* (New York: Pantheon, 2012); Thomas Frank, *What's the Matter with Kansas? How Conservatives Won the Heart of America* (New York: Metropolitan, 2004).

2   Barack Obama, "An Hour with Illinois Senator Barack Obama," *Charlie Rose*, PBS, November 23, 2004.

3   See in particular, Fredric Jameson, *Postmodernism, or, The Cultural Logic of Late Capitalism* (Durham, NC: Duke University Press, 1991): 38–54, and *The Geopolitical Aesthetic*: Cinema and Space in the World System (Bloomington, IN: British Film Institute, 1995): 11–19; David Harvey, *The Condition of Postmodernity: An Enquiry into the Origins of Cultural Change* (Cambridge, MA: Blackwell, 1989): 284–91.

4   Jameson, *Postmodernism, or, The Cultural Logic of Late Capitalism*, 53; Harvey, *The Condition of Postmodernity*, 328, 345.

5   Robert Young, "Putting Materialism Back into Race Theory: Toward a Transformative Theory of Race," *The Red Critique* 11 (Winter/Spring 2006) <http://www.redcritique.org/WinterSpring2006/index.html> Accessed March 5, 2007.

6   Edward Said describes this formalism as poststructuralist "textuality," in "The Problem of Textuality: Two Exemplary Positions," *Critical Inquiry* 4, 4 (Summer 1978): 673–714.

7   See Robert Irwin, *Dangerous Knowledge: Orientalism and Its Discontents*
    (New York: The Overlook Press, 2006). While I disagree with many of Irwin's
    conclusions, his arguments on this specific matter can be compelling.
8   See Lawrence Grossberg, "Cultural Studies vs. Political Economy: Is Anybody Else
    Bored with This Debate?" *Critical Studies in Mass Communication* 12, 1 (March
    1995): 72, and Angela McRobbie, "Post-Marxism and Cultural Studies:
    A Post-Script," *Cultural Studies*, ed. Lawrence Grossberg, Cary Nelson, and
    Paula A. Treichler (New York: Routledge, 1992): 719. McRobbie in particular was
    explicit in her distaste for the untenable "pre-postmodern Marxism as marked out
    by critics like Fredric Jameson and David Harvey."
9   Walter Benn Michaels, *The Trouble with Diversity: How We Learned to Love
    Identity and Ignore Inequality* (New York: Metropolitan Books, 2006): 107, 109.
    As such, the author follows both Fredric Jameson's judgment that politics of
    difference have "an essentially liberal, rather than radical, value," and Slavoj Žižek's
    view that multiculturalist pushes for diversity effectively imposes an Eurocentric
    distance that asserts superiority over the ethnic other by benevolently appreciating
    and "respecting" it. Fredric Jameson, *The Geopolitical Aesthetic* (Bloomington, IN:
    British Film Institute, 1995): 188 (referenced before at the start of the introductory
    chapter); Slavoj Žižek, "Multiculturalism, or, the Cultural Logic of Multinational
    Capitalism," *New Left Review* 225 (September/October 1997): 44.
10 Jane Tompkins, *West of Everything: The Inner Life of Westerns* (New York: Oxford
    University Press, 1992): 50–53.

Bibliography

Adorno, Theodor W. "On the Social Situation of Music." Wes Blomster, trans. *Telos* 35, 1978: 128–64.

—. *In Search of Wagner*. Rodney Livingstone, trans. London: NLB, 1981.

—. "Transparencies on Film." Thomas Y. Levin, trans. *New German Critique* 24–25 (Fall/Winter 1981–82): 199–205.

—. "On the Fetish-Character in Music and the Regression of Listening." Andrew Arato and Eike Gebhardt, eds. *The Essential Frankfurt School Reader*. New York: Continuum, 1982, 270–99.

—. "Culture Industry Reconsidered." J. M. Berstein, ed. *The Culture Industry: Selected Essays on Mass Culture*. London: Routledge, 1991, 98–106.

—. "Resignation." Henry W. Pickford, trans. *Critical Models*. New York: Columbia University Press, 1998, 289–93.

Adorno, Theodor W. and Hanns Eisler. *Composing for the Films*. London/Atlantic Highlands, NJ: The Althone Press, 1994.

Adorno, Theodor W. and Max Horkheimer. *Dialectic of Enlightenment*. John Cumming, trans. New York: Continuum, 1999.

Ahmad, Aijaz. *In Theory: Classes, Nations, Literatures*. London: Verso, 1992.

Alonso, Juan J. Badmen, Bandits, and Folk Heroes. *The Ambivalence of Mexican American Identity in Literature and Film*. Tuscon: University of Arizona Press, 2009.

Andrew, J. Dudley. *The Major Film Theories*. London: Oxford University Press, 1976.

Ansen, David. "Goodbye, Airhead." *Newsweek* (June 13, 1994): 52.

Anthony, George. "Is this Teen Scream the New DeNiro?" *Showcase (The Toronto Sun)* (July 5, 1987): COVER.

Artel, Linda and Susan Wengraf. *Positive Images: A Guide to Non-Sexist Films for Young People*. San Francisco: Booklegger Press, 1976.

Barr, Meghan. "One Year On, Occupy is in disarray; Spirit Lives On." *Yahoo! Finance* (September 18, 2012) <http://finance.yahoo.com/news/1-occupy-disarray-spirit-lives-161622760.html> Accessed April 26, 2013.

Barthes, Roland. "The Face of Garbo." *Mythologies*. Annette Lavers, trans. New York: Hill & Wang, 1975, 56–57.

Bayoumi, Moustafa. "Reconciliation without Duress: Said, Adorno, and the Autonomous Intellectual." *Alif: Journal of Comparative Poetics* 25 (2005): 46–64.

Beech, Hannah. "Eurasian Invasion." *Time* (April 16, 2001) <http://www.time.com/time/world/article/0,8599,106427,00.html> Accessed November 23, 2006.

Bellafonte, Ginia and Patrick E. Cole. "Generation X-cellent." *Time* (February 27, 1995): 62.

Beltran, Mary and Camilla Fojas (eds). *Mixed Race Hollywood.* New York: New York University Press, 2006.

Benjamin, Walter. "The Work of Art in the Age of Mechanical Reproduction." Harry Zohn, trans. *Illuminations: Essays and Reflections.* New York: Schocken, 1968, 217–52.

—. "A Short History of Photography." Phil Patton, trans. *Artforum* 15, 6 (February 1977): 46–51.

Berg, Charles Ramirez. "The Margin as Center: The Multicultural Dynamics of John Ford's Westerns." Gaylyn Studlar and Matthew Bernstein, eds. *John Ford Made Westerns.* Bloomington, IN: Indiana University Press, 2001, 75–101.

—. *Latino Images in Film: Stereotypes, Subversion and Resistance.* Austin: University of Texas Press, 2002.

Bernardi, Daniel. *Filming Difference: Actors, Directors, Writers and Producers on Gender, Race and Sexuality in Film.* Austin: University of Texas Press, 2009.

Bernardi, Daniel (ed.). *Classic Hollywood Classic Whiteness.* Minneapolis, MN: University of Minnesota Press, 2001.

Bernstein, Matthew and Gaylyn Studlar (ed.). *Visions of the East: Orientalism in Film.* New Brunswick, NJ: Rutgers University Press, 1997.

Bhabha, Homi. "The Other Question . . . " *Screen* 24, 6 (1983): 18–36.

—. *The Location of Culture.* London and New York: Routledge, 1994.

Bobo, Jacqueline. *Black Women as Cultural Readers.* New York: Columbia University Press, 1995.

Bogle, Donald. *Toms, Coons, Mulattoes, Mammies and Bucks: An Interpretive History of Blacks in American Films.* New York: The Viking Press, 1973.

Brennan, Timothy. "Edward Said: American Theory and the Politics of Knowledge." *Atlantic Studies* 2, 1 (2005): 93–103.

Brown, Joe. "*Little Buddha* (1994) Review." *The Washington Post* (May 27, 1994).

Brown, Wendy. *States of Injury: Power and Freedom in Late Modernity.* Princeton: Princeton University Press, 1995.

Buscombe, Edward. *The Searchers.* London: British Film Institute, 2000.

Cambridge, Massachusetts Police Department, Incident Report #9005127 (July 16, 2009).

Cameron, Ian and Douglas Pye (eds). *The Book of Westerns.* New York: Continuum, 1996.

Castañeda, Claudia. *Figurations: Child, Bodies, Worlds.* Durham: Duke University Press, 2002.

Chion, Michel. *Audio-Vision*. Claudia Gorbman, ed. and trans. New York: Columbia University Press, 1994.

Cho, Sumi. "Post-Racialism." *Iowa Law Review* 94–95 (2009): 1589–649.

Chow, Rey. *Ethics after Idealism: Theory, Culture, Ethnicity, Reading*. Bloomington, IN: Indiana University Press, 1998.

Clover, Joshua. *The Matrix*. London: BFI Publishing, 2004.

Cole, Mike. "'Racism' is about More than Colour." *Times Higher Education Supplement* (November 23, 2007) <http://www.timeshighereducation.co.uk/311222.article> Accessed March 30, 2013.

—. *Critical Race Theory and Education: A Marxist Response*. New York: Palgrave Macmillan, 2009.

Colonnese, Tom Grayson. "Native American Reactions to *The Searchers*." Arthur M. Eckstein and Peter Lehman, eds. *The Searchers: Essays and Reflections on John Ford's Classic Western*. Detroit, MI: Wayne State University Press, 2004, 335–42.

Cooper, Dennis. *All Ears: Cultural Criticism, Essays and Obituaries*. New York: Soft Skull Press, 1999.

Coupland, Douglas. *Generation X: Tales for an Accelerated Culture*. New York: St. Martin's Press, 1991.

—. "Generation X'd." *Details* (June 1995): 72.

Cowie, Elizabeth. "Women, Representation and the Image." *Screen Education* 23 (Summer 1977): 15–23.

Cripps, Thomas. *Slow Fade to Black: The Negro in American Film, 1900–1942*. New York: Oxford University Press, 1977.

Crosley, Hillary. "'Django Unchained': A Postracial Epic?" *The Root* (December 25, 2012) <http://www.theroot.com/views/django-unchained-postracial-epic> Accessed June 27, 2013.

Dallmayr, Fred. "The Politics of Non-Identity: Adorno, Postmodernism—And Edward Said." *Political Theory* 25, 1 (1997): 33–56.

Darder, Antonia and Rodolfo D. Torres. *After Race: Racism After Multiculturalism*. New York: New York University Press, 2004.

DeAngelis, Michael. *Gay Fandom and Crossover Stardom: James Dean, Mel Gibson and Keanu Reeves*. Durham: Duke University Press, 2001.

Debord, Guy. *The Society of the Spectacle*. Donald Nicholson-Smith, trans. New York: Zone Books, 1995.

deCordova, Richard. "Richard deCordova Responds to Miriam Hansen's 'Pleasure, Ambivalcence, Idenfication: Valentino and Female Spectatorship'." *Cinema Journal* 26, 3 (1987): 55–57.

Deggans, Eric. "Tarantino is the Baddest Black Filmmaker Working Today." *Salon* (December 27, 2012) <http://www.salon.com/2012/12/27/tarantino_is_the_baddest_black_filmmaker_working_today/> Accessed April 26, 2013.

Deis, Christopher. "May the Force (Not) be with You: 'Race Critical' Readings and the *Star Wars* Universe." Carl Silvio and Tony M. Vinci, eds. *Culture, Identities and Technology in the Star Wars Films: Essays on the Two Trilogies*. Jefferson, NC: McFarland and Company, 2007, 77–108.

Delgado, Richard. "Crossroads and Blind Alleys: A Critical Examination of Recent Writing about Race." *Texas Law Review* 82 (2003): 121–52.

Delgado, Richard and Jean Stefanic. *Critical Race Theory: An Introduction*, 2nd edn. New York: New York University Press, 2012.

Desser, David. "*The Geisha Boy*: Orientalizing the Jewish Man." Murray Pomerance, ed. *Enfant Terrible! Jerry Lewis in American Film*. New York: New York University Press, 2002, 153–65.

Diawara, Manthia. "Black Spectatorship: Problems of Identification and Resistance." *Screen* 29, 4 (1986): 66–76.

Dirlik, Arif. *The Postcolonial Aura*. Boulder, CO: Westview Press, 1997.

Dyer, Richard. "White." *Screen* 29, 4 (1988): 46–65.

—. "Into the Light: The Whiteness of the South in *The Birth of a Nation*." Richard H. King and Helen Taylor, eds. *Dixie Debates: Perspectives on Southern Culture*. New York: New York University Press, 1996, 165–76.

—. *White*. London: Routledge, 1997.

Eckstein, Arthur M. and Peter Lehman (eds). *The Searchers: Essays and Reflections on John Ford's Classic Western*. Detroit, MI: Wayne State University Press, 2004.

Eco, Umberto. *Travels in Hyperreality*. William Weaver, trans. New York: Harcourt Brace, 1986.

Edgerton, Gary. "'A Breed Apart': Hollywood, Racial Stereotyping, and the Promise of Revisionism in *The Last of the Mohicans*." *Journal of American Culture* 17, 2 (Summer 1994): 1–17.

Estrada, Gabriel S. "Star Wars Episodes I-VI: Coyote and the Force of White Narrative." Daniel Bernardi, ed. *The Persistence of Whiteness: Race and Contemporary Hollywood Cinema*. New York: Routledge, 2008, 69–90.

Feng, Peter X. *Identities in Motion: Asian American Film and Video*. Durham: Duke University Press, 2002.

Feng, Peter X. (ed.). *Screening Asian Americans*. New Brunswick: Rutgers University Press, 2002.

Field, Norma. *In the Realm of a Dying Emperor*. New York: Vintage, 1993.

Fish, Stanley. "Henry Louis Gates: Déjà Vu All Over Again." *The New York Times* (July 24, 2009) <http://fish.blogs.nytimes.com/2009/07/24/henry-louis-gates-deja-vu-all-over-again/> Accessed November 8, 2009.

Frank, Thomas. *What's the Matter with Kansas? How Conservatives Won the Heart of America*. New York: Metropolitan, 2004.

—. "To the Precinct Station." *The Baffler* 21 (2012) <http://thebaffler.com/past/to_the_precinct_station> Accessed April 26, 2013.

Fraser, Nancy. "Rethinking Recognition." *New Left Review* 3 (May/June 2000): 107–19.

Friedman, Lester (ed.). *Unspeakable Images: Ethnicity and the American Cinema.* Urbana, IL: University of Illinois Press, 1991.

Gates, Jr, Henry Louis. "The White Negro." *The New Yorker* (May 11, 1998): 62–65.

Gitlin, Todd. "Post-Modernism: The Stenography of Surfaces." *New Perspectives Quarterly* (Spring 1989): 56–59.

—. *Occupy Nation: The Roots, the Spirit, and the Promise of Occupy Wall Street.* New York: It Books, 2012.

González, Jennifer. "Envisioning Cyborg Bodies, Notes from Current Research." Chris Hables Gray, ed. *The Cyborg Handbook.* London, Routledge, 1995, 275–78.

Goodnough, Abby. "Harvard Professor Jailed; Officer Is Accused of Bias." *The New York Times* (July 20, 2009) <http://www.nytimes.com/2009/07/21/us/21gates.html> Accessed November 8, 2009.

Green, Tom. "Psst—This Snitch is Going Places in 'River.'" *USA Today* (May 20, 1987): 6D.

Grossberg, Lawrence. "Cultural Studies vs. Political Economy: Is Anybody Else Bored with this Debate?" *Critical Studies in Mass Communication* 12, 1 (March 1995): 72–81.

Guerrero, Ed. *Framing Blackness: The African Image in Film.* Philadelphia: Temple University Press, 1993.

Habib, Irfan. "Critical Notes on Edward Said." *International Socialism* 108 (2005) <http://www.isj.org.uk/index.php4?id=141&issue=108> Accessed March 25, 2011.

Haidt, Jonathan. *The Righteous Mind: Why Good People Are Divided by Politics and Religion.* New York: Pantheon, 2012.

Hall, Stuart. "Cultural Identity and Cinematic Representation." *Framework* 36 (1989): 68–81.

Hammnonds, Evelynn M. "New Technologies of Race." Jennifer Terry and Melodie Calvert, ed. *Processed Lives: Gender and Technology in Everyday Life.* New York: Routledge, 74–85.

Hansen, Miriam B. "Introduction to Adorno, 'Transparencies on Film' (1966)." *New German Critique* 24–25 (Fall/Winter 1981–82): 186–98.

—. *Babel and Babylon: Spectatorship in American Silent Film.* Cambridge, MA: Harvard University Press, 1991.

Haraway, Donna. "A Cyborg Manifesto: Science, Technology, and Socialist-Feminism in the Late Twentieth Century." *Simians, Cyborgs and Women: The Reinvention of Nature.* New York: Routledge, 1991, 149–81.

—. "Universal Donors in a Vampire Culture: It's All in the Family. Biological Kinship Categories in the Twentieth-Century United States." *Modest_Witness@Second_ Millenium.FemaleMan©_Meets_OncoMouse.* New York and London: Routledge, 1997, 213–65.

Harvey, David. *The Condition of Postmodernity: An Enquiry into the Origins of Cultural Change.* Cambridge, MA: Blackwell, 1989.

Haskell, Molly. *From Reverence to Rape: The Treatment of Women in the Movie*.
    New York: Holt, Rinehart and Winston, 1974.

Heath, Stephen. "Film and System: Terms of Analysis 2." *Screen* 16, 2 (1975): 91–113.

Henderson, Brian. "*The Searchers*: An American Dilemma." *Film Quarterly* 34 (1981):
    9–23.

Higashi, Sumiko. "Ethnicity, Class and Gender in Film: DeMille's *The Cheat*." Lester
    Friedman, ed. *Unspeakable Images: Ethnicity and the American Cinema*. Urbana, IL:
    University of Illinois Press, 1991, 112–39.

—. *Cecil B. DeMille and American Culture: The Silent Era*. Berkeley, CA: University of
    California Press, 1994.

Hilger, Michael. *From Savage to Nobleman: Images of Native Americans in Film*.
    Lanham, MD: The Scarecrow Press, 1995.

Hinson, Hal. "'Point Break': Wipeout!" *The Washington Post* (July 12, 1991): F6.

—. "Nothing Much about 'Ado'." *The Washington Post* (May 21, 1993): B7.

Hodges, Michael H. "Critics say 'Clones' has Racial Stereotypes." *The Detroit News* (May
    18, 2002).

Holmlund, Christine. "Displacing Limits of Difference: Gender, Race, and Colonialism
    in Edward Said and Homi Bhabha's Theoretical Models and Marguerite Duras's
    Experimental Films." *Quarterly Review of Film and Video* 13, 1–3 (1991): 1–22.

Homer, Sean. *Fredric Jameson: Marxism, Hermeneutics and Postmodernism*. New York:
    Routledge, 1998.

hooks, bell. "The Oppositional Gaze." *Black Looks: Race and Representation*. Boston,
    MA: South End Press, 1992, 115–31.

Howe, Desson. "Bram Stoker's Dracula (Review)." *The Washington Post* (November 13,
    1992): 44.

Howe, Stephen. "Edward Said and Marxism: Anxieties of Influence." *Cultural Critique*
    67 (Fall 2007): 50–87.

"Hunk on a Motorbike." *Mail and Guardian*. (July 19, 1996) <http://mg.co.za/
    article/1996–07–19-hunk-on-a-motorbike> Accessed June 6, 2013.

Hussein, Abdirahman A. *Edward Said: Criticism and Society*. New York: Verso, 2002.

Huyssen, Andreas. "Introduction to Adorno." *New German Critique* 6 (Fall 1975): 3–11.

Irwin, Robert. *Dangerous Knowledge: Orientalism and its Discontents*. New York: The
    Overlook Press, 2006.

Jameson, Fredric. *The Political Unconscious: Narrative as a Socially Symbolic Act*. Ithaca,
    NY: Cornell University Press, 1981.

—. "Postmodernism and Consumer Society." Hal Foster, ed. *The Anti-Aesthetic: Essays
    in Postmodern Culture*. Port Townsend: Bay Press, 1983, 111–25.

—. *Signatures of the Visible*. London: Routledge, 1990.

—. *Postmodernism, or, The Cultural Logic of Late Capitalism*. Durham, NC: Duke
    University Press, 1991.

—. "Actually Existing Marxism." *Polygraph* 6–7 (1993): 170–95.

—. *The Geopolitical Aesthetic: Cinema and Space in the World System*. Bloomington, IN: British Film Institute, 1995.

Jan, Tracy. "Harvard Professor Gates Arrested at Cambridge Home." *The Boston Globe* (July 20, 2009) <http://www.boston.com/news/local/breaking_news/2009/07/harvard.html> Accessed November 8, 2009.

Jay, Martin. *The Dialectical Imagination: A History of the Frankfurt School and the Institute of Social Research, 1923–1950*. Boston, MA: Little, Brown and Company, 1973.

—. *Adorno*. Cambridge, MA: Harvard University Press, 1984.

Jerome, V. J. *The Negro in Hollywood Films*. New York: Masses and Mainstream, 1952.

Johnston, Claire. "Feminist Politics and Film History." *Screen* 16, 3 (Summer 1975): 115–24.

Kalinak, Kathryn. "'Typically American': Music for *The Searchers*." Arthur M. Eckstein and Peter Lehman, eds. *The Searchers: Essays and Reflections on John Ford's Classic Western*. Detroit, MI: Wayne State University Press, 2004, 109–43.

Kamp, David. "The Importance of Being Hamlet." *Vanity Fair* (March 1995): 74–80.

Kaplan, Erin Aubry. "'Django' an Unsettling Experience for Many Blacks. *Los Angeles Times* (December 28, 2012) <http://articles.latimes.com/2012/dec/28/entertainment/la-et-django-reax-2-20121228> Accessed April 27, 2013.

Kelly, Richard. "Film Review: *Bulworth*." *Sight and Sound* 9, 2 (February 1999): 40–42.

Kempley, Rita. "*Johnny Mnemonic* (Review)." *The Washington Post* (May 27, 1995): C3.

Kilpatrick, Jacquelyn. *Celluloid Indians: Native Americans and Film*. Lincoln: University of Nebraska Press, 1999.

King, C. Richard and David Leonard. "Is Neo White? Reading Race, Watching the Trilogy." Matthew Kapell and William G. Doty, eds. *Jacking in to the Matrix: Cultural Reception and Interpretation*. New York: Continuum, 2004, 32–47.

Klady, Leonard. "Faces . . . 'Like a Chinese Menu.'" *Los Angeles Times* (October 1, 1988): Part V, page 1.

Kracauer, Siegfried. *Theory of Film*. New York: Oxford University Press, 1960.

Laclau, Ernesto and Chantal Mouffe. *Hegemony and Socialist Strategy: Towards a Radical Democratic Politic*. London: Verso Press, 1995 and 2001.

Larson, Stephanie Greco. *Media & Minorities: The Politics of Race in News and Entertainment*. Lanham, MD: Rowman & Littlefield, 2006.

Leab, Daniel J. *From Sambo to Superspade: The Black Experience in Motion Pictures*. London: Secker and Warburg, 1973.

Lehman, Peter. "'You Couldn't Hit It on the Nose': The Limits of Knowledge in and of *The Searchers*." Arthur M. Eckstein and Peter Lehman, eds. *The Searchers: Essays and Reflections on John Ford's Classic Western*. Detroit, MI: Wayne State University Press, 2004, 239–63.

List, Christine. "Self-Directed Stereotyping in the Films of Cheech Marin." Chon A. Noriega, ed. *Chicanos and Film*. New York: Garland Publishing, Inc, 1992, 205–17.

—. *Chicano Images: Refiguring Ethnicity in Mainstream Film*. New York: Garland Publishing, 1996.

Locke, Brian. *Racial Stigma on the Hollywood Screen from World War II to the Present: The Orientalist Buddy Film*. New York: Palgrave Macmillan, 2009.

Lott, Tommy L. *The Invention of Race: Black Culture and the Politics of Representation*. Oxford: Blackwell Publishers, 1999.

Maltby, Richard. "A Better Sense of History: John Ford and the Indians." Ian Cameron and Douglas Pye, eds. *The Book of Westerns*. New York: Continuum, 1996, 34–49.

Mapp, Edward. *Blacks in American Films: Today and Yesterday*. Metuchen, NJ: The Scarecrow Press, 1972.

Marchetti, Gina. *Romance and the "Yellow Peril": Race, Sex and Discursive Strategies in Hollywood Fiction*. Berkeley, CA: University of California Press, 1993.

—. "They Worship Money and Prejudice: The Certainties of Class and the Uncertainties of Race in *Son of the Gods*." Daniel Bernardi, ed. *Classic Hollywood Classic Whiteness*. Minneapolis, MN: University of Minnesota Press, 2001, 72–91.

Marcuse, Herbert. *One-Dimensional Man: Studies in the Ideology of Advanced Industrial Society*. Boston, MA: Beacon Press, 1964.

Marx, Karl. *A World without Jews*. Dagobert D. Runes, trans. New York: Philosophical Library, 1959.

McAlister, Melani. *Epic Encounters: Culture, Media, and U.S. Interests in the Middle East since 1945*. Berkeley, CA: University of California Press, 2005.

McKenna, Kristine. "Keanu's Eccentric Adventure." *The Los Angeles Times* (June 5, 1994): 3, 35–37.

McLean, Adrienne L. "The Thousand Ways There are to Move: Camp and Oriental Dance in the Hollywood Musicals of Jack Cole." Matthew Bernstein and Gaylyn Studlar, ed. *Visions of the East: Orientalism in Film*. New Brunswick, NJ: Rutgers University Press, 1997, 130–57.

McNay, Lois. *Against Recognition*. Malden, MA: Polity Press, 2008.

McRobbie, Angela. "Post-Marxism and Cultural Studies: A Post-Script." Lawrence Grossberg, Cary Nelson, and Paula A. Treichler, eds. *Cultural Studies*. New York: Routledge, 1992, 719–30.

"Michael Eric Dyson Blasted in Open Letter for Defending 'Django Unchained.'" *EurWeb* (December 30, 2012) <http://www.eurweb.com/2012/12/michael-eric-dyson-blasted-in-open-letter-for-defending-django-unchained/> Accessed June 27, 2013.

Michaels, Walter Benn. *Our America: Nativism, Modernism and Pluralism*. Durham, NC: Duke University Press, 1995.

—. *The Trouble with Diversity: How We Learned to Love Identity and Ignore Inequality*. New York: Metropolitan Books, 2006.

Mirowski, Philip. *Machine Dreams: Economics becomes a Cyborg Science*. Cambridge, MA: Cambridge University Press, 2002.

Morimoto, Marie Thorsten. "The 'Peace Dividend' in Japanese Cinema: Metaphors of a Demilitarized Nation." Wimal Dissanayake, ed. *Colonialism and Nationalism in Asian Cinema*. Bloomington, IN: Indiana University Press, 1994, 11–29.

Mulvey, Laura. "Visual Pleasure and Narrative Cinema." *Screen* 16, 3 (1975): 6–18.

Musser, Charles. "Divorce, DeMille and the Comedy of Remarriage." Kristine Brunovska Karnick and Henry Jenkins, eds. *Classical Hollywood Comedy*. London: Routledge, 1995, 282–313.

Neale, Steve. "The Same Old Story: Stereotypes and Difference." *Screen Education* 32, 3 (1979): 33–37.

—. "Vanishing Americans: Racial and Ethnic Issues in the Interpretation and Context of Post-War 'Pro-Indian' Westerns." Edward Buscombe and Roberta E. Pearson, eds. *Back in the Saddle Again: New Essays on the Western*. London: British Film Institute, 1998, 8–28.

Negra, Diane. *Off-White Hollywood: American Culture and Ethnic Female Stardom*. London: Routledge, 2001.

Nishime, LeiLani. "The Mulatto Cyborg: Imagining a Multiracial Future." *Cinema Journal* 44, 2 (Winter 2005): 34–49.

—. "Guilty Pleasures: Keanu Reeves, Superman and Racial Outing." Shilpa Dave, LeiLani Nishime, and Tasha G. Oren, eds. *East Main Street: Asian American Popular Culture*. New York: New York University Press, 2005, 273–91.

Noble, Peter. *The Negro in Films*. London: Skelton Robinson, 1948.

Nolley, Ken. "The Representation of Conquest: John Ford and the Hollywood Indian, 1939–1964." Peter C Rollins and John E. O'Connor, eds. *Hollywood's Indian: The Portrayal of the Native American in Film*. Lexington: The University Press of Kentucky, 2003, 73–90.

Noriega, Chon A. (ed.). *Chicanos and Film*. New York: Garland Publishing, Inc, 1992.

Nowell-Smith, Geoffrey. "Six Authors in Pursuit of *The Searchers*." *Screen* 17, 1 (Spring 1976): 26–33.

Obama, Barack. "An Hour with Illinois Senator Barack Obama." *Charlie Rose*. PBS. November 23, 2004.

Obenson, Tambay A. "Why Do You Think Mookie Threw a Trash Can into Sal's Pizzeria Window in 'Do The Right Thing?'" *Indiewire* (February 26, 2003) <http://blogs.indiewire.com/shadowandact/why-do-you-think-mookie-threw-a-trash-can-into-sals-pizzeria-window-in-do-the-right-thing> Accessed December 19, 2013.

Orlean, Susan. "Keanu Reeves (In Theory)." *The New Yorker* (March 21, 1994): 58.

Oshana, Maryann. "Native American Women in Westerns: Reality and Myth." *Film Reader* 5 (1982): 125–31.

Palumbo-Liu, David. *Asian/American: Historical Crossings of a Racial Frontier*. Palo Alto, CA: Stanford University Press, 1999.

Pearson, Roberta E. "Indianism? Classical Hollywood's Representation of Native Americans." Daniel Bernardi, ed. *Classic Hollywood Classic Whiteness*. Minneapolis, MN: University of Minnesota Press, 2001, 245–62.

Pye, Douglas. "Miscegenation and Point of View in *The Searchers*." Ian Cameron and Douglas Pye, eds. *The Book of Westerns*. New York: Continuum, 1996, 229–35.

Pyle, Forest. "Making Cyborgs, Making Humans." David Bell and Barbara Kennedy, eds. *The Cybercultures Reader*. New York: Routledge, 2000, 124–48.

Racevskis, Karlis. "Edward Said and Michel Foucault: Affinities and Dissonances." *Research in African Literatures* 36, 3 (2005): 83–97.

"Rebirth of a Nation: Computer Style." *Time* (Special Issue, Fall 1993): 66–67.

Rickey, Carrie. "The Importance of Being Keanu." *The Chicago Tribune* (June 26, 1994): 16–18.

Ritchie, Karen. "Get Ready for 'Generation X.'" *Advertising Age* (November 9, 1992): 21.

—. *Marketing to Generation X*. New York: Lexington Books, 1995.

Rollins, Peter C. and John E. O'Connor (eds). *Hollywood's Indian: The Portrayal of the Native American in Film*. Lexington: University Press of Kentucky, 1998.

Root, Maria P. P. "Within, Between, and Beyond Race." Maria P. P. Root, ed. *Racially Mixed People in America*. Newbury Park, CA: Sage Publications, 1992.

—. *The Multiracial Experience: Racial Borders as the New Frontier*. Thousand Oaks, CA: Sage, 1996.

Rosen, Marjorie. *Popcorn Venus: Women, Movies and the American Dream*. New York: Coward McCann and Geoghegan, 1973.

Rubin, Andrew. "Techniques of Trouble: Edward Said and the Dialectics of Cultural Philology." *The South Atlantic Quarterly* 102, 4 (2003): 861–76.

Rutsky, R. L. "Being Keanu." Jon Lewis, ed. *The End of Cinema as We Know It: American Film in the Nineties*. New York: New York University Press, 2001, 185–94.

Said, Edward. "Interview." *Diacritics* 6, 3 (1976): 30–47.

—. *Orientalism*. New York: Vintage Books, 1978.

—. "The Problem of Textuality: Two Exemplary Positions." *Critical Inquiry* 4, 4 (Summer 1978): 673–714.

—. *The World, the Text and the Critic*. Cambridge, MA: Harvard University Press, 1983.

—. "Response to Stanley Fish." *Critical Inquiry* 10, 2 (1983): 371–73.

—. "Orientalism Reconsidered." *Race and Class* 27, 2 (1985): 1–15.

—. "Edward Said." Imre Salusinzsky, ed. *Criticism in Society: Interviews with Jacques Derrida, Northrop Frye, Harold Bloom, Geoffrey Hartman, Frank Kermode, Edward Said, Barbara Johnson, Frank Lentricchia, and J. Hills Miller*. New York: Methuen, 1987, 123–48.

—. "Politics of Knowledge." Cameron McCarty and Warren Crichlow, eds. *Race Identity and Representation in Education*. New York: Routledge, 1993, 306–14.

San Juan, E. "Edward Said's Affiliations: Secular Humanism and Marxism." *Atlantic Studies* 3, 1 (April 2006): 43–61.

Sánchez, Rosaura. "Postmodernism and Chicano Literature." *Aztlán* 18, 2 (1992): 1–14.

Savlov, Michael. "*Bram Stoker's Dracula* (1993) Review." *Austin Chronicle* (November 20, 1992) <http://www.austinchronicle.com/gbase/Calendar/Film?Film=oid%3A139352> Accessed September 24, 2006.

Schwarzbaum, Lisa. "Techno Prisoners." *Entertainment Weekly* (April 9, 1999): 45–46.

—. "Fight Club." *Entertainment Weekly* (May 12, 2000): 47–48.

Shnayerson, Michael. "The Wild One: Keanu Reeves on Sex, Hollywood and Life on the Run." *Vanity Fair* (August 1995): 94–101, 146–48.

Shohat, Ella. *Israeli Cinema: East/West and the Politics of Representation*. Austin: University of Texas Press, 1989.

Shohat, Ella and Robert Stam. *Unthinking Eurocentrism: Multiculturism and the Media*. New York: Routledge, 1994.

Shulgasser, Barbara. "Much Ado about Keanu Reeves." *San Francisco Examiner* (August 12, 1995): 1.

Sklar, Robert. "*Oh! Althusser!*: Historiography and the Rise of Cinema Studies." Robert Sklar and Charles Musser, eds. *Resisting Images: Essays on Cinema and History*. Philadelphia: Temple University Press, 1990, 12–35.

Slack, Lyle. "Keanu's Excellent Adventure." *MacLean's* (January 23, 1995): 52.

Smith, Valerie (ed.). *Representing Blackness: Issues in Film and Video*. New Brunswick: Rutgers University Press, 1997.

Snead, James "Spectatorship and Capture in *King Kong*: The Guilty Look." Colin McCabe and Cornell West, eds. *White Screen, Black Images: Hollywood from the Dark Side*. New York: Routledge, 1994, 1–27.

Sollors, Werner. *Beyond Ethnicity: Consent and Descent in American Culture*. New York: Oxford University Press, 1986.

Spivak, Gayatri Chakravorty. *In Other Worlds: Essays in Cultural Politics*. New York/London: Methuen, 1987.

Stam, Robert. *Subversive Pleasures: Bakhtin, Cultural Criticism and Film*. Baltimore: Johns Hopkins University Press, 1989.

—. *Reflexivity in Film and Literature: From Don Quixote to Jean-Luc Godard*. New York: Columbia University Press, 1992.

—. *Film Theory: An Introduction*. Malden, MA: Blackwell Publishing, 2000.

Stam, Robert and Louis Spence. "Colonialism, Racism and Representation." *Screen* 24, 2 (1983): 2–20.

Steinem, Gloria. "Women are Never Front-Runners." *The New York Times* (January 8, 2008) <http://www.nytimes.com/2008/01/08/opinion/08steinem.html> Accessed November 16, 2009.

Stevens, Dana. "The Blur: On the Enlightened Fuzziness of Keanu Reeves." *Slate* (July 14, 2006) <http://www.slate.com/id/2145690/> Accessed September 22, 2006.

Stewart, Jacqueline Najuma. *Migrating to the Movies: Cinema and Black Urban Modernity*. Berkeley, CA: University of California Press, 2005.

Stoynoff, Natasha, Karen Brailsford, and Kristina Johnson. "A Most Excellent Enigma." *People* (July 11, 1994): 49.

Sweeting, Adam. "Hunk on a Motorbike." *Mail and Guardian* (July 19, 1996): 6–7.

Tarantino, Quentin. "Tarantino Talks to Gates: A Podcast Special." *The Root* (December 26, 2012) <http://www.theroot.com/multimedia/tarantino-talks-gates-podcast-special> Accessed June 27, 2013.

Taylor, Charles. "The Politics of Recognition." Amy Gutmann, ed. *Multiculturalism: Examining the Politics of Recognition.* Princeton, NJ: Princeton University Press, 1994, 25–73.

Taylor, Clyde. "The Re-Birth of the Aesthetic in Cinema." *Wide Angle* 13, 3/4 (July–October 1991): 12–30.

"*The Searchers* (Review)." *Variety* (March 14, 1956): 6.

Tillet, Salamishah. "Quentin Tarantino Creates an Exceptional Slave." *CNN In America* (December 25, 2012) <http://inamerica.blogs.cnn.com/2012/12/25/opinion-quentin-tarantino-creates-an-exceptional-slave/> Accessed June 27, 2013.

Tompkins, Jane. *West of Everything: The Inner Life of Westerns.* New York: Oxford University Press, 1992.

Travers, Peter. "*Much Ado About Nothing* Review." *Rolling Stone* (May 27, 1993): 56.

Tuska, Jon. *The American West in Film: Critical Approaches to the Wester.* Westport, CT: Greenwood Press, 1985.

Varadharajan, Asha. *Exotic Parodies: Subjectivity in Adorno, Spivak, and Said.* Minneapolis, MN: University of Minnesota Press, 1995.

Vasey, Ruth. *The World According to Hollywood.* Madison, WI: University of Wisconsin Press, 1997.

Waldman, Diane. "There's More to a Positive Image Than Meets the Eye." *Jump Cut* 18 (1978): 31–32.

Warner, Kristen. "Django Unchained As Post-Race Product." *Antenna* (December 28, 2012) <http://blog.commarts.wisc.edu/2012/12/28/django-unchained-as-post-race-product/> Accessed June 27, 2013.

Weber, Max. *The Rational and Social Foundations of Music.* Don Martindal, Johannes Riedel, and Gertrude Neuwirth, trans. Illinois: Southern Illinois University Press, 1958.

—. "Chapter V: Ethnic Groups." Guenther Roth and Claus Wittich, eds. *Economy and Society: An Outline of Interpretive Sociology.* New York: Bedminster Press, 1968, 385–98.

Widner, Cindy. "This is a Love Story." *The Austin Chronicle Online* (March 11, 2005) <http://www.austinchronicle.com/issues/dispatch/2005–03–11/screens_feature6.html> Accessed August 17, 2005.

Wiegman, Robin. "Race, Ethnicity, and Film." John Hill and Pamela Church Gibson, eds. *The Oxford Guide to Film Studies.* Oxford: Oxford University Press, 1998, 158–68.

Williams, Joseph. "Obama Scolds Cambridge Police." *The Boston Globe* (July 23, 2009) <http://www.boston.com/news/nation/washington/articles/2009/07/23/obama_scolds_cambridge_police/> Accessed November 8, 2009.

Williams, Raymond. *The Country and the City.* New York: Oxford University Press, 1973.

Xing, Jun. *Asian America through the Lens: History, Representations and Identity.* Walnut Creek, CA: AltaMira Press, 1998.

Young, Robert J. C. *Postcolonialism: An Historical Introduction.* Malden, MA: Blackwell, 2001.

Young, Robert M. "Putting Materialism Back into Race Theory: Toward a Transformative Theory of Race." *The Red Critique* 11 (Winter/Spring 2006) <http://www.redcritique.org/WinterSpring2006/index.html> Accessed March 5, 2007.

Žižek, Slavoj. "Multiculturalism, or, the Cultural Logic of Multinational Capitalism." *New Left Review* 225 (September/October 1997): 28–51.

Index

Page numbers in **bold** refer to illustrations.